Anti-*Dobbs*

Omar Swartz

Anti-*Dobbs*

An Interdisciplinary Polemic

PETER LANG
New York - Berlin - Bruxelles - Chennai - Lausanne - Oxford

Library of Congress Cataloging-in-Publication Control Number: 2024046967

Bibliographic information published by the Deutsche Nationalbibliothek.
The German National Library lists this publication in the German
National Bibliography; detailed bibliographic data is available
on the Internet at http://dnb.d-nb.de.

Cover design by Peter Lang Group AG

ISBN 9783034353878 (hardback)
ISBN 9783034353885 (ebook)
ISBN 9783034353892 (epub)
DOI 10.3726/b22499

Published by Peter Lang Publishing Inc., New York, USA
info@peterlang.com—www.peterlang.com

This publication has been peer reviewed.

DEDICATION

For Rui, the love of my life.

EPIGRAPH

There is in America a subject called civics, in which, perhaps more than in any other, the teaching is expected to be misleading. The young are taught a sort of copybook account of how public affairs are supposed to be conducted and are carefully shielded from all knowledge as to how in fact they are conducted.

Bertrand Russell, "The Functions of a Teacher," *Unpopular Essays* (New York: Routledge, [1950]/2009), 117.

CONTENTS

PREFACE

It is fair, in reading a book like this one on a controversial topic such as abortion, perhaps the *most* controversial topic in the United States today, to know something about the writer. For authority, I point to George Orwell who, in an autobiographical essay observed, "I do not think one can assess a writer's motives without knowing something of his early development."[1] This point is particularly salient for *critical* (or, in this case, *polemical*) scholarship, the type of writing that aspires, in Orwell's words, "to push the world in a certain direction, to alter other people's idea of the kind of society that they should drive after."[2] Orwell was a master of this type of writing, and an inspiration for me and many others who have some ideas about how to make the world a better place. All my education, all my reading, writing, and teaching have been directed toward that goal.

***

I am the son and only child of a single mother with only a lackluster secondary school education. I know that my mother was a poor and uninspired student because, after she died at the age of 81, I learned that she had a hoarding disorder. Of course, I suspected that something was wrong with her. When I was growing up, my mother was a "pack rat" who had an idiosyncratic collection of public street signs, old magazines and newspapers, and a bizarre array of knickknacks, tchotchkes, and fetishes, as well as innumerable succulents and other plants packed into our small apartment. Much later when I was in college and graduate school, my mother managed to buy an old house where she lived alone with her cats, and the "collecting" continued unabated. The disposal company that came to clear her house told me that, on a 5-point hoarding scale, my mother was a 4.5. I am sharing this because, while I was working through the physical rubble (and literal garbage) that was my mother's life, I came across her junior high and high school report cards and class assignments. Few things I have experienced have been as uncanny as reviewing those sad and depressing documents. When I asked my mother's lifelong friend (whom she knew from junior high school) about the grades, she told me that my mother "was no scholar."

Fundamentally, my mother was a good person. She struggled tirelessly and thanklessly for years to provide for us. We got by with the aid of a kind landlord who never raised her rent and a friend who brought over expired groceries from the market where she worked. My mother wanted a man in her life, someone to take care of us, but she seldom had dates and had fewer boyfriends. Sometimes she drank too much, and she often yelled and hit me. Not infrequently, I had to take refuge at a neighbor's or a friend's apartment. These were not good times for her or me, but we survived. My senior year of high school, I lived on my own and was never again particularly close to my mother, although we both tried. We were too different with too much shared trauma and opposing world views to understand each other well.

My mother was not a feminist; she made that clear to me throughout my childhood. She was against the Equal Rights Amendment because she believed that women should be treated "special" (i.e., entitled to certain "protections" and "benefits" from their husbands enforced by societal and legal norms), and she voted for Nixon, attracted to his "law and order" persona. Late in her life, my mother hated Hillary Clinton with a passion that went beyond any rational disagreement with Clinton's policies. Clinton was a woman with power who "allowed" her husband to cheat on her. Nothing, for my mother, was worse than that. It struck at the core of her identity. Above all, my mother wanted to be a wife and have a husband to "protect" her. Her entire life she remained, in sentiment, a child of the American 1950s.

My mother and my father divorced before I was 2 years old. By the time my mother was pregnant, she knew she was in a bad marriage (to put it mildly). My father was a huge narcissist who gambled and seldom held a steady job his entire life. He had the emotional maturity of a child. Abortion, however, was not an option for my mother. Had she been able to get a safe and legal abortion, her life would have been much different—better, as far as I can tell.[3] She lived her life, she told me (again and again), to be my mother. She was a dedicated (if not frustrated) mother.[4] While I do not doubt and appreciate her love for me, I cannot help but feel sorry for her, for her all-too-small vision of herself and the painful sacrifices she had to make to raise a son as a single mother in a social context in which she and I were clearly not wanted.

***

At some point, in most of my courses, I ask my students: What is it that becomes so universal among women—both conservative and liberal—that they have this common bond, this omnipresent sense that, as women, the world is not quite their own?[5] When I talk like this, the men, almost all of them, have no idea what I am saying. My words make no sense to them. It is as if I am speaking a foreign language, and in some sense I am. I have become foreign to their world views. They do not understand how a white male can be a feminist. They look at me *as if I were a woman*—that is, they look at me with suspicion and apprehension, discounting what I say. If I am not careful, I lose credibility with them altogether; they will think that, because I am a feminist, I am someone not to be trusted and probably gay. This is a common problem that teachers who deal with issues of gender and social justice in class must deal with.[6]

The women in class, however, almost all of them, nod their heads in recognition, and I often sense a low-level collective sigh as they experience some relief with the public utterance of something they thought no male could ever comprehend. But I do at least try, even if my understanding is imperfect (i.e., subject to bias and privilege). I recognize, along with Carole J. Sheffield, that "women's lives are bounded by the reality of pervasive sexual danger and the fear that reality engenders," and that men, even when they are not perpetuators of this fear, are largely oblivious to its existence.[7] By speaking of this danger and its gendered inequality, it perhaps grows easier to resist the cultural traits that perpetuate it. That is my hope, to help educate our way out of the terrible mess we have created for ourselves as women and men: "[T]he function of the writer is to act in such a way that nobody can be ignorant of the world and that nobody may say that he is innocent of what it's all about."[8]

There is clearly a divide in our society at least, if not in most societies, between the experiences of men and women grounded not in biological necessity, but in crude privilege or unequal power differentia. When men and women buy into this gendered thinking, it is all too easy to live one's life believing in the inevitability of social relationships as we experience them. All we must do is to act "naturally." For men, it is easy *not* to think about changing (why would we, we are doing just fine, enjoying enormous privileges under the current arrangements) and for women it is *dangerous* to do so. That danger led to women being named—and executed—as witches,[9] and today is expressed by men through domestic violence and sexual abuse, not to mention the more passive violence men do to women when they withdraw their financial support, so that women and their children all-to-commonly languish in neglect and poverty. As the feminist activist Gloria Steinem noted, "Most women are one man away from welfare."[10]

While "well-behaved women rarely make history," women who violate the expectations of their gender often pay a heavy price. With *Dobbs v. Jackson Women's Health Organization*,[11] the Supreme Court of the United States has made the price and burden of being a woman much heavier. The suffocating smog of oppression against women grows thicker. It is my position in this book that the *Dobbs* decision was wrong, immoral, and unjust, and it perpetuates the sad legacy of misogyny that destroyed my mother (and millions of women like her) who did the best she could with what she had and that, while that was maybe enough to survive, this legacy of misogyny broke her in the process.

An earlier reviewer thought this claim about my mother and other women being "destroyed" by a society hostile to women seems "more than a bit sweeping" and that it removes agency from them. Perhaps it does. The problem, however, is less my characterization and more the fact that many women in our society become so hurt by ill-treatment, misogynistic attitudes, and structural inequality that their subjectivities become damaged or deformed out of terror, hopelessness, or neglect, greatly limiting their opportunities. Nevertheless, I acknowledge that my language here, and throughout this book, is somewhat polemical in style. But as I articulate and defend in the Introduction, this book is a *polemic* in the full sense of the term. Using an interdisciplinary array of sources and arguments (mostly legal, historical, and philosophical), I am making the strongest case possible for how the abortion issue is a shadow cast by the law over a more fundamental and important issue: the status of and respect for women as human beings and equal citizens of the United States. Obviously, many people are going to disagree with this, both in terms of the substance and style of my writing. That's okay, I expect no less. However, through years of dedicated study and teaching, I have earned the right to speak on this important issue, no matter how imperfectly, and to prod an intelligent public (my primary audience) to rethink their positions and understandings provoked by my unique contribution to the subject. I do not offer the final word; no one can. I offer only a perspective, grounded in anger and frustration to be sure, but one passionately committed to bettering the lives of women and men by pushing back against outdated legal and religious views that impact life in the United States in a variety of ways.

I insist on being "radical" in the sense of getting to the *root of the problem* and not with merely alleviating symptoms. To be "pro-women" in this sense, as exemplified in this book, is to be *radical*, as the "woman question" is the question, world-wide, upon which our world depends, and the answer to this question is full and unapologetic equality. Even climate change and environmental threats cannot be understood outside of the prevalence of gender inequality: men simply act upon the world what they have forever done to women. Moreover, as the "root" of American legal culture is the Constitution, that is where I direct my ire on this essential question. The U.S. Constitution has often failed us, but not always and not necessarily. With hard work, it can be a tool for good.

Again, to quote Orwell, who had this to say about writing a book: "My starting point is always a feeling of partisanship, a sense of injustice [. . .]. I write it because there is some lie that I want to expose, some fact to which I want to draw attention, and my initial concern is to get a hearing."[12] Is anyone listening? For those of us who are paying attention, what are we going to do about it?

Notes

1 *Why I Write* (New York: Penguin Books, [1946]/2005), 4.

2 Ibid., 5.

3 I was asked recently how I felt about the idea of my mother aborting me nearly 60 years ago. "I wish she had," I responded. While I appreciate being alive, and I am grateful for all that I have with my own family and career, I know that my *mother's life* was what mattered at the time, not mine. As I will argue throughout this book, abortion does *end* a developing life, and there is something sad and tragic about that. But *not* having an abortion when wanted or needed also has consequences that matter for the mother. In the unhappy event that a woman and her fetus encounter a divergence in their interests and a decision must be made on whether or not to carry the fetus to term, that decision belongs to the pregnant woman alone. Her life takes precedence over her fetus in any example I can imagine, even against the interest of the father.

4 When not fretting over my radical politics or my teenage rebelliousness (she once tried to have me declared "incorrigible" and incarcerated for challenging her authority), my mother searched for indications that I might be gay, including surreptitiously reading my diary and complaining to her friends about what she found. Apparently, questioning gender, parental, and other societal norms leads a person to become morally suspect and a social threat. Being white and male helped me with the authorities who pushed back against my mother's efforts. Young women and people of color tend not to be so lucky. For a historical account of criminalizing young women for acting independently, see Mary Conyngton, *Senate Report on Condition of Woman and Child Wage-Earners in the United States v. 15: Relation Between Occupation and Criminality of Women* (Washington, DC: Government Printing Office, 1911). Retrieved from https://fraser.stlouisfed.org/title/summary-report-condition-woman-child-wage-earners-united-states-3830?page=375.

5 At my university, where I have taught for almost 25 years, the overwhelming student population is "liberal" or even further to the left. This is very different from when I taught in North Carolina for three years and in Indiana as a graduate student before that. The North Carolina students were far less accepting of my critical pedagogy and critique of the status quo. One undergraduate told me, "you are the professor that my parents and pastor warned me about when I went off to college."

6 See Kate Dube, "What Feminism Means to Today's Undergraduates," *Chronicle of Higher Education* 50, no. 41 (June 2004), http://chronicle.com/article/What-Feminism-Means-to-Todays/8838/.

7 "Sexual Terrorism," in *Women: A Feminist Perspective*, 5th ed., ed. Jo Freeman (Mountain View, CA: Mayfield Publishing, 1995), 2.

8 Jean Paul Sartre, "What Is Writing?" *What Is Literature?* (New York: Routledge, 2001), 15.

9 In Europe between approximately 1450–1700 CE there were more than 50,000 judicial (as many as 100,000) executions of witches. People (mostly women) accused of being witches were tortured, tried, and executed under the color of law. For the judicial suppression of Witchcraft in the New England context, see Cotton Mather, *Wonders of the Invisible World* (New York: Bell Publishing Company, [1693]/1900).

10 Quoted in Lorraine Ali and Lisa Miller, "The Secret Lives of Wives," *Newsweek*, July 12, 2004, 46.

11 142 S.Ct. 2228 (2022).

12 *Why I Write*, 8.

ACKNOWLEDGMENTS

I wrote this book out of angst for the future of the United States where I live with my family, Rui Zhao, Avi Swartz, and Mia Swartz. They all experienced secondhand angst as I developed this manuscript, and they did so with great love, forgiveness, and understanding. I hope that they—and all families—benefit politically, socially, and culturally from the results.

This book has much improved from the conscientious feedback I received from Karen Breslin, Sharon Coggan, and Jeff Schweinfest, three individuals deeply committed to education and social change.

INTRODUCTION

> [I]n general people experience their present naively, as it were, without being able to form an estimate of its contents; they have first to put themselves at a distance from it—the present, that is to say, must have become the past—before it can yield points of vantage from which to judge the future.[1]

The U.S. presidential election of 2016, which resulted in Donald Trump becoming the 45th President of the United States, was a watershed moment in our recent history as a nation. It marked what appears to be the eclipse of the social and constitutional liberalism—often challenged and imperfectly realized—that defined the U.S. in the post-World War II era. Such liberalism, often taken for granted and assumed to be a part of our national heritage, was itself a *break* from the pattern of historical intolerance and moral exclusion that has defined the United States from the beginning of our nation's existence.[2]

The tumultuous 2020 and 2022 elections, while perhaps pausing the pace of our regression and providing some welcome (and perhaps temporary) breathing space for reflection and regrouping, have not promoted much in the way of *solutions* to our fundamental problems as a society and what this has meant for the "social justice" aspirations embedded in the post-war liberal era (our collective self-image as a nation). Moreover, the upcoming 2024 elections, a sorry repeat of 2020, could mean a return of a greatly empowered Presidential Trump. In short, the so-called "cultural wars" (the socio-political-legal conflicts revolving around *who we are* and *what kind of a nation* we should be) of the past few decades seem as intractable, dangerous, and destructive as ever.[3]

The term "social justice," I acknowledge, is notoriously difficult to define authoritatively, as few people, even those further to the right on the political spectrum, are for social *injustice* per se. In general, the concept of social justice is evoked in individual, collective, and organizational attempts at promoting change and equality relative to communities that are disenfranchised, marginalized, and/or oppressed (in the case of this book I will be primarily discussing women, although I recognize that much of what I have to say cuts across socioeconomic, racial, and queer identities as well). The term "social justice" has been applied to progressive movements with the aim of empowering individuals who have been subjected to inequity as far as access to resources, opportunities, and further bearing burdens of harm and negative impacts that are not felt proportionately by other more privileged groups (e.g., in environmental racism). Social justice discourse is a radical form of challenging oppression, with the goal of addressing and dismantling structures, policies, and institutions that contribute to avoidable human suffering, often the result of extreme poverty. As used in this book, social justice is the "process of communicating, inspiring, advocating, organizing, and working with others of similar and diverse organizational affiliations to help all people gain respect and participate fully in society in a way that benefits the community as well as the individual."[4]

As President, and with the help of Senate Leader Mitch McConnell's base Machiavellianism,[5] Trump made good on his promise to appoint Supreme Court Justices to overturn *Roe v. Wade*.[6] *Roe*, along with *Planned Parenthood of Southeastern Pennsylvania v. Casey*,[7] guaranteed, within certain reasonable (but highly contested) parameters, a woman's right to terminate her pregnancy. *Roe's* long-expected demise came on June 24, 2022, when the Supreme Court issued *Dobbs v. Jackson Women's Health Organization*.[8] "Turning back the clock" 50 years, the *Dobbs* Court held that the U.S. Constitution does *not* confer on a woman the right to terminate an unwanted and perhaps health-threatening pregnancy, that the government can force her to suffer motherhood with all its consequences.[9] With *Dobbs*, the legal, political, and cultural subordination of women, long a bane on women's lives, grew worse. This sickening, suffocating blanket of misogyny and its historical embodiment in the law is the great concern of this book.[10]

Specifically, I will argue that the abortion issue, important as it may be, is a *shadow* cast by the law over a more *fundamental* and important issue: the status of and respect for women as human beings and equal citizens in the United States. I maintain that generous abortion rights (perhaps with some qualification) are fundamental to the liberty and equality of women, and that *Dobbs* was grotesquely wrong in both the legal and moral sense. Moreover, the decision was grounded in an unarticulated—that is, *suppressed*—misogyny and patriarchy[11] in the Court's historical narrative, stretching back for centuries in the Common Law Tradition. As I will demonstrate, the Court knew full well what it was doing when it arrogantly, egregiously, callously, and at times gleefully attacked womenkind in their most vulnerable condition. In so doing, the Court attacked us all. The Court knew it was *endorsing a repulsive anti-women ideology and practice as courts earlier in our history endorsed and propped up white supremacy and heteronormativity. For these reasons, and because of the sheer magnitude of the people involved and the primal suffering it ordained,* the *Dobbs* decision has led to my loss of faith in the integrity of the current United States Supreme Court and the important role (and hope) that it plays in our lives.[12]

The phrase, "Common Law Tradition," will be used frequently throughout this book. By this, I simply mean the legal tradition originating in England after 1066 which was integrated into the United States during the seventeenth and eighteenth centuries, largely under the influence of Sir William Blackstone's four volumes, *Commentaries on the Laws of England*, published between the years 1765 and 1770. Other major contributors to our contemporary understanding of the Common Law Tradition include Sir Edward Coke, Sir Matthew Hale, and, in the United States, James Kent and Joseph Story, to name only a few.

The original title to this book was an accurate but unwieldy, "History, Abortion, and (Elusive) Gender Equality: Uncovering and Engaging the Suppressed Misogyny of *Dobbs v. Jackson Women's Health Organization*." The more I wrote on this topic, the more I was incensed by the *Dobbs* decision. The more I thought about the legal history I have studied and taught for more than two decades, the more I understand how present the hold of legal history and its intersection with other cultural forms remains, and that too many Americans are content with their ignorance of it. We have to understand this history in order to engage with it and use it to fight for a better world. That fight cannot come from a place of ignorance. Thus, this book is both anti-*Dobbs* and all it represents, and a *polemic* for the total equality of women and respect for women in U.S. society.[13] I both name and condemn the forces that oppose the full equality for women.

A Path Through the Thicket

This book consists of five chapters. While each engages the *Dobbs* decision, I am not providing a line-by-line textual analysis of the case. With some fairness, it could be said that this book is an outrage *to* the *Dobbs* decision while not being *about* the decision per se. *Dobbs* provided me a focus to write an interdisciplinary polemic addressing what I see is the persistence of misogyny in law, and in culture more generally. In other words, I am not providing a purely legal analysis, but something different (perhaps a ruthless "cultural criticism" is a more accurate description of this work). In a sense I am wearing two hats, writing from different perspectives. I am, of course, a student of law, having graduated *magna cum laude* from Duke University in 2001.

I am, however, more than a legal scholar. Before attending law school, I earned a doctorate in communication (emphasis in rhetorical studies) and have, for nearly 25 years, been a professor who has taught a variety of courses in law, rhetoric, and critical theory in a college of liberal arts and sciences, not in a law school. I have never practiced law. Moreover, I identify as a *critic* in the tradition of Freud, Marx, and Nietzsche, all of whom waged a "war" of sorts against certain ideas prevalent during their time that they correctly thought were unreasonable.[14] More so than others who shared similar concerns, these theorists (generally speaking) were able to bring to their inquiry a brilliant and uncompromising focus which, while controversial and hyperbolic at times, moved society forward in some important liberalizing ways. To these theorists I add the work of feminist, philosopher, and human rights activist Catharine A. MacKinnon, arguing that, in the fight for women's equality, she is as important as Freud, Marx, and Nietzsche in their respective realms.

Chapter 1 provides a critique of judicial philosophy. It engages with the "originalist" and conservative views that hamstring the *Dobbs* majority's moral and political vision, allowing it to strip, for the first time in history, a fundamental Constitutional right from the American people. *Dobbs*' originalist and conservative orientation represents a clear example of how the institutional and imaginative orders of U.S. society are often limited by the legal apparatuses in ways that make social justice and substantive equality difficult to achieve. The very legal norms that are proclaimed to be just, fair, and self-evident work in less visible ways to discourage alternative thinking about the structure of society and the feasibility of more inclusive social and economic communities.[15]

In contrast to the originalist view is a constructivist (or liberal) type of interpretation, which is an attempt to adapt the Constitution to the needs of each generation anew, making it responsive to the experience of Americans living in the twenty-first century. The poetic terms of Ralph Waldo Emerson, from his great 1837 "declaration" of American intellectual independence,[16] are apropos here. In his celebrated address, "The American Scholar," Emerson urged that the intellectual life of our great nation needed to be freed from the fetters of the old-world way of thinking. He argued that America's intellectual and moral strength had to match its material strength and that could only come by thinking in uniquely American ways as befitting an eclectic, youthful, and dynamic nation. As he cautioned: "Each age must write its own books [. . .]. The books of an older period will not fit this."[17]

The U.S. Constitution, I offer, is such a "book" that Emerson evokes with his call for forward-thinking and American ingenuity in response to what was then European "backwardness." The Constitution is an important text, no doubt, central to the identity of the United States. It is a serious text written with great care and deliberation at an important juncture in our history. But it is just a *text*, words on a piece of paper, without flesh and blood, and without life. Moreover, a text is only as valuable as it is drafted, interpreted, and applied. As James Boyd White notes, "What matters is always what place, if any, such an instrument will have in the lives of those it is intended to regulate."[18]

The Constitution was articulated by people trying to create a nation during heady and difficult times, doing (perhaps) the best they could, when we today know they could (and *should*) have done better. Like any text, the Constitution has its strengths and its weaknesses situated within the context and exigencies that birthed it and enabled it to *persevere* for as long as it has. (While this perseverance has not been easy, it was much more difficult than it needed to be, the Civil War being an obvious example.) Twenty-first-century American society, however, is morally and socially as different from American society in the eighteenth century as spacecraft is to the horse and buggy that transported our nation's founders to and from the Constitutional Convention in 1787. It is time that we stop misperceiving or idolizing our founding era. It was the *beginning*, not the end, of our democratic consciousness. To borrow from the ethos of Martin Luther King Jr., expressed at a pivotal movement during the Civil Rights Movement: "[I]f America is to be a great nation this must become true."[19] *America is not "great" when it* countenances *slavery, racism, homophobia or, in the case of my study, the second-class citizenship of women.*

It can, however, become great (if not better) had it the wherewithal to live up to its most noble aspirations. Against the national rising tide of cultural and political reactionism, this is becoming increasingly necessary.

Chapter 2 reviews MacKinnon's argument that women have been socially constructed as man's inferior and systematically subordinated by the law which, substantially, represents men's interest. This is contrasted with "liberal" feminism, as represented by *Roe* ("a global symbol of feminist triumph over patriarchy"),[20] in which people work through legal and democratic methods toward political and social autonomy for women in the context of a pluralistic and democratic society, where everyone has an equal role to play. Liberal feminism encourages the use of public resources for, among other things, affordable abortion access (long prohibited by the federal Hyde Amendment), comprehensive anti-discrimination and sexual harassment laws in the educational and workplace environments, anti-poverty programs to help working-class women and their children, and equal protection of the laws, generally. *Roe*, while imperfect, was a vindication of that liberal interest and partial fulfillment of a long unrecognized American promise, opening what the poet Walt Whitman called, in a different context, "democratic vistas."[21]

I argue that MacKinnon's "radical" approach to feminism remains relevant today, profoundly so, because liberal feminism and the movement which surrounded it has, in part, *stalled*. If *Dobbs* is to be taken as a bellwether, as I believe it is, liberal feminism may be in *retreat*, the victim in some sense of its own success. As Jennifer Baumgardner and Amy Richards note, feminism during the past 30 years was "like fluoride. We scarcely notice we have it—it's simply in the water."[22] While feminism, broadly speaking, is larger than the quest for legal equality and sexual autonomy, it must at least be grounded in equality and autonomy, or else it is nothing. And, as described in this book, outside of *Roe* (whatever its limitations or shortcomings), women have *never* had legal equality and sexual autonomy throughout the long history of the Common Law Tradition.

Chapters 3 and 4 are broken into a number of thematic sections, consisting of the empirical/historical evidence I have gathered from more than 20 years of teaching a university course titled "Law and Diversity in United States History." I use this evidence to back MacKinnon's general claim that the law negatively and systemically impacts women's lives, and also to support my own argument that the decision in *Dobbs* is profoundly steeped in a religiously tainted, patriarchally infused, long-lived, and deeply rooted animosity to strong, independent women who live outside of *patriarchal* limitations—the precise class of women who need and benefit from abortion rights. Traditionalist women (a small but substantial sliver of our nation) do not need *Dobbs*, for their agency is already protected by their decision, for whatever reason, to become mothers and/or to subordinate themselves to their men—but the rest of us (and poor women more than ever) need *Roe* and *Casey* to flourish in our lives and on our terms. Through these examples, I explore how the Common Law Tradition intersects with both Christianity and the *Patria Potestas* power of the husband/father/state.

Chapter 5 argues that anti-abortion regulations are objectively and subjectively anti-woman and that there are no good arguments for prohibiting abortion that does not in some fashion denigrate women for being women and "punish" them for their reproductive capabilities (or for their sexual activity).[23] To do so, I first engage with the *Dobbs* Court's preemptive objection to this argument when, early in its decision, it dismissed the view that the goal of preventing abortion constitutes "invidiously discriminatory animus against women," dissociating a woman's interest from that of her fetus, pitting the two against each other and privileging the fetus.[24] By doing so, the *Dobbs* majority rendered laws regulating or prohibiting abortion to "mere rational review," the lowest standard of judicial scrutiny, and to hold that the state's interest in "prenatal life" is a rational interest against the interest of the woman's bodily and social autonomy, which *Dobbs* strips of legal cognizance. As a result, women are reduced to being little more than forced "fetal containers" under the regulation of men with the backing of the state. This strikes me as the antithesis of freedom, something akin to slavery. If nothing else, it is ugly, unkind, and unnecessary. Ultimately, I consider, "who gets to define the fetus?" and conclude, as I have suggested here, that that power resides in the pregnant woman alone.[25]

Collectively, the above sections show how, throughout the past 200 years of American legal history (at least), women have been subject to the degradation, humiliation, and lack of legal identity that we typically associate with involuntary servitude in this country, and that this history sheds important light on the legal and social condition of women today. Throughout, I review the profound misogyny of the Common Law Tradition, one which the *Dobbs* majority held up as authority for its position that, since women had no common law right to abortion, the tradition was resolutely "pro-life," and, therefore, the constitutional right to an abortion should not exist now.

Ignored from the Court's narrative is how, both within and outside of *coverture*, the formal collection of laws subjecting a married woman to the servitude and authority of her husband, there were hundreds of ways in which women (and their children) were considered the property of their husbands and treated accordingly. Moreover, common-law legal and religious views supported, and were in turn supported by, the sexist views imbedded in medicine, philosophy, and other cultural discourses, creating a circular, self-reinforcing environment in which women were defined in ways that "justified" their second-class citizenship (at best) and sexual servitude to men. Many women, such as my mother, bought into this epistemology as evidenced by female resistance to the Equal Rights Amendment, which led to its defeat in 1982 after decades of feminist organizing with significant male support.[26]

As a result of the arguments made in the above-previewed sections, I can conclude that the Court's holding in *Dobbs* was an untimely expression of deeply religious and conservative biases and hatred against independent women and the important role they play in our liberal, democratic, and multicultural *secular* society grounded in creative cooperation and civic fraternity among citizens. *Dobbs* was a *backwards* step from an increasingly backwards and reactionary Court, during a period in the United States when forward-thinking laws, judgments, and political commitments were increasingly needed to improve our democratic and social institutions and the overall quality of our lives. Women (and men) deserve better.

***

One final point before I begin. The concept of "religion" is salient in this book, and I will mostly be critical of it, particularly in some of its Christian forms, as implicated in the Common Law Tradition and in U.S. society, generally. However, I want to note at the outset that religion is not a monolithic entity that can be good or bad. Rather, following philosophers William James[27] and John Dewey,[28] "religion" is a word that we use to describe an outlook that some people take toward the world and a type of practice that may flow from that outlook. It means as many different things as there are people who think that religion is important. Moreover, as James notes, "Religious fermentation is always a symptom of the intellectual vigor of a society; and it is only when they forget that they are hypotheses and put on rationalistic and authoritative pretensions, that our faiths do harm."[29]

I am not anti-religion—that would be like being anti-poetry (or anti-myth), which is as impossible as it is undesirable. People form communities and define their lives through sharing a particular meaning regarding some specific terminology and/or a particular ideology or world view. Such communities' collective common narratives develop histories, as well as habits of practice, which make up their world. The wonderful diversity of human life can be found here. Nothing could be more human. The word "religion" does not and cannot capture the plethora of these experiences. Its absence would render human beings two-dimensional. What is important from an intellectual point of view are the *expressions* and *practices* (the lived poetry) of these communities, which vary widely across time, place, and culture. It is not possible to talk meaningfully about religion without discussing a specific literature or a specific group during a specific time, which is what I intend to do here, as difficult as it may be. Much like Paul Ricoeur's three "masters of suspicion,"[30] I tend to reflexively sneer at religious expression, but that may say more about me than religious discourse in general. As the philosopher Bertrand Russell pointed out, "we must be skeptical even of our skepticism."[31]

A similar point is true when discussing political ideologies: "Left," "Right," "Democrat," "Republican," "Liberal," "Conservative," etc. These are words that often suggest an essentialized and well-understood meaning but, in fact, have none outside of a specific context. Like religion, this makes discussing politics difficult and it becomes all-to-easy to demonize our political opponents. In neither case, however, do we have to be silent, but we must be *sensitive* as we are talking about other people's most personal self-identifications and their lives (this concern includes that of the fetus as well). As sensitive as I try to be, however, I am self-consciously positioning this book as an interdisciplinary polemic, avoiding dry, sterile academic objectivity and precise disciplinary boundaries in the interest of the topic's seriousness and profound immediate importance, demanding an informed and intelligent response.[32]

I realize, along with Michel Foucault, that polemical critique is not without its limitations, particularly in comparison to the more measured and invitational disciplinary "dialogue" demarcating normalized and disciplined scholarship. "On principle," writes Foucault, polemical writing "possesses rights authorizing him to wage war and making that struggle a just undertaking; the person he confronts is not a partner in the search for the truth, but an adversary, an enemy who is wrong, which is harmful and whose very existence constitutes a threat."[33]

Polemics disallows possibility "of an equal discussion: it examines a case; it isn't dealing with an interlocutor, it is processing a suspect; it collects the proofs and his guilt, designated the infraction that he has committed, and pronounces the verdict and sentences him."[34] Polemics is a war on an enemy made into a threat to be abolished. Without being overly dramatic, that is precisely *my intent*. Like Nietzsche, I want to wage war against an idea and, in so doing, "[s]ometimes the cruel word of censure must be uttered."[35] My enemies are *not* those individuals with whom I disagree on political or religious grounds, but legalized (and cultural) misogyny, so long tolerated, and now emergent in *Dobbs*.

Foucault warns that "new ideas" seldom come from polemics, but my idea is not new; rather, it is politically pressing and necessary for resisting the ascendant anti-democratic forces we face as a nation. Embodying this polemical stance means that I might not always be *surgically precise*. I am a *critic*, after all, not a social scientist. Nevertheless, I apologize in advance for any overstatements or inappropriate aspersions and recognize, along with critic Edward Said, that "[r]eal intellectual analysis forbids calling one side innocent, the other evil. Indeed, the notion of a side is, where cultures are at issue, highly problematic, since most cultures aren't watertight little packages, all homogenous, and all either good or evil."[36] If it helps my audience appreciate my authorial persona, do not view me as an academic. Rather, see me as an intelligent and engaged citizen with bias and passion who, nevertheless, has something to contribute on an important national controversy.

I believe in our national motto, *E pluribus unum*, but that means the states, in coming together to form one union, must be held accountable for upholding the rights of *all* its citizens, Black and white, women and men, Jew and gentile. As columnist Jamelle Bouie notes, the "repressive turn" of the post-Obama U.S. society comes not from the federal government, but from *state* legislatures (primarily led by Republicans), adding, "Americans have a long history with various forms of sub-national authoritarianism: state and local tyrannies that sustained themselves through exclusion, violence and the political security provided by the federal structure of the American political system."[37] He correctly concludes, "In many respects, the history of American political life is the story of the struggle to unravel those sub-national units of oppression and establish a universal and inviolable grant of political and civil rights, backed by the force of the national government."[38]

Sadly, although we have been improving over the centuries, the liberal grand vision of nationally-backed civil rights continues to be imperfect, and there is much backsliding on the racial front. Life in the United States is likely to worsen still, including for LGBT people. For the purposes of this book, my claim is that, until a woman in Mississippi or Massachusetts can have the same fundamental rights to control her own body free from government coercion, the great U.S. experiment in democracy will remain under actualized.

Notes

1 Sigmund Freud, *The Future of an Illusion* (New York: W.W. Norton & Company, 1961/1927), 5.
2 Howard Zinn, A *People's History of the United States* (New York: Harper Perennial Modern Classics, [1980]/2015).
3 According to James Davison Hunter, "the culture war emerges over fundamentally different conceptions of moral authority, over different ideas, and beliefs about truth, the good, obligation to one another, the nature of community, and so on. It is, therefore, cultural conflict at its deepest level." *Culture Wars: The Struggle to Define America* (New York; Basic Books, 1991), 49.
4 Phillip K. Tompkins, "Using Communication Research to Mitigate Homelessness: Emergence from Outreach Work," *Spectra* 47, no. 1, May 2011: 10.
5 Readers may note that throughout this book I employ derogatory-seeming language (such as the term "Machiavellianism") or ascribe unflattering adjectives (i.e., "misogynist," "homophobic," "racist") to the rhetoric or leadership style of national leaders or cultural agents who have actively engaged in the effort to curb or eliminate abortion rights. I do this for two reasons. First, as discussed below, I have self-consciously chosen a polemical writing style. Second, and more importantly, I believe that these are not *ad hominem* attacks. While readers can take issue with any particular characterization I make, the people I am writing about in this book (or at least their world views) are known to have discernable misogynist, homophobic, and racist tendencies. Moreover, Republican leadership over the past 10 years has been strongly Machiavellian and hateful, at least in comparison to Democratic politicians.
6 410 U.S. 113 (1973).
7 505 U.S. 833 (1992).
8 142 S.Ct. 2228 (2022).
9 I recognize my phrase "suffering motherhood" may seem unnecessarily emotive, as I discussed in footnote #5. While some women *do* find themselves in this position, 60 percent of women who have abortions in recent years *already* have children. Their choice to terminate their pregnancy was in part so that they could be *better* mothers to the children they already have. Additionally, only 9 percent of women in the United States denied an abortion end up putting their children up for adoption once given birth, which suggests an agency overlooked in my phrase "suffering motherhood." See Diana Greene Foster, *The Turnaway Study: Ten Years, a Thousand Women, and the Consequences of Having—or Being Denied—an Abortion* (New York: Simon and Schuster, 2020). Foster's study reveals that people who are denied abortion suffer the ills of increased poverty, relationship to violent men, and more physical health consequences. This suggests that many women do not seek abortions to reject motherhood per se, but rather out of economic and social necessity.
10 Throughout I will be championing a vision of *Roe* and *Casey* privileging what they accomplished and am less focused with their shortcomings, which were significant. While lamenting the demise of both cases, I recognize that they were more complicated in their legal and cultural implications for women in terms of race, sociological class, and the physician-centeredness of their holdings. In short, both *Roe* and *Casey* can be read as

containing elements of the very misogyny I am in this book critiquing. See Paula Abrams, "The Scarlet Letter: The Supreme Court and the Language of Abortion Stigma," *Michigan Journal of Gender & Law* 19, no. 2 (2013): 293–337; Kimberly Mutcherson, "Beyond Roe: Imagining the Future of Scholarship on Reproduction," *Women's Rights Law Reporter* 35 (2013): i–viii; as well as the collection of essays in *What* Roe v. Wade *Should Have Said: The Nation's Top Legal Experts Rewrite America's Most Controversial Decision*, ed. Jack M. Balkin (New York: New York University Press, 2023).

Moreover, Justice Ruth Bader Ginsburg's criticism of *Roe*, made before she was appointed to the Court, is well known. She thought that the *Roe* Court "ventured too far" and, thus, was counter-productive, imposing on the various states (which, like now, had a range of views on the issue of abortion), in broad, sweeping terms. Ginsburg, "Some Thoughts on Autonomy and Equality in Relation to *Roe v. Wade*," *North Carolina Law Review* 63, no. 2 (1985): 375–386. She also wrote that *Roe* precluded "dialogue" with state legislators, pre-empting change that was in the process of occurring because of evolving social attitudes in the 1960s and 1970s. "Speaking in a Judicial Voice," *New York University Law Review* 67 (1992): 1185. For all their shortcomings, *Roe* and *Casey* were, and continues to be, about what *kind* of society and world we want to have, and who is privileged, who makes the decisions, and who is hurt by such a constitution.

11 The definition of "patriarchy" that I will be using comes from Gerda Lerner, who defines it as "the manifestation and institutionalization of male dominance over women and children in the family and the extension of male dominance over women in society in general." *The Creation of Patriarchy* (New York: Oxford University Press, 1986), 238–239.

12 This "faith" was not the result of my "privilege" (which I undoubtedly have as a white male) but of hard work and an open mind. I went to law school thinking the worst of our legal system, viewing the Court through a Marxist-inspired lens. Studying law, however, transformed me intellectually and won me over to the thought that *maybe* there was something about the legal system that was hopeful. I found it, or thought I found it, in mid-to-late twentieth century jurisprudence and politics. I discuss this and the profound sadness I feel as an American in this book's conclusion.

13 Polemical scholarship is critical and necessary when it engages with the social and legal discourse that serves to reify a degrading status quo grounded in histories of inequality and inhumanity. As critical sociologist C. Wright Mills noted, "Neither the life of an individual nor the history of a society can be understood without understanding both." *The Sociological Imagination* (New York: Oxford University Press, [1959]/2000), 3. Simply, scholars pick sides in contentious social issues and fight, from their subjective standpoints informed by their education, research, and professional training, as well as their American sense of justice and fair play, for an effect as a form of speaking truth to power. See Omar Swartz, *In Defense of Partisan Criticism: Communication Studies, Law, & Social Analysis* (New York: Peter Lang, 2005). Not picking a side in substantial political issues condemns one to support the politics of the status quo, which is unacceptable. As many noteworthy activists observed, "If you are neutral in situations of injustice, you have chosen the side of the oppressor." Quoted in Gary Younge, "Archbishop Desmond Tutu: The Secrets of a Peacemaker," *The Guardian*, May 22, 2009, https://www.theguardian.com/books/2009/may/23/interview-desmond-tutu.

14 For my project, criticism is crucial to this process of preserving and extending democracy by seeking out its weaknesses and providing a corrective, filling in its lacunas, suggesting alternatives, and provoking change. As John Greenway observes, "The emergence of American democracy was not a continuous process, but a series of localized movements, impelled by oppressed groups who saw their own situation incompatible with the principles of democracy." *American Folksongs of Protest* (Philadelphia: University of Pennsylvania Press, 1953), 27. Such criticism, therefore, is suspicious of everything we take for granted and ruthless in its commitment to edify. Above all, such criticism is *melioristic* in seeking social change. Criticism, as I envision it here, is a profoundly humanistic, atheistic approach that believes society can be made better by individuals working together through concerted intelligent action, social cooperation, and critical engagement, often known as *praxis*. Praxis requires the type of inspired, engaged, and at times idiosyncratic study such as I am supplying. We need to not only know and understand, but to be compelled to become engaged. For that we need outrage as well as awareness of the cause of our feelings. This is what I attempt to provide.

15 This idea is discussed at length in my "Toward a Critique of Normative Justice: Human Rights and the Rule of Law," *Socialism & Democracy* 18 (2004): 185–209.

16 Kenneth S. Sacks, *Understanding Emerson: "The American Scholar" and His Struggle for Self-Reliance* (Princeton, NJ: Princeton University Press, 2003).

17 *Essays and Addresses* (Chicago: Scott, Foresman and Company 1907), 259.

18 *When Words Lose Their Meaning: Constitutions and Reconstitutions of Language, Character, and Community* (Chicago: University of Chicago Press, 1984), 245.

19 "I Have a Dream," *Negro History Bulletin* 31, no. 5 (May 1, 1968): 17. The "this" in King's sentence refers to the "dream" he beautifully elucidates in the preceding paragraphs, one that resolves the contradictions implicit in American society and reified by law.

20 Julie Suk, *After Misogyny: How the Law Fails Women and What to Do About It* (Berkely, CA: University of California Press, 2023), 87.

21 *The Portable Walt Whitman* (New York: Penguin Classics, [1871]/2003), 315–384.

22 *Manifesta: Young Women, Feminism, and the Future* (New York: Farrar, Straus & Giroux, 2000), 17.

23 To be clear, this is my position, not the position of either *Roe* or *Casey*.

24 Again, I do not want my argument to imply that I care nothing for a developing fetus. Far from it. I share with my religious opponents a gleeful joy and sense of wonderment over the emergence of a new human being. Babies, I believe, are goods; they literally are our future as a species. I have both a biological and an adopted child. These children mean the world to me. But all goods must be balanced against each other contextually. When it comes to gestation and parenthood, the agent capable of striking a balance must be the mother "to undertake her maternities in freedom." Simone de Beauvoir, *The Second Sex* (New York: Vintage, [1952]/1989), 492. In this context, I find it difficult to perceive any significant male interest that warrants their veto power over a woman's bodily autonomy. As Leah Willingham notes, state legislatures, particularly in conservative states, are "male-dominated" and often lack meaningful minority participation, and these men are responsible for advancing abortion restrictions as well as dictate the terms of women's sexual health, generally. "Gender Divide Prominent as Male-Dominated Legislatures Debate

Abortion," *PBS*, September 24, 2022, https://www.pbs.org/newshour/politics/gender-divide-prominent-as-male-dominated-legislatures-debate-abortion.

25 Readers need to realize that the lens I am engaging in this book comes from the tradition of Second Wave feminism and that this tradition is not without its limitations, as critiqued by Third Wave feminism as well as by racial and post-colonial scholars (e.g., the sentence above can read that I am denying rights over a pregnancy to transmen or others who do not identify as "women."). I do not wish to enter the sometimes-bitter "war" between the two traditions, both of which I value, because they enrich feminism generally. For criticism of the "universalizing" idea of "women" that is attributed to Second Wave feminism and evidenced in my writing, see Angela Davis, *Women, Race & Class* (New York: Vintage, 1983); Kimberly W. Crenshaw, *On Intersectionality: Essential Writings* (New York: The New Press, 2017); and Patricia Hill Collins, *Black Feminist Thought: Knowledge, Consciousness, and the Politics of Empowerment* (New York: Routledge, [1990]/2022).

26 Jane J. Mansbridge, *Why We Lost the ERA* (Chicago: University of Chicago Press), 1986. I acknowledge that women may reject abortion and equality rights for reasons that make sense to them. I do not intend to strip these women of their agency in defining themselves how they prefer and living the lives they wish to live. What I object to is their placing of limitations on *other* women who wish to make different choices. Nor, in this book, do I intend to blame the women who fought, or continue to fight, for equality and sexual autonomy for any failures to achieve it. I want to inspire all of us, women and men, to reengage the fight for full equality for women by understanding better the historical reasons for its importance.

27 *The Will to Believe* (New York: Longmans, Green and Co., 1897).

28 *A Common Faith* (New Haven, CT: Yale University Press, 1934).

29 *Will to Believe*, xiii.

30 Ricoeur identified Freud, Marx, and Nietzsche as "masters of suspicion," people who discerned problems (illusions) with the status quo and taught humanity how to see the world through a different, less encumbered lens. If nothing else, their views were fresh and stimulating. They represent a useful "hermeneutics of suspicion." *Freud and Philosophy: An Essay on Interpretation* (New Haven, CT: Yale University Press, 1970), 32–36. Additionally, psychiatrist Karl Stern views this critical trivium as heirs of an emergent yet reductive humanism that was, nevertheless, an exhortation and expression of "ascetic courage" made possible by the post-enlightenment "loss of metaphysical sense." All three theorists were rebelling against the "hypocrisy" and the "compliancy" of their times. *The Flight from Woman* (Paragon House: St. Paul, MN, [1965]/1985), 65–66. Yet it was *their* times. New times require new thinkers, perhaps modeled on those of the past.

31 *Skeptical Essays* (London: Routledge, 1993/1928), 109.

32 As Howard Zinn notes, "That a metalsmith uses reliable measuring instruments is a condition for doing good work, but does not answer the crucial question: will he now forge a sword or a plowshare with his instruments?" Both require the same commitment to undistorted facticity. *The Politics of History*, 2nd ed. (Urbana: University of Illinois Press, 1990), 10.

33 "Polemics, Politics, and Problemizations," *The Foucault Reader* (New York: Vintage Books, 2010), 381–383.

34 Ibid.

35 Reinhold Niebuhr, "Leaves from the Notebook of a Tamed Cynic," *Major Works on Religion and Politics* (New York: The Library of America, 2015), 66.

36 Edward W. Said, *Representations of the Intellectual* (New York: Vintage 1994), 119.

37 "The Real Threat to Freedom Is Coming from the States," *The New York Times*, May 26, 2023, https://www.nytimes.com/2023/05/26/opinion/freedom-states-rights.html#:~:text=Across%20the%20country%2C%20we%20are,is%20coming%20from%20the%20states.

38 Ibid.

· 1 ·

A CRITIQUE OF JUDICIAL PHILOSOPHY

> *Stare decisis* is like wine. If it's really new, you don't want to drink it, it has to age for a while. If it's really old, it is very valuable, or it has possibly turned to vinegar. There's this magical period in between. It is not difficult for a judge to make the stare decisis inquiry come out however the judge wants it to come out.[1]

In this chapter I consider the matter of judicial philosophy; that is, the methods and perspectives that ground a judge or justice's approach to constitutional interpretation. In it, I review two popular approaches courts use for interpreting the Constitution, loosely called "originalism" and "constructivism." I explore both perspectives with an eye toward which approach "works better" for increasing social inclusion in the United States, particularly gender equality within the law. Both perspectives, I note at the outset, are more complex than I can represent fully here, as I engage with them in a somewhat truncated form to make my point about the insufficiency of the Court's reasoning in *Dobbs v. Jackson Women's Health Organization*[2] and the harm it has inflicted on society.

Originalism maintains that there are fixed, stable meanings contained in the Constitution which were defined centuries ago that demand allegiance from contemporary courts. New claims for justice, novel advancements in moral reasoning, new poetic visions of the good, and the pressures of contemporary life, such as the exigencies of climate change, have little bearing in the Court's reasoning.

Constructivism, on the other hand, maintains that Constitutional meaning and understanding adapts, evolves, and changes by considering current controversies and pressures when deciding important constitutional questions. Constructivism eschews the formalism and dogmatism that characterize originalist orthodoxy and keeps a steady eye on the *effects* or *outcomes* of an interpretation. It asks, what are the *consequences* for interpreting the Constitution in a particular way? Because the law is an expression and determinative of community life which is always changing, outcomes matter in ways that originalists ignore. Constructionism replaces fealty to the past with a careful, principled concern for the present.

After discussing both interpretative practices, I then trace the effects of each judicial philosophy on our unfinished struggle in this country for gender equality and find one, originalism, to be lacking in integrity, morality, and usefulness. As it turns out, to nobody's surprise, originalism was the legal theory behind the Court's disastrous *Dobbs* decision and its dystopian world view. Further, the unethical political maneuvering of Republican Senators of the Supreme Court nomination process in the lead-up to *Dobbs* was a major enabling factor in the decision, further delegitimizing the Court and any respect we have for its decision.

Politics of Exclusion: Originalism

While not necessarily tied to judicial theories of constitutional interpretation, my argument is that the institutional and imaginative orders of U.S. society are often limited by the legal apparatuses in ways that make social justice difficult to achieve. This becomes particularly noticeable in the context of so-called "originalist" types of reading the Constitution, such as *Dobbs*. I use the phrase "originalist types of reading" to denote the fact that there is no *one* school of "originalism." As the preeminent constitutional scholar Erwin Chemerinsky notes, there are "many variations of originalism" which "all share a central belief that the meaning of a constitutional provision is fixed when it is adopted and can be changed only by amendment."[3] Moreover, Chemerinsky notes, three propositions characterize the originalist approach to constitutional analysis:

> (1) the meaning of the constitutional text is fixed at the time of ratification; (2) judges should give the meaning a primary role in constitutional interpretation; and (3) pragmatic concerns and consequences are not allowed to trump discoverable original meaning.[4]

Generally, an originalist position maintains that, when interpreting the Constitution, we should do so as it was originally written using the text as it would have been understood by people living at the time it was conceived. "In interpreting the Constitution," declared successful Supreme Court nominee Samuel A. Alito Jr.:

> I think we should proceed in the way we proceed in interpreting other important legal authorities. In interpreting statutes, for example, I think we should look to the text of the Constitution and we should look to the meaning that someone would have taken from the text of the Constitution at the time of its adoption.[5]

Supreme Court nominee Amy Coney Barrett spoke similarly at her confirmation hearings: "I interpret the Constitution as a law, that I interpret its text as text, and I understand it to have the meaning it had at the time people ratified it. So that meaning doesn't change over time. And it's not up to me to update it or infuse my own policy views into it."[6] The late Justice Antonin Scalia argued, "What the Constitution meant when it was adopted is what it means today, and its meaning doesn't change just because we think that meaning is no longer adequate to our times."[7] And Supreme Court Justice Clarence Thomas claimed, "Our country was founded on the view that a correct understanding of the nature of God and the human person is critical to preserving the liberty that we so enjoy."[8] As articulated by these four justices, the originalist view assumes a fixed meaning for the text that can somehow be definitively known and that does not change over time and circumstance, a sort of supra-constitutional rule that has primacy and unquestionable status over all else.[9] In short, for originalists, the constitution is what it is—judges *find* it, they do not *make* it through the interpretive act, which is how we normally think of a "judgment." With a "judgment," as opposed to, say, an edict, someone with specialized training and a discerning eye must often reconcile the irreconcilable, making the best of a bad situation, or harmonize different conflicting interests. This is an important reason why we use human beings, and not computers, to operate our judiciary. Judges and Justices are tasked with making a *choice* from a set of limited, perhaps less-than-ideal, outcomes justifying that choice to others in the judiciary, the other branches of government, and to the public. In the often-repeated words of Justice Felix Frankfurter, "The

Court's authority—possessed of neither the purse nor the sword—ultimately rests on sustained public confidence in its moral sanction."[10]

In other words, courts must *own* their decisions, and accept responsibility for all its consequences. Justice is not the mechanical or passive application of legal rules and principles. Such applications, when blindly followed or haphazardly executed, frequently lead to unjust results and autocratic political outcomes. While the rules and principles of constitutional government matter, only with *context* can they have meaning. The weight and the saliency of the rules and principles fluctuate, which is why judging is an *art*, not a science, and the art of judging takes this into consideration. As the influential federal appellate court Judge Learned Hand once noted,

> I like to think that the work of a judge is an art [. . .]. It is a bit of craftsmanship [. . .]. It is what a poet does, it is what a sculptor does. He [or she] has some vague purposes and he has an indefinite number of what you might call frames of preferences among which he must choose; for choose he has to, and he does.[11]

Originalists disagree profoundly with this point I am making. For them, the meaning of the Constitution is *a priori* and beyond discussion and debate, something lesser minds than their own cannot see or appreciate, which is why they must *declare* what it is and shut down all alternative discussions. In the end, Justices Scalia, Thomas, Alito, and Barrett know best (this is a truncated list). This makes me wonder why we even need a nine-person Court. Any one originalist who is sufficiently pious would be enough, as the interpretative theory of originalism makes all "true-seeing" justices fungible. After all, absent a successful amendment process, the literal Constitution does *not* change ever, for any reason. If the text reads "men" it means men, not *women*. If the Constitution states that slaves are to be counted as "three-fifths" of a "free" citizen for the purposes of determining congressional representation, then that is what we have.[12] If we the people, who must live under the Constitution and depend upon it for our liberty and dignity, do not like the meaning that exists in the Constitution, the originalists tell us that we are free to *amend* the Constitution. That is our only recourse and our responsibility.

This suggestion of amending the Constitution to rid it of things we do not like, say, racism, sexism, homophobia/transphobia, or economic oligarchy, however, is profoundly disingenuous. Proponents of this originalist view ignore how amending the Constitution is an incredibly difficult task (Chemerinsky calls this "*the* defining characteristic" of the document)[13] given Article V and the complexity and politics of this ideologically divided nation.

Article V provides two ways to amend the Federal Constitution: (1) A vote of two-thirds of both the House of Representatives and the Senate followed by a ratification of three-fourths of the various state legislatures (i.e., ratification by 38 states), and (2) A Convention called for this purpose by two-thirds of the state legislatures, if the Convention's proposed amendments are later ratified by three-fourths of the state legislatures.[14] Drew DeSilver notes, "Of the roughly 12,000 amendments proposed since the Constitutional Convention, only 33 have gone to the states for ratification, and just 27 have made it all the way into the Constitution."[15]

Seen from a liberal perspective, the most important amendments to the Constitution are those that buttress our democratic commitments by protecting fundamental principles of liberty and self-government, particularly the Bill of Rights (Amendments 1–10) and the Civil War Amendments (#'s 13–15). Other amendments address defects or issues not envisioned in 1789, such as Presidential disability and succession (Amendment 25) or popular election of U.S. Senators (Amendment 17). While these amendments have helped modernize and liberalize the Constitution with great social impact, its limitations remain in that it is a conservative document that often places property interests ahead of human needs, making it difficult for government to create solutions to pressing problems such as systemic poverty, de facto discrimination, and global warming.[16]

While a stabilizing force politically (relative to other political systems), the Constitution often reifies an unjust social order, serving as a roadblock from democratic change. Some of its harshness has been mediated by liberal Supreme Court readings, particularly in the twentieth century[17] and by the politics of dissent, which often provide political cover for more progressive Courts in their reasoning. In other words, absent Supreme Court interpretation (or with it from an originalist Court), we are stuck with the default position of the Framers, with all their social, moral, and epistemological blinders; shortcomings; and idiosyncrasies; as well as their idealization of the beneficence of state government. How hopeless things appear, as they do now, if we remove the potential for a progressive judiciary from the picture. Absent catastrophic or existential threats to our nation (as perhaps perceived on the morning of September 11, 2001), national unity on even the most worthwhile of topics is highly unlikely (e.g., the inability of the states to ratify the Equal Rights Amendment).

What goes unanswered by originalists is *why*, precisely, should we give the Framers such deference, especially when all their faults, bigotries, and bias are glaringly obvious and become more so with the passage of time? Why re-entrench the backward, socially exclusive, and downright offensive views of the genocidal, slaveholding, bigoted, religiously intolerant, sexist, wealthy, and proto-homophobic individuals and communities who founded our nation? We are so much better than they were. Where they had good ideas, we should use them (which we have to our benefit), but why treat the Constitution like fundamentalists of any religion treat their respective holy texts? Regardless of how we may feel about such pious people (they may be respectable or contemptible, saints or fools), nobody mistakes religiously pious people for being open-minded, flexible, and socially inclusive. To the contrary, such people are often blinded by their pigheadedness. While it was once common, few jurisprudentially-minded people today (outside of Natural Law theorists in the Catholic tradition)[18] think that making theocratic or neo-theocratic arguments is a good basis for legal reasoning or a good way to organize society. Such arguments and ways of governance do not model or enhance the critical thinking and moral openness that we expect from a secular judiciary in a modern age which must balance and reconcile competing interests in ways that religious devotees are not capable. Religion, in particular fundamentalist or orthodox religion, is mostly Manichean; the law, as described here in progressive terms, its antithesis.

People who advance an originalist position argue that their view comports with the "nature" of a constitution, which was intended to bind and limit any one generation from ruling according to the "passion of the times." I understand this concern. Such "passions" may be terrifying, especially when they conjure up racial or other types of demons that turn people into mobs bent on lynching or destroying property (e.g., The Tulsa Race Massacre in 1921), which, in fact, were common in this country despite the Rule of Law, and with government complicity when such violence served the interests of white supremacy. But if the "passion of the times" is to *abrogate* slavery, for example, and to fight *for* political and social inclusion for women and minorities, then we do not want constitutional or political roadblocks. In the face of such progressive effort, constitutional recalcitrance itself becomes the problem. In the language of the jurist Learned Hand, "If we are able to keep our democracy, there must be one commandment: Thou Shalt Not Ration Justice."[19] In my terms, we *want* decisive federal action to counter state-level injustice, just as we want it to fight the causes and effects of climate change and other existential threats to our survival. Intelligent collective action, in service of goals unachievable at the local level, is a good thing. If done conscientiously, it may be the *only thing* that can save us from ourselves. Conservative obsolescence in the face of illogical premises, deep-seated irrational fears, or outworn beliefs and religious dogma keeps us from doing what needs to be done, with tragic consequences.

The same principle for federal action applies to efforts to eradicate sexism and homophobia. States that practice, or encourage its citizens to practice such harms, need to be stopped, their "sovereignty" notwithstanding. The question, therefore, is *not* "limited or unlimited government" or "strong or weak government," but what *kind* of government will we have and who gets included in "the people." Any government that pits one class of people against another or uses the mechanism of power to enrich its own privileges at the expense of others, is *not* a government worth defending, no matter how "democratic" it appears on paper. "We the People" means *all* of us and that we fight, collectively, toward this end.

Originalism ignores this question of "the people" because it knows the answer (i.e., "the people") is exclusive and limited (white men, property owners, Christians of a particular sect, etc.). It further ensures limited government by constricting citizenship as much as possible to the ideal represented by these "types" and demonizes all others. And it elevates to a "biblical" level authority for these historical choices. The Framers defined what they thought was the proper scope of government once and for all, according to their experience, and that becomes the final word. According to originalists all the "balancing" that is needed in constitutional adjudication was done by the Framers: they "fixed the limits." Originalism, therefore, constricts the judiciary, whose job (absent this arbitrary restraint) is to *balance* and *weigh* competing interests as it appears to us today.[20] With originalism, however, such balance and weighing are off the table.

Originalists claim that they are preventing the court from asserting its "will," one perceived as "elitist" and "undemocratic." Originalists do not trust judges who are "unelected" and "disconnected" from "the people." They prefer what they see as the "careful mix" of institutional arrangements set up by the Framers that are charged with making policy, each accountable, in some ways, to the electorate, as defined minimally (i.e., restricted by social class, race, gender, and religion[21]). This point was made by Robert Bork who, in 1971, set the tone for the modern discussion of originalism.[22] Bork championed a restricted review of juridical interpretation and protection in the First Amendment context, holding it to a neutered form of political speech, protecting only political *debate* among social and economic *equals* ("elites" in the true negative sense of the word) but not political *dissent* (i.e., what the rest of us think). In it he explained that only rights that can be explicitly found in the text of the Constitution or "clearly intended" should be recognized.

Politics of Inclusion: Constructivism

This originalist/conservative view can be contrasted with a constructivist/liberal perspective which is an attempt to interpret the Constitution to adapt it to the needs of each generation with its rapidly changing demographics, thus making it supple and adaptable, giving it a poetic Emersonian hue. "It is an inadmissibly narrow conception of American constitutional law to confine it to the words of the Constitution and to disregard the gloss which life has written upon them."[23] Such an approach also helps guard against the stultifying effects of orthodoxy (religious, legal, or otherwise) with its drab dogmas, crusty blinders, false dichotomies, and dubious weights. As George Orwell observed, "Orthodoxy of whatever color seems to demand a lifeless, imitative style."[24] This is true in law as in life. An "orthodox" Constitution is, in many respects, a cruel one, exalting form over function, giving the "dead hand" of the Framers a zombie-like presence to continue their ancient prejudices. As Thomas Jefferson wisely noted:

> [L]aws and institutions must go hand in hand with the progress of the human mind. As that becomes more developed, more enlightened, as new discoveries are made, new truths disclosed, and manners and opinions change with the change of circumstances, institutions must advance also, and keep pace with the times. We might as well require a man to wear the coat which fitted him when a boy, as civilized society to remain ever under the regimen of their barbarous ancestors.[25]

Like orthodox religion, an orthodox constitution is a type of prison for the mind, if not the heart. Such stance shrinks the terrain and truncates the spirit upon which human freedom and happiness can flourish. This critique of orthodoxy is apropos of originalist writing style. In *Dobbs*, for example, we could predict the outcome and reasoning of the opinion before a single line of the decision was written.

In contrast, constructivists maintain that the Constitution has relevant meaning beyond the "original text." They argue that articulations/assertions of textual meaning are often historically misleading and laden with contemporary meaning in the mind of the interpreter (i.e., Scalia's views of the past are not *the* past, they are his achronistic/idealistic reconstruction of it which, intentionally or not, fits his political world view). Rather, what the constitution means can only be determined when it is viewed as an evolving and dynamic document that changes over time in relationship to new contingencies, new understandings of old issues, and new ethical or moral dilemmas. A constructivist mindset, one like the philosophy of law known as Legal Realism, views law as not simply a result of a written text, but a product of the views of judicial decision-makers, as well as social, economic, and contextual influences that wash over all of our lives.[26]

For constructivists, law functions "organically," adapting itself to the changing dynamics of society. It recognizes that common law and constitutional adjudication is an inherently subjective system that produces inconsistent and sometimes incoherent and unjust results that are largely based on the political, social, and moral predilections of state and federal judges.[27] Recall how slavery, in particular, received significant protection in the original Constitution, while at the same time the Constitution loudly and proudly proclaimed a new era of liberty and equality for all men. Therefore, the views and needs of present society, along with its experience of the past, should be considered when interpreting key constitutional provisions. As Justice William J. Brennan Jr. explained:

> The Framers discerned fundamental principles through struggles against particular malefactions of the Crown; the struggle shapes the particular contours of the articulated principles. But our acceptance of the fundamental principles has not and should not bind us to those precise, at times anachronistic, contours.[28]

In other words, the Constitution is at its most valuable when it is read to embody important values, not literal prescriptions, as the prescriptions it does offer are contextualized by the exigencies from which they emerged. For example, it is no longer the literal "desk drawer" in the study of the lord or master that is off limits to a warrantless search, but the Global Positioning System (GPS) devices attached to the cars, luggage, and phones of everyday people that receive consideration. As Brennan notes:

> Successive generations of Americans have continued to respect these fundamental choices and adopt them as their own guide to evaluating quite different historical practices. Each generation has the choice to overrule or add to the fundamental principles enunciated by the Framers; the Constitution can be amended or it can be ignored. Yet with respect to its fundamental principles, the text has suffered neither fate.[29]

This constructionist view is sometimes called the "Living Document" approach which views the Constitution holistically as a dynamic organism meaningful in the context of modern contemporary problems. It can be seen exemplified by Justice Oliver Wendell Holmes Jr. when he noted that

> the provisions of the Constitution are not mathematical formulas having their essence in their form; they are organic, living institutions transplanted from English soil. Their significance is vital, not formal; it is to be gathered not simply by taking the words and a dictionary, but by considering their origin and the line of their growth.[30]

Period dictionaries, it should be noted, are the preferred resource of originalists who use them to understand what the text of the Constitution means. In dictionaries, originalists claim to find the crystallization or the essence of a text's "eternal" meaning. What they fail to realize, however, is that period dictionaries are little more than museums or mausoleums containing remnants, fragments of what was (or what we *think* was). The materials of such institutions have long shed their flesh or relevance (they are as dead as stone) and exist only as suggestions of what *could* be, which would be the pragmatic constructionist approach to the issue.

Constructionists understand that the past has life for us only to the extent that it causes us to *think* or *be* in a certain way, one qualitatively different than the past. Society is not static; one way or another it will change, and efforts to keep it *one* way is a type of violence with implications for specific groups of people (usually those with the least amount of power). Law must grow from, and with, society. As Holmes noted, past constitutional text-making has

> called into life a being the development of which could not have been foreseen completely by the most gifted of its begetters. It was enough for them to realize or to hope they had created an organism; it has taken a century and has cost their successors much sweat and blood to prove that they created a nation. The case before us must be considered in the light of *our whole experience* and not merely in that of what was said a hundred years ago.[31]

In the context discussed above, we can understand what President Woodrow Wilson meant when he wrote that "Government is not a machine, but a living thing."[32] Wilson argues that government is "Darwinian" (dynamic, growing, evolving) and not "Newtonian" (mechanical, locked in, predictable) in nature due to its ability to modify itself in relationship to its environment which is constantly changing under what Wilson calls the "sheer pressure of life."[33] As life is dependent on its environment, government is dependent on its interactions with others and its "community of purpose." Government consists of a body of people, not "blind forces" that make the decisions upon which we structure our lives.[34] Such "purpose" is necessarily vague and can only be understood experientially. This is what Holmes meant when he called the constitution "an experiment, as all life is an experiment. Every year, if not every day, we have to wager our salvation upon some prophecy based upon imperfect knowledge."[35] Thus, Wilson concludes, "Living political constitutions must be Darwinian in structure and in practice. Society is a living organism and must obey the laws of life, not of mechanics; it must develop."[36] Step by step, society progresses (or tries to progress) against the stubborn headwinds of a recalcitrant Court.

An important idea animating constructivism is that interpreting the Constitution in accordance with long outdated (and horrendous) views can lead to unacceptable outcomes. These include, for example, endorsing the doctrine of military conquest to legitimize the forced dispossession of Native American lands,[37] the forced return by federal forces of runaway slaves seeking sanctuary in free states,[38] the sanctioning of racial apartheid,[39] the banning of interracial intimacy,[40] second-class status for residents of our captured territories abroad (American Samoa, Guam, the Northern Mariana Islands, Puerto Rico, the U.S. Virgin Islands, and formally the Philippines),[41] white supremacist racial laws generally,[42] the outlawing of same-sex sexual relationships,[43] and denying associational and familial rights to non-nuclear or non-traditional families.[44] These and other intolerable legislation have long existed in this country, with significant degrees of popular and political support.

Thus, I remain puzzled by Justice Scalia when he asks:

> What secret knowledge ... is breathed into lawyers when they become Justices of this Court, that enables them to discern that a practice which the text of the Constitution does not clearly proscribe, and which our people have regarded as constitutional for 200 years, is in fact unconstitutional?[45]

Such knowledge is no secret: I call it an evolved sense of justice and equality, the result of a sharper national moral imagination. So when Scalia laments, "Day by day, case by case, [the Court] is busy designing a Constitution for a country I do not recognize,"[46] I reply, "I should hope so." Things such as sexism, racism, imperialism, and discriminatory heterosexuality, which have long defined the nation, need to be challenged and removed. This is no less true when, in our diverse and geographically large society, many places in our nation (in the South, for example) hold racist, sexist, nativist, and homophobic sentiments, sometimes nakedly but often clothed in religious dress. Anyone who pays attention to what occurs each day across this country can see this.

Even today, in a growing number of places, the above contemptible, despicable views are resurfacing and flexing their muscles, as exemplified in Donald Trump's "Make America Great Again" movement with all the hatred and resentment it amplified and continues to presage. Unfortunately, the *Dobbs* decision has provided political and legal cover for this way of thinking, rewarding the forces of intolerance and reactionism. This is unacceptable because the Constitution and the Courts are supposed to *protect* us from prejudice and discrimination by authoritarian majorities. To cite Chemerinsky again, the "preeminent purposes of the Court are to protect the rights of minorities who cannot rely on the political process and to uphold the Constitution in the face of repressive desires of political majorities."[47] Without such protection, the Rule of Law and the Constitution itself are *meaningless*, as the U.S. history of what white supremacy used to call "racial relations" attests.

To avoid such outcomes, we can articulate constitutional contemporary meaning in the context of everyday people from the broad and flexible terms in which the text of the constitution is situated. The terms "equality," "liberty," and "due process of law" are only unnecessarily made complicated by legal scholasticism, draining the concepts of their important (and obvious) meaning. We know *what* freedom looks like, and slavery and segregation are *not* it. Neither is the harassment of sexual minorities. Likewise, forcing women to carry an unwanted fetus to term is *neither* freedom *nor* liberty. It is boorish barbarianism.

In the above sense, U.S. constitutionalism in its broadest ethos means finding ways to balance fundamental interests (e.g., between "privacy" and "security" or "freedom" and "equality") among diverse populations. It means not privileging religion over non-religion, business profit over workers and the environment, men over women, straights over queers, and whites over blacks and other minorities. This means that religious biases remain with the holder and are not imposed on others (in other words, religious exemptions to generally applicable laws intended to prevent discrimination are per se unacceptable).[48] It means removing (or reducing as much as possible) the hierarchical and structural inequality that prevents all citizens from interacting meaningfully in the public sphere. Social justice is not "rocket science," but it does require an open mind and a willingness to consider the subjectivities of others, a trait more grounded in liberalism than conservativism (and among atheists than religionists).[49]

In short, liberal constitutionalism, in its American expression, means creating space for everyone to thrive on their own terms so long as they do not infringe on the rights of others. This is not a difficult concept to understand. Those of us who have been paying attention to recent events, both in the United States and in many places throughout the world, wonder why, with growing concern, liberalism is under such attack. Liberalism seems natural, normative, and inevitable in any society that aspires to be democratic. Of course, not every society has such aspirations, and many want to define themselves on ethnic or religious terms which carry with them an array of deleterious outcomes. For those societies, democracy is threatening, although, I will argue, still a moral imperative. Of those nations that practice (or strive to practice) democracy, its people recognize (or ought to recognize) that liberalism is a desirable and reasonable response to religious warfare and racial persecution that plagued Western nations for centuries. Such communities should also be welcoming of immigrants fleeing from illiberal societies.[50]

While the Drafters of the Constitution feared a "powerful central government," as they should, they also wanted state government to address the needs of "the people" (at least as they defined it, which was narrowly and rigidly). With national maturity, however, and after great struggle and sacrifice, we have learned as a nation to relax the boundaries of that exclusion to be more welcoming and generous with the franchise and the so-called "blessings of liberty." Even if it was not the intention of the Framers, it has become clear that, without meaningful federal oversight, local and state governments can, and often do, act as hatefully, irrationally and illiberally as the old-world European powers that the Founders of our nation fled. We must not forget that old-world illiberalism was the foundation of the great (meaning terrible) imperial empires, perpetual war throughout Europe and beyond, leading up to two catastrophic world wars and the continuing threat of total nuclear annihilation. That bloody, intolerant world finally collapsed, for the most part, in 1945 and from the ruins rose degrees of political and social liberalism. In many cases, democracy spread and "the people" of the many European nations increasingly gained a voice and a place at their respective tables.

Constitutional Interpretation and White Male Supremacy

Back home following the war, the rising tide of liberalism fought against deep-seated American racism over the questions: Who are "the people" that our Constitution serves? Who among us Americans is included in the document which claims to be for all, as represented in that seldom achieved aspiration, "equal justice under the law?" We today would like to think the Constitution serves all of us who live in this country, but it does not.[51] This may appear shocking to many of us twenty-first-century able-bodied, cis-gendered, cosmopolitan, liberal, professional, middle-class, and above all, *white male* heterosexual members of post-World War II liberalism whose inclusion in the liberal state we take for granted. It is *less* shocking for everyone else: women, immigrants, ethnic and religious minorities, blue-collar workers, the poor, and queer people who feel (and are, in fact) excluded from many of the constitutional values and legal opportunities that protect majority subjectivities. They may be "citizens," but they are not *of* "the people" who receive equal justice or equal rights under the law.

Obviously, Black people were long denied the status of "the people" under the U.S. Constitution. This was reiterated in the infamous *Dred Scott v. Sandford* decision of 1857, holding that Black people, descendants of Africans who were captured and brought in chains to America for slavery, were excluded from constitutional considerations and protections. The Court read the relevant history and concluded that the Constitution simply was not written for Black Americans. The Court could thus disclaim its own responsibility in perpetrating an egregious historical wrong, giving American slavery an extended lease on life.

According to the *Dred Scott* Court, they were simply acquiescing to the "will" of the Framers who carefully and conscientiously crafted a document that entrenched and protected the institutionalized slavery of Black people. They disclaimed, as originalist courts are apt to do, that "[i]t is not the province of the court to decide upon the justice or injustice, the policy or impolicy, of these laws [of slavery]. The decision of that question belonged to the political or law-making power; to those who formed the sovereignty and framed the Constitution."[52] This situation, of course, changed with the North's victory in the bloody Civil War, and with the subsequent Reconstruction Amendments to the Constitution (1865–1870) which were hoisted by bayonets upon an unwilling and resentful South.[53] As a result, even originalist courts acknowledged the change in the legal landscape and came to treat Black people with an iota of more respect, at least within the extremely limited parameters established by the *Slaughter-House Cases* and its progeny.[54]

In recent years, because of the Civil Rights Movement (1954–1968) and the heyday of Second Wave feminism (circa 1960–1980), the federal government tried to make life better for Black people and women. Modest successes, however, were met with massive popular and political backlash, often with the Court's blessing, using a newly honed originalist perspective courtesy of jurists like Bork and Scalia. For example, so-called "colorblind" restrictions on *ameliorative* social programs dealing with poverty and education, as championed by Bork, Scalia, and others on the current Supreme Court, serve to reinforce and perpetuate the legal, political, and social inequalities of the past. Justice Scalia also rejected so-called "racial preferences" for administrators to ameliorate social inequality, calling it "a historic trivialization of the Constitution."[55] More recently, Chief Justice Roberts noted, in a case where the Court ruled it unconstitutional for school officials to consider race as a *factor* in assigning students to a particular school to reflect a balanced racial composition among the district's schools that "[t]he way to stop discrimination on the basis of race is to stop discriminating on the basis of race."[56] Such cheap, misleading, simplistic tautology is designed to eviscerate thought and remediative action necessary for social justice.[57]

At the same time, Scalia and other originalists, with their reverence for the "Founding Fathers," their generation of morals, statesmanship, and values, show little appreciation for the *other* ways throughout history in which the Constitution has been (and continues to be) "trivialized" in *support of racial inequality* grounded in "race" and "blood" or principles of "white supremacy" (the words of the Court in *Loving v. Virginia*).[58] Scalia, without any apparent appreciation for the not-so-subtle nuances of legal history, confidently states:

> [U]nder our Constitution there can be no such thing as either a creditor or a debtor race. That concept is alien to the Constitution's focus upon the individual, and its rejection of dispositions based on race, or based on blood. To pursue the concept of racial entitlement—even for the most admirable and benign of purposes—is to reinforce and preserve for future mischief the way of thinking that produced race slavery, race privilege and race hatred. In the eyes of government, we are just one race here. It is American.[59]

While nominally and intuitively fair and commonsensical on its face, this colorblind, do-not-look-at-the-past-as-if-it-is-immaterial view, at the expense of a social justice or critical perspective, is problematic. It ignores and reifies the racially unjust realities of life in this nation by drawing away attention from communities of color that are ignored, dehumanized, and suffering in the *present* due to their non-normative status and condition of disempowerment. Scalia's view denies the fact that such marginalization and alienation that exists for vast swaths of the American population is the result of *centuries* of oppression, reinvented and updated as the times and circumstances of national life change, which has created nearly insurmountable barriers to their success. As expressed by President Lyndon B. Johnson in 1965:

> You do not wipe away the scars of centuries by saying: Now you are free to go where you want, and do as you desire, and choose the leaders you please. You do not take a person who, for years, has been hobbled by chains and liberate him, bring him up to the starting line of a race and then say, "you are free to compete with all the others," and still justly believe that you have been completely fair.[60]

"Color-blindness" ideology in today's America is a self-serving defense of inequality and an attempt to absolve ourselves of responsibility for the profoundly racist world we have inherited and the colossal economic disparities that exist among our citizens. It is an excuse not to change and to embrace a reactionary ignorance over an informed cultural intelligence and policies designed to make a difference. Simply, to be "color blind" is to selfishly cling to one's own inherited privileges and to mistakenly believe that one has achieved success *solely* on one's merits.[61]

While race, of course, does not matter in terms of a person's status as a citizen and abilities as an individual, the inconvenient fact is that race *does* matter in ways that reinforce the social inequities baked into our system by the legacy of white supremacy. In effect, such a "colorblind" approach as advocated by Justice Scalia and others reifies the historical inequities that ground current social inequality while ignoring the *actual* ways in which people are discriminated against because of their race.[62] While we, living in the United States sometimes for generations, are all, colloquially, "American," we have been constructed socially and legally into categories of different *value*. This value is grounded in an economic and ideological superstructure that limits our agency and life potential. Man/woman, white/black, straight/gay, Christian/Jew, able/disabled and the intersections among these categories (and with different racial/ethnic groups), along with variations of social class, access to health care, and educational opportunities, have a great deal to do with how much "freedom" we experience, how much agency we can express in our lives.

While the law is not responsible for all variation and malleability of a person's status per se (obviously, an individual's choices and happenstance play an important role), the law *is* responsible to the extent that it ignores the historical reification of these as legal categories with certain social privilege, granting them the veneer of inevitability—for example, in the context of race.[63] More practically, the law *is* the problem when it is interpreted as *preventing* positive statutory remedial action that could make a difference in improving the lives of individuals. Much has been written on the continuing effects of slavery and racism in our society and more needs to be done, particularly in the face of so-called anti-Critical Race Theory legislation and educational pushback among Republican politicians who want Americans to remain blissfully ignorant of the reason why there has been an outpouring of calls for racial and social justice in recent years.[64] This history is real, and denialism and parochial, petty politics does not change that fact, just as sexism (as I show in Chapters 3 and 4) has been real throughout our history with similar lingering consequences. The implications of *both* need to be addressed if the American experiment in democracy is to succeed. The fight over the *history* of racism (or sexism) in the United States is the fight over the continuing *presence* and *practice* of racism (and sexism) in the United States. The legacies of both remain salient in preventing social opportunity among large segments of the population, and the degrees to which the law takes *cognizance* of it and provides tools for combating it can and should be addressed.

Sexism is real, although its persistence in society is often underappreciated and *naturalized* under the belief that there is something "real" (and by "real," I mean, "essentially important") about *sex distinctions* that justify treating women and men differently, which is what we see throughout the Common Law Tradition, to the detriment of women. Confronting this essentialism regarding women and the gendered legacies with which they live is an important legal and political task: the gaining of an Equal Rights Amendment (ERA). With the absence of an ERA, however, first proposed in 1923 but never ratified by the states, courts are allowed to attach difference and draw legal conclusions between men and women which, in most every case I can think of, is little more than a reassertion of ancient sexist assumptions that privilege men and disadvantage women. In one extreme case, for example, Justice Scalia maintains that women are *not* included in the Fourteenth Amendment because that amendment was clearly written to address the rights of formerly enslaved Black *men* (recall Black *women* were excluded from the Fifteenth

Amendment) at a time in which the Common Law Tradition's biases against women were particularly pervasive.[65]

A critical, constructivist perspective, one grounded in the needs of the present as well as in an understanding of the experience of the past (with all of its obfuscations and mystifications), is concerned with those who exist on the margins of society, often as dispensable, unwanted people (i.e., "surplus population," poor people of color, or immigrants)[66] or as "second-class" citizens in the case of women, generally, which is the subject matter of this book. This critical focus inspires and requires advocates to identify and to engage the structures that place certain communities in the periphery of society and keep them there across generations (or centuries, as in the case of women).

Conclusion

My bone of contention with *Dobbs* is not that the Court can, and did, provide an "originalist reading" on the topic of reproductive freedom, which is of course, *a* way of reading the law. Yet, while they try to make it seem that way, originalism is *not* a privileged method of interpretation under the Constitution. According to Chemerinsky, "Originalism's adherents do not provide an explanation of why it is desirable to follow the views and understandings from centuries ago."[67] Nor does it do what it purports to do, "preventing judges from deciding cases according to their personal moral references."[68] As far as originalist judges go, their decisions, claimed to be "objectively obtained," align well with their political and religious ideology.[69]

This point was noticed by Stephen Eric Bronner. An originalist constitutionalism, he argues,

> mirrors the true believer's interpretation of the Bible, how the interests of strict constructionists advocated by "originalists" mirror those of the chauvinist, and how the refusal to redress pressing issues of difference and equality is justified by reliance on the supposedly timeless decisions of "great men" and the conservative disposition of elitists.[70]

Moreover, "originalism," continues Bronner, "serves as a vehicle for rolling back the advances made by subaltern groups."[71] He concludes, "Rather than adapt law to new circumstances, and highlight its critical and historical character, the originalist interpretation presupposes a mythical community in which the privileges and prejudices of white males were taken for granted."[72]

Along with many other scholars, I maintain that, for the above reasons, an originalist reading is not a good way to interpret the Constitution. Chemerinsky notes that, while tradition is "an important source that can inform decisions," it "should not limit the meaning of the Constitution."[73] But such limited perspective is precisely the *point* of originalist jurisprudence:

> For an originalist, nothing matters except what was thought when the provision was adopted. This limitation denies our ability to learn from all that has happened since, including from long-standing traditions of protecting rights and advancing equality, as well as from rethinking traditions that we should renounce.[74]

Or, as explained by the *Dobbs* dissent:

> As a matter of constitutional method, the majority's commitment to replicate in 2022 every view about the meaning of liberty held in 1868 has precious little to recommend it. Our law in this constitutional sphere, as in most, has for decades upon decades proceeded differently. It has considered fundamental constitutional principles, the whole course of the Nation's history and traditions, and the step-by-step evolution of the Court's precedents. It is disciplined but not static. It relies on accumulated judgments, not just the sentiments of one long-ago generation of men (who themselves believed, and drafted the Constitution to reflect, that the world progresses). And by doing so, it includes those excluded from that olden conversation, rather than perpetuating its bounds.[75]

Unfortunately, the integrity of the dissent's reasoning was lost on the *Dobbs* majority which ruthlessly pursued its own dogmatic agenda, hidden as it was as a piece of reasoned jurisprudent analysis. Recognizing this ruse is the first step for combating it.

Notes

1 Samuel A. Alito Jr., "Justice Alito Reflects on His Tenth Anniversary on #SCOTUS" (lecture, Federalist Society's Texas Chapters Conference, September 21, 2015). Retrieved from https://joshblackman.com/blog/2015/09/21/justice-alito-reflects-on-his-tenth-anniversary-on-scotus/. Readers should recall that Justice Alito was the author of the Court's *Dobbs* decision.

2 142 S.Ct. 2228 (2022).

3 *Worse Than Nothing: The Dangerous Fallacy of Originalism* (New Haven: Yale University Press, 2022), 14.

4 Ibid. Chemerinsky attributes this insight to Eric J. Segall, *Originalism as Faith* (New York: Cambridge University Press, 2018), 8.

5 *Confirmation Hearing on the Nomination of Samuel A. Alito Jr. to be an Associate Justice of the Supreme Court of the United States*, 109th Cong. (2006), 465.
6 Cited in Chemerinsky, 9. Justice Barrett was also a member of the *Dobbs* majority.
7 "Judicial Adherence to the Text of Our Basic Law: A Theory of Constitutional Interpretation" (lecture, Catholic University of America, October 18, 1996). Retrieved from https://www.proconservative.net/PCVol5Is225ScaliaTheoryConstlInterpretation.shtml.
8 "Faith and Reasoning are Mutually Reinforcing," in *Imprimis: A 50th Anniversary Collection*, ed. Douglas A. Jeffrey (Hillsdale College Press, 2022), 136. Thomas was also a member of the *Dobbs* majority.
9 For some reason, only religious (often Catholic, as in these four examples) conservatives can discern these meanings and the rest of us are denied an understanding, no matter how much constitutional law we may have studied. In writing this, I acknowledge that Justice Sonia Sotomayor is Catholic and part of the *Dobbs* dissent. I also want to acknowledge that there are many American Catholics, including high ranking U.S. government officials, who are Democrats and support reproductive freedom for women (e.g., President Joe Biden and former House Speaker Nancy Pelosi). That said, I am a legally trained liberal Jew and, thus, I am particularly sensitive to the threat posed by conservative Catholics, with their history of antisemitism and sympathy for fascist government. See J. F. Pollard, "Fascism and Catholicism," in *The Oxford Handbook of Fascism*, ed. R. J. B. Bosworth (Oxford University Press 2019), 166–184. I feel similarly about *any* person, no matter what religion, who uses their orthodoxy to limit other people's choices by imposing their religious values on the Constitution.
10 *Baker v. Carr*, 369 U.S. 186 (1962), 267, dissent.
11 *Remarks at Proceedings of a Special Session of the United States Court of Appeals for the Second Circuit in Commemoration of Judge Learned Hand's Completion of Fifty Years of Federal Service* (1959), 28–29.
12 Article 1. Section 2.
13 *The Case Against the Supreme Court* (New York: Penguin Books, 2014), 8.
14 See David E. Kyvig, *Explicit and Authentic Acts: Amending the U.S. Constitution, 1776–1995* (Lawrence, KS: University Press of Kansas, 1996).
15 "Proposed Amendments to the U.S. Constitution Seldom Go Anywhere," *Pew Research Center*, April 12, 2018, https://www.pewresearch.org/fact-tank/2018/04/12/a-look-at-proposed-constitutional-amendments-and-how-seldom-they-go-anywhere/#:~:text=Of%20the%20roughly%2012.
16 For example, the current Court's attack on the Administrative State. See Vicki Lens, "'Deconstructing the Administrative State': Legal Trends and Consequences," *Journal of Sociology & Social Welfare* 50, no. 2 (2023): 35–51. This attack was recently exemplified in *Loper Bright Enterprises v. Raimondo*, 143 S.Ct. 2429 (2024) which overturned the 40-year tradition of "agency deference," which commanded courts to defer to a regulatory agency's "reasonable interpretation" of legal ambiguity within a law enforced by that agency. Now, at the bequest of an industry subject to regulation, conservative courts with zero scientific expertise or environmental concern are empowered to second-guess and veto the discerning expertise of professional regulators.
17 Peter Irons, A *People's History of the Supreme Court* (New York: Penguin, 2006).
18 Stuart Banner, *The Decline of Natural Law* (New York: Oxford University Press, 2021).

19 "75th Anniversary Address to the Legal Aid Society of New York" (February 16, 1951). Retrieved from https://orinkerrblog.files.wordpress.com/2018/06/learned-hand-address-1.pdf.

20 A non-originalist but free speech absolutist position is chillingly similar in its effect on society, illustrating that, in many things, it is the *dogmatic* nature of the reasoning rather than the politics itself that creates problems for society. There are few absolutes in constitutional law, and efforts to create absolutes have negative implications in the daily lives of people. Case-in-point, the liberal Justice Hugo Black famously argued that "the First Amendment's unequivocal command that there shall be no abridgment of the rights of free speech and assembly shows that the men who drafted our Bill of Rights did all the 'balancing' that was to be done in this field." *Konigsberg v. State Bar of California*, 366 U.S. 36 (1961), 56. Black elaborates on this position in "Justice Black and First Amendment Absolutes: A Public Interview," *New York University Law Review* 37 (1962): 552–554. The social import of Black's position is that only literal speech is protected, not symbolic speech or actions, protests, or even much art.

21 See Alexander Keyssar, *The Right to Vote: The Contested History of Democracy in the United States* (New York: Basic Books, 2000), tracking the history of suffrage in the United States, noting state restrictions based on religious affiliation. To this day, the constitution of seven states (Arkansas, Maryland, Mississippi, North Carolina, South Carolina, Tennessee, and Texas) *ban* atheists from holding public office. As recently as 1997, the South Carolina Supreme Court ruled in *Silverman v. Campbell*, 486 S.E.2d, that its state constitutional ban on atheists holding public office was unenforceable on First Amendment Grounds and on Article VI, section 3 of the U.S. Constitution, prohibiting religious tests for public office. Decades earlier, in *Torcaso v. Watkins*, 367 U.S. 488 (1961), the U.S. Supreme Court ruled similarly, but these seven states, most of which are staunchly anti-abortion, did not seem to notice or care.

22 "Neutral Principles and Some First Amendment Problems," *Indiana Law Journal* 47, no. 1 (1971): 1–35.

23 Justice Felix Frankfurter, *Youngstown Sheet & Tube Co. v. Sawyer* 343 U.S. 579 (1952), concurrence.

24 "Politics and the English Language," *Horizon* 13, no. 73 (January 1946): 261.

25 Letter to Samuel Kercheval, July 12, 1816, in "American History from Revolution and Reconstruction to Beyond: The Letters of Thomas Jefferson 1743–1826," https://www.let.rug.nl/usa/presidents/thomas-jefferson/letters-of-thomas-jefferson/.

26 Justin Zaremby, *Legal Realism and American Law* (New York: Bloomsbury Academic, 2014).

27 See Karl Llewellyn, *The Bramble Bush* (New York: Oceana Publications, 1930).

28 Justice William J. Brennan Jr., "To the Text and Teaching Symposium" (speech, Georgetown University, October 12, 1985, Washington, DC); (Occasional Paper No. 2, The Federalist Society, Washington, DC, 1986), in *The Great Debate: Interpreting Our Written Constitution* (Washington, DC: The Federalist Society, 2010). Retrieved from https://fedsoc.org/commentary/publications/the-great-debate-justice-william-j-brennan-jr-october-12-1985.

29 Ibid.

30 *Gompers v. United States*, 233 U.S. 604 (1914), 610.

31 *Missouri v. Holland*, 252 U.S. 416 (1920), 433. Italics added.

32 *The New Freedom: A Call for the Emancipation of the Generous Energies of a People* (New York: Doubleday, Page, and Company, 1913), 47.

33 Ibid.
34 Ibid.
35 *Abrams v. United States*, 250 U.S. 616 (1919), 630.
36 *The New Freedom*, 48.
37 *Johnson v. McIntosh*, 21 U.S. 543 (1823), voiding land transfers from Native Americans to private individuals. The Court held that indigenous peoples were mere inhabitants with no ownership rights in the land, which had been vested in the United States as a result of independence from Britain, which had acquired the land rights previously through "discovery" and the "law of the sword."
38 *Prigg v. Pennsylvania*, 41 U.S. 539 (1842). The Court held that the Fugitive Slave Act of 1793, intending to effectuate Article IV, Section 2, Clause 3 of the U.S. Constitution ("The Fugitive Slave Clause"), precluded a free state and its citizens from helping escaped blacks avoid being forcibly removed and returned to servitude in a slave state by agents of their owners.
39 *Plessy v. Ferguson*, 163 U.S. 537 (1896), holding that the Fourteenth Amendment was not intended to promote social equality among the races and that state-imposed racial segregation was not per se unconstitutional.
40 *Loving v. Virginia*, 388 U.S. 1 (1967). The Court *struck down* state laws (16 states had such laws at the time) banning marriage between individuals of different races, holding that anti-miscegenation statutes violated the Due Process and the Equal Protection Clauses of the Fourteenth Amendment. Anti-miscegenation laws were routinely held against constitutional attack until *Perez v. Sharp* 198 P.2d 17 (1948), issued by the Supreme Court of California.
41 *The Insular Cases*, a collection of Supreme Court cases addressing the status of overseas U.S. lands (and people) taken from Spain as the spoils of war. See Tom C. W. Lin, "Americans, Almost and Forgotten," *California Law Review* 107, no. 4 (2019): 1249–1302.
42 Racial Integrity Act, Va. Stat. § 219 (passed March 8, 1924). See https://encyclopediavirginia.org/primary-documents/preservation-of-racial-integrity-1924/. For a discussion of how this act—intended to protect "white blood" from racial contamination—and U.S. racial attitudes in general influenced the racial laws of Nazi Germany, see James Q. Whitman, *Hitler's American Model: The United States and the Making of Nazi Race Law* (Princeton: Princeton University Press, 2017).
43 *Bowers v. Hardwick*, 478 U.S. 186 (1986), upholding state anti-sodomy laws for private consensual contact against the privacy claims of homosexuals.
44 Changed somewhat in *Moore v. City of East Cleveland*, 431 U.S. 494 (1977). The Court struck down a city zoning ordinance prohibiting a black grandmother from living with her grandchild and his cousin. It recognized the importance of a broader conceptualization of "family" than that limited to the "nuclear family."
45 Dissent, *Board of County Commissioners v. Umbehr*, 518 U.S. 668 (1996), 688–689.
46 Ibid.
47 *The Case Against the Supreme Court*, 298.

48 In *303 Creative v. Elenis*, 143 S.Ct. 2298 (2023), the Court did *exactly* this, permitting an exception to public accommodation laws for religious objectors on First Amendment grounds.

49 Liberalism, notes James L. Richardson, "resists sharp definition." Nevertheless, Richardson provides a "cluster of values" representing the liberal idea: political rationalism; hostility to autocracy and hierarchy; distaste for arbitrary authority and appeals to "tradition"; and tolerance, individualism, egalitarianism, meliorism, privacy, reason, science, and progress. *Contending Liberalisms in World Politics* (Boulder, CO: Lynne Rienner Publishers, 2001), 17–18.

50 See Omar Swartz, and Lucy W. McGuffey, "Migrating Pedagogy in American Universities: Cultivating Moral Imagination and Social Justice," *Communication Education* 67, no. 1 (2018): 102–109. I recognize that not everyone in the nation is onboard with my optimistic view of diversity, inclusion, and the importance to showing sensitivity to the needs of others. For example, Edward J. Erler writes, "Greater diversity means inevitably that we have less in common, and the more we encourage diversity the less we honor the common good. Any honest and clear-sighted observer should be able to see that diversity is a solvent that dissolves the unity and cohesiveness of a nation." "Does Diversity Really Unite Us? Citizenship and Immigration," in *Imprimis: A 50th Anniversary Collection*, ed. Douglas A. Jeffrey (Hillsdale College Press, 2022), 232.

51 Throughout most of his writing, philosopher Richard Rorty maintained a cautiously upbeat view of the potential of the United States to learn from its mistakes and serve to expand the cause of human decency. See, Rorty, *Achieving Our Country* (Cambridge, MA: Harvard University Press, 1998). By the end of his life in 2007, however, Rorty grew less optimistic, more caustic and disappointed, more fearful that he put his faith in a society no longer able or willing to create the culture he felt us capable of achieving. See Danny Postel, "Last Words from Richard Rorty," *The Progressive*, June 2007, 15.

52 60 U.S. (19 How.) 393.

53 Scholars have recognized two sources of objections that can be raised to the adoption of these amendments. First, whether or not the defeated confederate states had the legal competency to assent to ratification and, second, the extent to which the ratifications extorted assent by threat of force. These are discussed in John Harrison, "The Lawfulness of the Reconstruction Amendments," *The University of Colorado Law Review* 68 (2001): 375–462.

54 83 U.S. 36 (1873). The Supreme Court narrowed the Fourteenth Amendment by distinguishing between *federal* and *state* citizenship, giving responsibility for protecting civil rights to the *states*, making the Fourteenth Amendment a "dead letter" for almost a century. Federal privileges and immunities that existed at the time afforded to black citizens were few, including free access to seaports for purposes of foreign commerce; protection of life, liberty, and property on the high seas or within a foreign country; and the right of habeas corpus. In the *Civil Rights Cases*, 109 U.S. 3 (1883), the Court further held that the Thirteenth and Fourteenth Amendments were not a mechanism for Congress to pass laws protecting African-Americans from discrimination by private parties.

55 "The Disease as Cure: 'In Order to Get beyond Racism, We Must First Take Account of Race,'" *Washington University Law Quarterly* 147 (1979): 148.

56 *Parents Involved in Community Schools v. Seattle School District*, 551 U.S. 701 (2007), 748.

57 Building upon these views, affirmative action was finally ruled unconstitutional by the Court in *Students for Fair Admissions v. Harvard*, 600 U.S. 181 (2023).

58 388 U.S. 1 (1967), 7.

59 Concurrence, *Adarand Constructors, Inc. v. Peña*, 515 U.S. 200 (1995), 239.

60 "To Fulfill These Rights" (commencement address, Howard University, June 4, 1965). Retrieved from https://www.presidency.ucsb.edu/documents/commencement-address-howard-university-fulfill-these-rights. While the tactics of affirmative action need to change in response how racism is expressed today (U.S. society has changed since 1965 and our policies in addressing it need to change), ignoring or denying the problem is *not* a solution.

61 Pamela Walker Laird challenges this deeply entrenched national myth. See, *Pull: Networking and Success Since Benjamin Franklin* (Cambridge, MA Harvard University Press, 2007).

62 Eduardo Bonilla-Silva, *Racism Without Racists: Color-Blind Racism and the Persistence of Racial Inequality in America*, 6th ed. (New York: Rowman & Littlefield Publisher, 2021).

63 Ian Haney López, *White by Law: The Legal Construction of Race* (New York: New York University Press, 2006).

64 Critical Race Theory, which started in the 1970s, and the more recent *1619 Project*, grew out of prominent eras of police brutality against Black men, the despondency of the "school-to-prison" pipeline, and the intractability of the "new" Jim Crow. Michelle Alexander, *The New Jim Crow: Mass Incarceration in the Age of Colorblindness* (New York: The New Press, 2010). The significant economic and health disparities that exist between whites and People of Color (POC) further fueled these movements. For many Americans (and not just POC), our country's racist, sexist, and homophobic past continues to seem all-to-present. Outraged POC and their allies have started (once again) to organize against it. President Trump's tone-deaf public relations debacles when he addressed well publicized acts of racial/social violence/injustice resulted in widespread protests. In response, Trump and his media enablers spent months whipping the nation into an orgy of fear over progressive education policies. Christopher F. Rufo is the person most responsible for weaponizing dissatisfaction with CRT. See Benjamin Wallace-Wells, "How a Conservative Activist Invented the Conflict Over Critical Race Theory," *The New Yorker*, June 18, 2021, https://www.newyorker.com/news/annals-of-inquiry/how-a-conservative-activist-invented-the-conflict-over-critical-race-theory. Such policies, it was claimed (often without knowledge of the pedagogy involved), constituted "a harmful and divisive ideology" and a "warped, distorted" view of the United States which "promoted division" by teaching that the "United States of America is fundamentally racist or sexist." Critics also claimed that liberal attempts to teach history through the lens of the struggle for racial justice and inclusion "tries to make [white] kids feel bad." These quotes come from Char Adams, "How Trump Ignited the Fight Over Critical Race Theory in Schools," *NBC News*, May 10, 2021, https://www.nbcnews.com/news/nbcblk/how-trump-ignited-fight-over-critical-race-theory-schools-n1266701. For context and overview, see Francesca López, Alex Molnar, Royel Johnson, Ashley Patterson, LaWanda Ward, and Kevin Kumashiro, "Understanding the Attacks on Critical Race Theory" (Boulder, CO: *National Education Policy Center*, 2021), http://nepc.colorado.edu/publication/crt.

65 Max Fisher, "Scalia Says Constitution Doesn't Protect Women from Gender Discrimination," *The Atlantic*, January 4, 2011, https://www.theatlantic.com/politics/archive/2011/01/scalia-says-constitution-doesn-t-protect-women-from-gender-discrimination/342789/.

66 Tim Christiaens, "Financial Neoliberalism and Exclusion with and Beyond Foucault," *Theory, Culture & Society* 36, no. 4 (2019): 95–116.

67 *Worse Than Nothing*, xi.

68 Ibid.

69 I cannot help noticing that, of the eight Jewish Supreme Court justices who have sat on the bench (Louis D. Brandeis, Benjamin Cardozo, Felix Frankfurter, Arthur Goldberg, Abe Fortas, Ruth Bader Ginsburg, Stephen G. Breyer, and Elena Kagan), none of them are originalists and all of them were liberal. David G. Dalin, *Jewish Justices of the Supreme Court: From Brandeis to Kagan* (Waltham, MA: Brandeis University Press, 2017).

70 *The Bigot: Why Prejudice Persists* (New Haven, CT: Yale University Press, 2015), 183.

71 Ibid., 184.

72 Ibid.

73 *Worse Than Nothing*, 173.

74 Ibid.

75 *Dobbs*, 2333.

· 2 ·

LIBERAL AND RADICAL FEMINISM REVISITED

An important theme throughout the chapters of this book is that together, women and men clearly have their work cut out for them as we continue to create a culture of gender equality, one that is substantial and total, stripped of its masculinist assumptions, patriarchal ideology, and sexual exploitation.[1] In other words, we need to confront collectively our nation's embedded misogyny. In light of this task, it is important for men, particularly the men who write and support laws limiting a woman's access to birth control or reproductive health, to understand that "[w]omen consent to unwanted sex out of a sense of duty, or out of a need for material support if they are economically dependent upon the relationship for their own or their children's survival. Sometimes, women consent to unwanted sex out of a fear of future violence."[2] Simply, "When men have the power to make or destroy women's livelihoods, economic security, and other prospects for a decent life, women lack the power to refuse or prevent men's sexual advances."[3]

This critique of misogyny must be complete and uncompromising. It must be economic and must be grounded in a more realistic understanding of how female agency operates in the world under patriarchy. This *starts*, in short, with abortion rights:

> The basic freedom of the world is woman's freedom. A free race cannot be born of slave mothers. A woman enchained cannot choose but give a measure of that bondage to her sons and daughters. No woman can call herself free who does not own and control her body. No woman can call herself free until she can choose consciously whether she will or will not be a mother.[4]

The bulk of this effort, however, must be by women themselves. The great message of feminism as a social and political movement is to remake society by rejecting patriarchy in all its forms. While it is imperative that men help preserve for women the breathing space they need to grow and thrive, and while unjust laws can and are changed (and sometimes changed back again), women need to see themselves as fully fledged and equal members of society and to demand to be accepted as such, even, and particularly, when the law denies this. Admittedly, this can be difficult:

> Traditional female wisdom teaches us that a woman's face is her fortune, her sex appeal the bait, her body the promised payoff. Appearance, we learn, will either assure or deny a woman access to lust, love, acceptance, protection, social position and security. How can she then look at her body with a non-judgmental eye or see sex as a pleasurable end in itself?[5]

Women must learn to see themselves as equal to men and to live their lives on their terms, not those of men, and men need to be supportive of that goal. Then women can demand, as they have been doing, the equality which the law can then force men to respect. While some men are willing allies of women, many are not. Foundational to this respect is bodily autonomy, something men have seldom, if ever, granted women willingly.

We cannot assume, however, that all women have agreement on this task. Some women, of course, are feminists of one sort or another and take this message to heart and are willing to fight (again and again). These women tend to be college-educated or the children of college-educated parents. Some women, however, are *anti-feminist* and resist this change, often passionately and with political effectiveness (Phyllis Schlafly and Ann Coulter being notable examples). And some women simply do not think about these issues at all, as they live and struggle through their busy lives, focusing on their immediate needs or individualizing their situation. Men, however, and the masculinist assumptions baked into the law, are not going to give women the respect they deserve until women stand up and demand it, which, of course, has been the purpose of the feminist movement over the past 150 years, with remarkable success. Unfortunately, that movement has stalled in some respects, and many women continue to have internalized some of the very biases, prejudices, and oppressions that feminist scholars have tried hard to bring into the open and defeat.[6]

As Gail Pheterson notes, internalized oppression is the mechanism within an oppressive system for perpetuating domination not only by external control but also by building subservience into the minds of the oppressed groups, the "incorporation and acceptance by individuals within an oppressed group of the prejudices against them within the dominant society."[7] As she notes, internalized oppression involves varieties of self-hatred, self-concealment, fear of violence and feelings of inferiority, resignation, isolation, powerlessness, and gratefulness for being "allowed" to survive. This may lead women to express anger at other marginalized people (projection) rather than at the group that is oppressing them (men), which explains, in part, white, female racism. With this understanding in mind, this chapter seeks to highlight some of the various resources for resistance and change offered by two divergent strands of feminist thought: liberal and radical feminism.

MacKinnon, "Stalled" Liberal Feminism, and the Law

Before discussing Catharine A. MacKinnon's feminism we need to understand whom we can call a "feminist" (liberal, radical, or otherwise). Feminists are those of us who recognize that women have been, and continue to be, systemically and structurally disfavored by the law (and by most every other social institution) for most of recorded history, and likely before. We feminists not only recognize this condition as wrong but as a profoundly grave and egregious wrong in the way that we feel that racism, homophobia, and antisemitism are wrong. We believe that the continuing legal, political, and social subordination of women to men in law and in social practice is fundamentally and unequivocally unacceptable. Such status is sexist, chauvinistic, and anachronistic, and we feel motivated to do something about it through teaching, writing, protesting, and by enacting contrary, emancipatory values in our families and lives. Social justice begins at home, and if we cannot be kind and just to members of our own families, how can we expect to enact these values in the larger world? In short, we stand for a progressive and inclusive future for *all* people and stand opposed to the advocates of social, political, and legal intolerance.

One form of feminism, liberal feminism, works toward political and social autonomy for women in the context of a pluralistic and democratic society by encouraging state resources and public policy goals to increase health care access for all (including abortion and reproductive health access), mental health services, anti-discrimination laws in educational and workplace environments, anti-poverty programs, and equal protection. Liberal feminism works within the existing economic, political, and social frameworks of this country to incrementally improve the lives of women and their families. It urges our nation to live up to its highest ideals, championing those who fall through our society's many cracks while attempting to reduce the size and prevalence of such cracks. With all its faults, liberal feminism deserves much credit for the changes in the law and society since the 1970s that I will be discussing. This is, of course, not the only way to think of feminism.

MacKinnon, a widely known and prominent scholar and public intellectual in the 1980s and 1990s, provides a contrast to the liberal perspective. She had a significant legal and cultural impact on sexual harassment law, which we now take for granted. MacKinnon successfully advanced a legal theory, designed from the standpoint of women in their experience of work-life, for the purpose of helping them to resist the impact of patriarchal and sexist hierarchies in workplace relationships that took advantage of the vulnerabilities of female employees. She argued that injustices experienced by working women stemmed from their subordination to men in society and its parallel legal culture of patriarchy. For example, a man may think his behaviors toward women at work are affectionate, friendly, or fun while his female coworkers experience his conduct as threatening, demeaning, and damaging. These perceptions by women, MacKinnon maintained, are not idiosyncratic or psychological outliers, or something asocial about the women involved, but widespread and costly for women, and reflect what the law should, and now does, recognize as "sex discrimination," requiring deterrence and, when that does not work, punishment and victim compensation.[8]

MacKinnon's style of thinking is encouraging, relentless, and powerful. It is bold, provocative, and deeply insightful, even if some of her arguments have weaknesses or appear extreme. Her critique of pornography, for example, which stems from her work in sexual harassment law, and her recognition of power differentials between women and men is both conceptually and theoretically profound on the one hand, and practically, legally, and socially flawed on the other. MacKinnon, along with feminist activists Andrea Dworkin and Robin Morgan, views pornography as the "theory" of rape, sexualizing violence against women which demonizes all men and inherently victimizes all women, rejecting female agency and imposing government censorship over not just the adult entertainment industry (broadly construed), but over art, literature, and a wide range of communicative and social activity, generally.[9]

The strengths and weaknesses of MacKinnon's theory can be found highlighted by the U.S. Court of Appeals (Seventh Circuit) in *American Booksellers Association v. Hudnut.*[10] In striking down MacKinnon and Dworkin's model pornography ordinance enacted by the city of Indianapolis, the court praises MacKinnon's theoretical veracity while forcefully pointing out its sweeping negative effects on society, imposing a state-approved vision of sex, reminiscent of the disruptive draconian and irrational Comstockian laws (named for the psychotic regime of Anthony Comstock) of the nineteenth to mid-twentieth centuries to which few people would want our society to return.

Comstock (1844–1915) was one of this country's most successful moral entrepreneurs who exemplifies the dangerous nexus between religion, law, and misogyny that I am critiquing. A tireless crusader for "Christian values" and a stanch anti-feminist who "capitalized on a wave of anti-feminist sentiment," Comstock successfully campaigned and petitioned Congress for tough national censorship laws and installed himself as the enforcer of those laws. For decades, Comstock was our nation's official censor, who pursued his job with remarkable energy and enthusiasm.[11] His goal was to not only suppress erotic subject matter in art and literature, but to prevent information about sexuality, reproduction, and birth control from being circulated, setting back the birth-control movement many decades. His organization, *The New York Society for the Suppression of Vice* had, as its seal, two pictures: one, a policeman thrusting a hapless prisoner behind bars, and two, a burning pyre of books. As U.S. Postal Inspector, Comstock is reputed to have destroyed 15 tons of books and nearly 4,000,000 pictures. Comstock boasted that he was responsible for 4,000 arrests and 15 suicides.[12]

In my courses when I mention MacKinnon, few students know who she is. I am unsure of the reason (although Third Wave feminist critique of her work may have something to do with it). Is it because MacKinnon identifies as a "radical feminist," a term which upsets many people? Is it because MacKinnon's "dominance approach" to feminism asks us to think twice about common assumptions regarding sexuality, religion, family, the media, workplace relationships, interpersonal relationships, and the paternal presence of the state in our lives? Whatever the reason, people do not want to think about her anymore. Apologists for post-feminism certainly do not.

I suspect, however, that much of our amnesia involves MacKinnon's attack on "liberal feminism," which, to the extent that people identify with feminism at all, seems to be a more privileged (or safe) position to embody. She grounds her critique of liberalism in her feminist theory of power in which she describes power as "male." She writes, "Women and men are divided by gender, made into the sexes as we know them, by the social requirements of heterosexuality, which institutionalizes male sexual dominance and female sexual submission."[13] In other words, society is constituted through male domination in which women are systematically subordinated sexually in a sexualized, totalized order.[14]

Often called the "dominance approach," MacKinnon theorizes that the entire structure of society is a gendered hierarchy in which a woman's experience as victim is deeply structural. Women suffer not because of unintentional happenstance, for example, the timing of Supreme Court deaths, retirements, replacements and the politics surrounding these events,[15] but because society has been *specifically* and *intentionally* arranged this way by men—that society is skewed in the interests of men as a class and that buried bias operates fundamentally on how we interact with one another as women and men. Male dominance and privilege are protected politically, philosophically, and through the law. It is not any one impediment that is the problem, such as sexual harassment, domestic violence, the feminization of poverty, or oppressive beauty norms, but the very way we take what it means to be "men" and "women," and how we experience ourselves as such, that makes patriarchy so difficult to defeat. Resistance to this situation involves deconstructing and reimagining what it means to be gendered. It is about replacing the "male" standard with something more inclusive.

MacKinnon's approach, in other words, is a critique of the *system* of male hegemony, its comprehensive matrix of power and influence, the process by which the interests of *males* become asserted and internalized as the *human* interest. This plays out in various ways in society. In this concept, a woman is defined as only a "thing" that exists in relationship to the male power that constructed her.[16] It follows that women have little agency in a society in which men hold all the power. According to MacKinnon,

> Women often do not control the conditions under which they become pregnant; systematically denied meaningful control over the reproductive uses of their bodies through sex, it is exceptional when they do. Women are socially disadvantaged in controlling sexual access to their bodies through socialization to customs that define

> a woman's body as for sexual use by men. Sexual access is regularly forced or pressured or routinized beyond denial.[17]

In other words, "When sex is violent, women may have lost control of what is done to us, but absence of force does not ensure the presence of that control."[18]

MacKinnon's views are no doubt extreme and can reasonably be attacked as essentialist and determinative (affrontive to the notion of female agency), nobly attempting to address vital issues of life, law, and liberty but with a plethora of important nuance or sensitivity omitted. However, it is not my intention to critique MacKinnon here (others have adequately done so), as her work—or at least her militant attitude—is tremendously useful in a post-*Roe* world. MacKinnon is one of those rare thinkers who is important, in part, *because* of her faults, the excesses of her genius, and the intensity of her expression, embodying Nietzsche's observation (couched in predictably nineteenth-century chauvinistic language) that "[t]he errors of great men are venerable because they are more fruitful than the truths of little men."[19] MacKinnon is *great*. Few people are able to have a positive impact on the law as she has.

Moreover, MacKinnon, as a radical feminist, remains profoundly relevant today because liberal feminism and the movement which surrounded it has *stalled* and, if *Dobbs* is to be taken as a bellwether, as I believe it is, liberal feminism may be in retreat.[20] Thus, the conservative/religious reaction that has long dogged liberal feminism is gaining ground, along with other reactionary and intolerant forces which embody not only misogyny, but also racism, homophobia, antisemitism, anti-intellectualism, and what we are seeing today as forms of "Christian nationalism."[21]

With *Dobbs* we have been put on notice: no longer can we close our eyes and hope for the best. With *Dobbs* the tide has (apparently) turned. In time, the implications of this sea change will grow more dire and increasing numbers of will women suffer.[22] It is time to return to the barricades, to the vitalism of the 1960s and its wonderful legacy of outrage, protest, and dissent. While the activism of the 1960s did not solve the problems of racism, sexism, homophobia, and poverty, it got us to face these problems and to fight for their solutions. Today, the gloves need to come off in our mass movements for social change. In this context, *law is the problem*, not the solution to our nation's failure to live up to its rhetorical commitment to freedom and equality, and judges must decide: to stand *for* or *against* total equality for women and must step down from the bench if they stand against it. The fact that the *Dobbs* majority ruled as it did speak volumes to its own internalized misogyny.

The attack on liberalism in the United States and abroad has been obvious for some time.[23] In the context of this book, my fear of illiberal forces in law and society is that I see the highwater mark of liberal feminism exemplified in *Roe*. I know we cannot reduce everything about liberal feminism or women's rights to *Roe*. I also want to recognize that *Roe* was *problematic* in the context of the Reproductive Justice Movement and women of color who, with good reason, felt *left out* of the liberal feminist agenda.[24] *Roe* was not the end-all, be-all of women's liberation, no single court case can achieve that;[25] *Roe*, however, was significant, if not the *most* significant advancement for women, in my lifetime, as important as *Loving v. Virginia*[26] was for racial equality. As the dissent in *Dobbs* explained:

> For half a century *Roe* and *Casey* have protected the liberty and equality of women. *Roe* held, and *Casey* reaffirmed, that the Constitution safeguards a woman's right to decide for herself whether to bear a child . . . that in the first stages of pregnancy, the government could not make that choice for women. The government could not control a woman's body or the course of a woman's life: It could not determine what the woman's future would be. Respecting a woman as an autonomous being, and granting her full equality, meant giving her substantial choice over this most personal and most consequential of all life decisions.[27]

The following quote that I want to emphasize from MacKinnon helps to focus my critical tone. It is inherited from "the masters of suspicion" legacy of Freud, Marx, and Nietzsche and grounded in their profound humanism and faith in the power of critical intelligence. MacKinnon explains that, in "a democracy, a constitution . . . has to legitimate itself with people, and so to women it has quite a lot to answer for [. . .]. [F]idelity, in law as in life, is a relationship, a two-way street: our fidelity to the Constitution is bound up with its fidelity to us."[28] In a different mythical context, the word "us" paired with the word "constitution," could mean "We the People," that honorific but misleading abstraction basic to American self-congratulatory narratives and pop-patriotism so prevalent in society. Such narrative falsely postulates a national unity of civic equals whose voices contribute meaningfully to the construction of society.[29] MacKinnon, however, has a specific audience in mind. She is speaking to *women*, a group conspicuously *absent* from "We the People," in the Preamble to the U.S. Constitution, and from much subsequent legal and political discourse, including, most prominently, the *Dobbs* majority.

Against the backdrop of her work fighting for human rights for women and gender equality here and abroad,[30] MacKinnon is challenging American women to take a hard look at the U.S. Constitution and to assess their place in our nation's history and present, to not take it for granted.[31] Our mere presence in this country does not necessarily mean we are included as equal members of the political community, as many minorities can attest to. MacKinnon is challenging women to drop their assumptions about what the United States means to them *as women* (as opposed to, say, as citizens, wives, workers, Christians, etc.) and to look at their *lived* experiences, in which far too many of them are abused, poor, degraded, insulted, preyed upon, objectified, manipulated, ignored, and whose interest society seldom considers.[32]

Wealthy white women are, of course, going to experience gender differently than poor women of color. For example, such women are likely to think of themselves as normatively "special" (meaning, "better than" other women) in terms of educational status, religious beliefs, occupation, and through their status of being married to a successful white male spouse (doctor, lawyer, professor, CEO, etc.) who embodies social privilege. Some women "have it all" and more, but often at a cost. As MacKinnon notes, such elite women (or women who aspire to be elite) "benefit greatly from standing with the forces that keep women down."[33] Such women will thus not appreciate the extent to which their status as *women* (separate from their other status) affects them in ways that are like that of other women who appear different because of a plethora of cultural, racial, or socioeconomic factors. The "other," however, is always closer to us than we think.

While the privileges of wealth soften life's rough edges, few women can escape the bonds of patriarchy in relationship to their own social class and peers. It is less about how any specific woman *acts* and more about the way she is *acted upon* by others, as well as the omnipresence of masculinity and patriarchy in society. The hurt may be delivered in different forms and with different levels of intensity and consequences depending on a woman's relative economic or social privilege, but it is *structured* into her relationship with the men in her life and the legal norms prescribing the conditions of her existence. Gilded cages are still cages, although there are obvious differences between a palace and a hovel, and between being a woman now and being one in the nineteenth century.

In other words, regardless of her wealth, religion, race, or any other factor—that by being a woman and *for no other reason*—her way of being in the world is covered by a mask of sorts separating (burdening) who they are inside and distorting how others see them.[34] This mask may be so tight and so old that women mistake it for their face, or else they may be young enough to remember how it chafes, even as they tell themselves that they must learn to live with this chafing as part of what it means to be alive. This "feeling" is part of what activist Betty Friedan called "the problem that has no name." Early in her path-breaking 1963 book, *The Feminine Mystique*, Friedan described a felt condition "which is simply the fact that American women are kept from growing to their full human capacities" which "is taking a far greater toll on the physical and mental health of our country than any known disease."[35]

Women, Friedan noted, felt miserable, as if something deep inside them was dying. They felt stunted, even *amputated*, like they had lost some part of themselves without understanding what was happening to them. Other writers have called this "normative discontent."[36] I prefer the term *alienation*. This is the feeling that one is out of place in one's own skin, that one is "boxed in" and suffocating, stunted and unable to grow as a human being. It is the gnawing, inescapable feeling that one's life is not one's own. It is being disconnected, isolated, and alone in a community of people or in one's family, like Gregor Samsa (Franz Kafka's cockroach-man) in his room listening longingly to the sounds of daily life by his terrified family below, knowing that he is forever after to be excluded from them.[37] Above all, it is to be a stranger to oneself. Friedan's great accomplishment was to bring this discontent into focus so (at least some) women could see it for what it was, understand its many causes, and learn to fight it. In her interview with Terry Gross on NPR's Fresh Air, author Carol Shields provides a typical reaction that (white middle-class) woman had to Friedan's book: "[I]t was like a thunderbolt. I was astonished. I had no idea women thought like that, or that woman could be anything other than what they were [. . .]. It gave me courage."[38]

In her work, MacKinnon directly engages this alienation obliquely identified in Friedan's book by stripping away these other "add-on" identities from women (who, certainly, do not act as a monolithic block) to highlight the importance of the "situatedness" of being a *woman-qua-woman* in this society. Her argument is that the lives of many women do not match up with the public rhetoric and stated goals of our civic and legal institutions proclaiming their equality and recognizing their value and agency as human beings. Simply, our *talk* about women's equality does not match our *action* in creating policies that treat women as equal to men. Indeed, on the international level, the United States often ranks low in terms of maternal health and women's rights, generally.[39]

Take, for instance, an important international treaty intended to address the type of concerns raised in my book. In 1979 the United Nations (UN) established the Convention on the Elimination of All Forms of Discrimination against Women (CEDAW). Discrimination is defined in the CEDAW as:

> Any distinction, exclusion or restriction made on the basis of sex which has the effect or purpose of impairing or nullifying the recognition, enjoyment or exercise by women, irrespective of their marital status, on a basis of equality of men and women, of human rights and fundamental freedoms in the political, economic, social, cultural, civil or any other field.[40]

The United States, alone among industrialized nations, has not ratified the CEDAW. Reluctance to ratification is related to many of the things I have been discussing: claims it would destroy the traditional family structure in the United States by redefining "family" and the respective roles of men and women, or that it could be used to usurp the proper role of parents in child-rearing, that it supports abortion rights, and furthers same-sex marriage, or that it will give too much power to the international community over "states' rights." Further, suspicion of the United Nations is rampant among cultural conservatives and religious extremists who bitterly resent the humanistic norms and international cooperation or cosmopolitanism that represents the best spirit of the UN.[41]

While it is not difficult to ignore the ways in which, by international comparisons, the United States lets women down (most people focus more on local issues affecting them, or else individualize the misogyny they experience, thinking they brought it on themselves), it is *less difficult to ignore* that we still do not have an Equal Rights Amendment. So whatever rights women do have come from positive law, which can be changed at the will of Congress, an institution with a discernable misogynistic (and homophobic) streak among its many Republican members. The same is true at the state level, with more than a little racism thrown into the mix, particularly in the South.[42] Nor do we, after *Dobbs*, have a constitutional right to abortion, and the right to privacy upon which it was situated has been hollowed out by right-wing ideologues. Thus, in a legal sense, women *remain* vulnerable to political oppression in ways that men are not. So much for lauded "equal protection" and "equality of opportunity" we hear so much about by conservatives who claim we have nothing to be complaining about.

As MacKinnon observes, and the *Dobbs* decision confirms, "most women feel that the law is not about them, has no idea who they are or what they face or how they think or feel, has nothing to say to them, and can do nothing for them. When the law and their life collide, it is their life that gets the worst of it."[43] This is nowhere as true as when the state denies a woman the right to terminate her pregnancy. Under international law, specifically the Rome Statute of the International Criminal Court of 1998, forced pregnancy is a war crime.[44] To be clear, because of influence by the Holy See (an anachronism if there ever was one) and resistance by other member states, the statute prohibiting forced pregnancy was narrowly limited to "a subset of violations of sexual and reproductive rights committed during armed conflicts or during other human rights crises involving widespread and systematic attacks against civilian populations" to avoid conflicting with the domestic anti-abortion policies.[45] That distinction, however, between "enemy forces" and one's own "government forces," is likely to be lost on the woman forced to undergo an unwanted pregnancy; under the patriarchy that exists within our laws, the two become virtually indistinguishable. In the patriarchal war on women, rape and forced pregnancy are just another day without the ERA and within the persistence of Constitutional structural inequality.

ERA's Legacy of Defeat and Anti-Feminist Women

The defeat of the ERA in 1982 is nothing short of tragic (although expected under MacKinnon's "dominance" perspective), as evident now that the political winds have turned against liberal feminist objectives. The ERA's demise came during a period in which women's rights were *advancing*, most notably abortion rights in *Roe* in 1973, and the promise of equal protection in *Reed v. Reed* and its subsequent line of cases.[46] Thus, much of the defeat of the ERA was perceived as symbolic and not fully threatening to liberal values. Elsewhere, civil rights statutes were filling in the gap, and many states stepped up to interpret their own constitutions in line with the ERA or adopted "little ERAs" to the same effect. Society was changing for the better. The great social movements of the 1950s, 1960s, and 1970s were having a welcomed positive effect. In terms of abortion, however, we now know we were living on borrowed time. This great, liberal achievement turned out to *not* be sustainable against the massive backlash and the rise of the political "Christian Right" *Roe* inadvertently helped to energize. At their most robust, abortion rights were never secure, particularly for poor and minority women. We now understand that, while Constitutional protections *do* matter, they still do not matter *enough*. The sentiment by judge Learned Hand from 1944 remains true today:

> I often wonder whether we do not rest our hopes too much upon constitutions, upon law and upon courts. These are false hopes [. . .]. Liberty lies in the hearts of men and women; when it dies there, no constitution, no law, no court can save it; no constitution, no law, no court can even do much to help it.[47]

I am scared. What else are we posed to lose in the decades ahead now that the Court has given up any pretext of caring about our liberty?[48]

Generally, the ERA was defeated because two demographics organized against it: conservative churches/political organizations and older-generation women, the people most threatened by gender equality. The first group consisted of Catholics, Mormons, and fundamentalist Christians who rallied their support behind the anti-ERA movement, using the same tired arguments that gender inequality was part of "God's plan," and was a function of good government and a stable society. For these opponents, inequality was baked into their world view. Second, an older generation of white women feared the ERA, seeing it as a threat to the only identity that had ever been respectable to them—housewife and mother. Such was the perceived culture of female identity expected of women.

Writing in 2020, neo-conservative journalist Christopher Caldwell takes note on how political and social norms have changed for women. Rather than celebrate this change, he complains that now "there are two cultures of American womanhood—the culture of married women and then culture of single women."[49] These are, he claims, "diametrically" opposed politically as if women were being psychologically pulled in conflicting directions. Caldwell argues that these "two cultures" represent a weakening of women as a class, hurting them by raising expectations of something other than marriage. The cause of this "rupture was feminism, which taught women to be discontent with their lot in life." In contrast, Caldwell assures us that back in the Kennedy Era, "there was one culture of femininity, and it united women from cradle to grave."[50] Implicit in Caldwell's argument is that life was better for women during this time.

I doubt that a single culture of "femininity" is a good thing, and I would hope that, well into the twenty-first century, there would be more than *two* cultures of "American womanhood," as women, like men, can be as diverse as their imaginations and self-confidence allow them to be. No one should be trapped in stifling straightjackets of conformity. But many are, even today. In resisting the ERA, many women fought to maintain traditional gender roles and legal status, just as many women now reject feminism or do not see the value of reproductive rights. They define themselves in terms of their relationship with men and align themselves with the masculinist beliefs found in religion or in other aspects of conservative ideology. For these women, obedience to an imposed and fixed "moral law," written by and for men, trumps their own agency in defining for themselves their relationships with society. The argument and tone of the ERA's critics exemplify the essentialist approach to gender and the intellectual and literal straightjacket it placed on women embodied in the Common Law Tradition that I am here critiquing.

Marion Olson, chairwoman of a right-wing Minnesota political party, declared, "We don't want to turn our daughters into tigers and our sons into pansies. Nature did not intend men and women to be equal."[51] Critics warned that the "strongest sign of the decay of a nation is the feminization of men and the masculinization of women" and that this was, bizarrely, considered a sign of "communism."[52] For these critics, women in particular, gender equality was perceived by some as threat to their status of the woman as a "homemaker" which "excuses" women from earning money, engaging in politics, and serving in the military.[53] In more detailed terms, progressive writers Barbara Ehrenreich and Deirdre English explain that a

> conservative woman may be pursuing the ever-fleeting chimera of male protection. From her point of view, every advance in women's legal status may represent a further erosion of male responsibility. "Equal rights" might threaten the only security she has left should her husband's sexual interest wane—the sanctity of marriage. Abortion is threatening simply because it makes pregnancy a "woman's choice," rather than something that men must be held responsible for. So it is women who have provided the main constituency of the "family values" movement, even though its political and religious leadership is often male.[54]

Opponents of the ERA claimed, among other things, that it would lead to gay marriage, civil rights for the LGBT community, and unisex toilets. From a legal perspective, the only argument that seems to me to have some validity is the "states' rights" argument which saw the ERA as a federal "power grab," just as the *Dobbs'* majority saw abortion rights, LGBT rights, and protections for racial minorities as federal "power grabs" when they come from Washington or from the federal courts. These critics point out that (scare quotes and all), traditionally, the federal government had only limited jurisdiction over family law, divorce, and child custody as well as no general "police power" interests in overseeing "morality" or behaviors of state citizens. *Obergefell v. Hodges*, the great "marriage equality" case, for example, overruled the little-known *Baker v. Nelson*, in which, in a single sentence, the Supreme Court turned down an appeal from a same-sex couple who had been denied a marriage license "for want of a substantial federal question."[55]

From an originalist perspective, this is correct. Even so, this "hands off" approach reflected a time in which discernible differences in culture and identity existed among the states in America (slavery in the Southern states is one glaring example), which were viewed as "laboratories" of democracy in a phrase coined by Justice Louis Brandeis. According to Brandeis, it "is one of the happy incidents of the federal system that a single courageous State may, if its citizens choose, serve as a laboratory; and try novel social and economic experiments without risk to the rest of the country."[56] These geographical and cultural differences no longer exist in any substantive manner, and the so-called "states' rights" argument has pretty much turned into the right of the political majority of a state to oppress any minority it wants, which is the one thing that the federal government and Americans from across the nation should never accept. A nation is only as strong as its "weakest links" and a morally weak and intellectually challenged state (i.e., those known as the "Bible Belt" states),[57] beyond being a political embarrassment (repeatedly) to the nation, is an existential threat to the dignity of all Americans.[58]

As a lawyer I understand the textual grounds for the "states' rights" argument. It may look good on paper to leave as much power as possible with local governments with little meaningful federal oversight, what state elites call "meddling in our internal affairs," but I see it as anachronistic as much else in the original Constitution, particularly when it comes to individual rights and liberties. When nations such as China make this complaint of "outside meddling" to deflect international criticism of its grisly human rights record, the world sees it for what it is: a claim for unaccountable power to act beastly and ruthlessly against its own people. Denying states in our federalist structure such power seems to me to be a *minimal* constitutional requirement as well as a fundamental aspect of our nationhood, so we do not allow so-called "pariah" states to exist in our community.[59] These states, at their worst, are America at its worst, something that no American should tolerate.

Moreover, the extreme "states' rights" position is no good *practically*, and states' rights proponents overlook the fact that the country is very different than it was in 1789. The great success of the United States lies in its strong federal government, one reflecting a forward-thinking liberal cosmopolitanism rather than parochial and insular state values, imposing accountability and protections against different forms of discrimination and other socially backward thinking found in many of the anti-abortion states. This is particularly more important today, than ever, in trying to tackle the difficult environmental and geo-political issues of the twenty-first century. The United States gives up on its liberalist aspirations at its peril to its international relevance and reputation. An illiberal United States is, in many ways, an anemic one unbefitting of respect.

States are important, however; they are closer and more accountable to their citizens than a distant Washington bureaucracy. I understand and appreciate the (partially accurate) view that "all politics is local." However, the *sad* (my apologies to Brandeis) history of many states' "laboratories," particularly those in the South and in Western states during the era of the powerful railroad and mining companies, often produced government-sanctioned monstrosities. Corporate wealth and white supremacy corrupted state government,[60] as politicians often led by preaching and practicing a racial and/or economic oligarchy that is antithetical to Constitutional government and to the values of a free and socially inclusive society. White supremacy, patriarchy, and naked capitalist denigration as seen during the industrial period of the United States required a *national* response, which the judiciary bitterly resisted for decades and conservatives, to their shame, continue to abhor.

The woman most instrumental in leading the fight against the ERA was conservative activist Phyllis Schlafly, a powerful speaker, writer, and organizer. While already politically active (a member of the John Birch Society, a fringe extremist ultra-conversative hate group) and deeply committed to the (failed) campaign to elect Barry Goldwater president in 1964, Schlafly found her calling in the early 1970s with the fight to defeat the ERA. Throughout her efforts in organizing and publishing, Schlafly exemplified the essentialist approach to gender embodied in the Common Law Tradition that I am here critiquing. Men and women are *not* the same, she insists, and ignoring the differences cannot make it so: "It is based on the fact of life—which no legislation or agitation can erase—that women have babies and men don't."[61] Because of women's reproductive capabilities, Schlafly argues, they have what she calls an "innate maternal instinct" which she defines as an "overriding psychological need of a woman [to] love something alive."[62] Women make natural teachers and nurses for this reason and terrible soldiers or leaders. If a woman cannot "lavish her maternal love so that it doesn't well up inside her" it will cause her "psychological frustration."[63] What she calls "feminism," she claims, "is doomed to failure because it is based on an attempt to repeal and restructure human nature."[64] In Chapters 3 and 4, we will see how this argument was made throughout much of the legal, scientific, philosophical, and other cultural literatures of the late nineteenth and early-to-mid-twentieth centuries with devasting consequences on women's psyche and educational opportunities.

As a result of entrenched conservative and traditional assumptions regarding women and men (Schlafly herself preached a Catholic-nationalism common to the hysterical anti-Communism of the period),[65] and how they have long been embodied in the law, *Dobbs* was written as if women did not matter at all in the eyes of the law. A woman's interest as a human being is eviscerated by the Court and she has once again been turned into an object to be controlled (or handled) by often Catholic men (and some Catholic women, such as Justice Barrett) whose allegiance to a socially backward, historically abhorrent, and still intolerant Church should not have legal significance on how they govern. This statement only *appears* extreme because most people do not read MacKinnon (or any feminist, for that matter), nor do they pay attention to the nuances of constitutional history and the Common Law Tradition where nearly *all* women, particularly married women, were under the control of men, whether they agreed to it or not. They were the *de facto* or literal servants or slaves in a masculinist political economy that profited from their servitude, labor, and sexuality. In many ways, this is still true today.[66]

Testifying in 1970 before the Senate Subcommittee on the Equal Rights Amendment, Marjorie Longwell, chairman of the National Women's Party, noted that the Common Law Tradition placed the stigma of inferiority and bondage on women (as it did on Blacks and non-Christians generally) and that it "is vitally important to remember that our Founding Fathers wrote the U.S. constitution in THE LIGHT OF THE OLD ENGLISH COMMON LAW AND THE OLD ENGLISH COMMON LAW did not recognize women as PERSONS."[67] This is not hyperbole, nor is it a particularly new observation. According to one legal treatise author in 1837, the "whole theory" of marriage under the Common Law is "slavish ... a disgrace to any civilized nation."[68] It degrades females "almost to the level of slaves."[69] The author adds, "With regard to political rights," females form a "positive exception to the general doctrine of equality."[70]

I have always wondered, even as a child, how "general" such a doctrine of equality could be when it excluded half of the population on gender grounds and also excluded people based on religion, ethnicity, race, and social class. Who, other than white Christian heterosexual men of means, is left to enjoy the "blessings" of liberty? When I spoke this way, people told me to "hush," that "you don't understand." Maybe, as I was a child, these adults knew something I did not? Now I have a doctorate and a law degree and have spent decades studying this issue. I feel the same way now as I did then. I think the adults in my life were telling me "not to rock the boat" and "just get along" with how things were. I could never do that, and I am surprised and dismayed that others do.

Indeed, so-called "political liberty" has never meant what most people believe it means now. Writing early in the twentieth century, Alfred B. Cruikshank provides a spirited defense of the early national practice of "property suffrage"[71] used to exclude poor whites along with racial and gender exclusion that were pervasive at the beginning of this nation and lasted in some form until the Voting Rights Act (VRA) of 1965. In 2013, however, the VRA was gutted by the Supreme Court in *Shelby County v. Holder* on "state sovereignty" and "equality" grounds.[72] So much for progress. By declaring the "end" of *de jure* racial discrimination, the Court ruled unconstitutional the use of the coverage formula in Section 4(b) of the VRA to determine which jurisdictions are subject to the preclearance requirement of Section 5. *Shelby* thus frees jurisdictions identified by the coverage formula in Section 4(b) from seeking preclearance for new voting changes. In other words, the states and counties that were most vehement in practicing racial discrimination prior to the VRA are now free to practice it again. Equality among the *states* trumped equality among the *people* living in those states. Such political fetishism and hollow formalism are no longer worthy of our democracy.

Conclusion

This chapter has explored the work of Catharine A. MacKinnon in relationship to contemporary threats against liberal feminism, which, I argue has "stalled," and the *Dobbs* decision which presages even further rollbacks for women's rights and their status in our society. Also discussed in this context is the ERA's legacy of defeat and the influence of powerful anti-feminist women in pushing back against the gains women have made since the late 1960s (there seems to be no shortage of outspoken anti-feminist Republican women leaders or talking heads at Fox News). In the next two chapters, I provide a close reading of the historical record to reveal the *hundreds* of ways in which women were legally, socially, medically, and philosophically deemed to be inferior to men and how society conspired to deny women the status of being fully human and the political equal to men throughout all walks of life.

Notes

1 As I mentioned earlier, my feminist lens comes from Second Wave feminism with which I engage some of its radical and liberal trends. I do this while engaging simultaneously (but not privileging), when appropriate, the intersectional analysis characteristic of Third Wave feminism. Further, I realize that my choice of Catharine A. MacKinnon to aid me in this chapter will alienate some readers who reject her somewhat universalizing approaches and absence of racial considerations. For Third Wave critiques of the feminist assumptions I am engaging in this chapter, see Amanda Cawston, "The Feminist Case Against Pornography: A Review and Re-evaluation," *Inquiry* 62, no. 6 (2019): 624–658; Marlee Kline, "Race, Racism, and Feminist Legal Theory," *Harvard Women's Law Journal* 12 (1989): 115–150; and Susan Archer Mann and Douglas J. Huffman, "The Decentering of Second Wave Feminism and the Rise of the Third Wave," *Science & Society* 69, no. 1 (2005): 56–91.

2 Julie Suk, *After Misogyny: How the Law Fails Women and What to Do About It* (Berkely, CA: University of California Press, 2023), 14.

3 Ibid., 74.

4 Margaret Sanger, *Woman and the New Race* (New York: Brentano's Publisher, 1920), 94. Some readers (understandably) object to Sanger in light of her well-known eugenicist sentiments. This shortcoming in her work, however, should not distract us from the profundity of her conviction that human freedom cannot exist without female reproductive freedom. In writing this, however, I recognize that Sanger herself has a complicated engagement with the issue of abortion and never actively supported legalization. While Sanger established Planned Parenthood, an organization subsequently most associated with the provision of (and fight for) legal and safe abortion, she herself did not openly support legal abortion. See "Margaret Sanger Answers Questions on Abortion-An MSPP Exclusive," *Margaret Sanger Papers Project, no.* 60 (Spring 2012), https://sanger.hosting.nyu.edu/articles/ms_abortion/.

5 Wendy Chapkis, *Beauty Secrets: Women and the Politics of Appearance* (Boston: South End Press, 1986), 139.

6 For example, conservative author Heather Mac Donald argues that the way to fight the sexual exploitation and abuse of women is not *with* feminism, but *without* it. She accuses feminism of "denying the differences between men and women, and . . . ridiculing the manly virtues of gentlemanliness and chicory and the female virtues of modesty and prudence." In effect, she, and those that feel similarly, argue that women are responsible for their own victimization. The cause is feminism, which "dissolved the civilizational restraints on the male libido." Against all the evidence of history, Mac Donald concludes that the "boorish behavior that pervades society today would have been unthinkable in the past, when a traditional understanding of sexual propriety prevailed." "The Negative Impact of the #MeToo Movement," in *Imprimis: A 50th Anniversary Collection*, ed. Douglas A. Jeffrey (Hillsdale College Press, 2022), 125.

7 "Alliances Between Women: Overcoming Internalized Oppression and Internalized Domination," *Signs* 12 (1986): 148.

8 See *Sexual Harassment of Working Women: A Case of Sex Discrimination* (New Haven: Yale University Press, 1979).

9 See Andrea Dworkin, *Intercourse* (New York: Basic Books, 1987). Robin Morgan coined the phrase, "Pornography is the theory, and rape is the practice" in her essay, "Theory and Practice: Pornography and Rape," from her *Going Too Far: The Personal Chronicle of a Feminist* (New York: Vintage Books, 1978), 163–169.

10 771 F.2d 323 (1985).

11 Amy Sohn, *The Man Who Hated Women: Sex, Censorship, and Civil Liberties in the Gilded Age* (New York: Farrar, Straus and Giroux, 2021).

12 The facts in this paragraph came from "The Hypocrites' Club," *The Economist*, March 13, 2008, https://www.economist.com/united-states/2008/03/13/the-hypocrites-club; Devin Leonard, *Neither Snow Nor Rain: A History of the United States Postal Service* (New York: Grove Press, 2016); Edward de Grazia, *Girls Lean Back Everywhere: The Law of Obscenity and the Assault on Genius* (New York: Vintage; 2nd ed., 1993), 5; and Annalee Newitz, "The 19th-Century Troll Who Hated Dirty Postcards and Sex Toys," *The New York Times*, September 20, 2019, https://www.nytimes.com/2019/09/20/opinion/sunday/mens-rights-activists-comstock.html. Comstock's social views are expressed in several of the books he published, including *Traps for the Young* (New York: Funk & Wagnalls Co., 1884).

13 "Feminism, Marxism, Method, and the State: An Agenda for Theory," *Signs* 7, no. 3 (1982): 553.

14 *Toward a Feminist Theory of the State* (Cambridge, MA: Harvard University Press, 1991), 113.

15 Recall how in 2016, upon the death of Justice Scalia, President Barak Obama nominated Judge Merrick Garland for a seat on the Supreme Court. However, Senate Majority Leader Mitch McConnell, a Republican ideologue, refused to hold a hearing on the nomination, arguing that the Presidential election, some 8 months away, necessitated a delay ("the people should decide," he declared). His blockage of the nomination, a naked power move with no legal justification or precedent, gave the seat to President Donald Trump after the next election. The hypocrisy and cheating continued with the nomination of Brett M. Kavanaugh (who was hugely unpopular) and reached fruition, weeks before the 2020 election, after the death of Ruth Bader Ginsberg and the ascension of Amy Coney Barrett to the high bench. Barrett was seated without *any* democratic votes *after* McConnell refused to follow his own reasoning, allowing her to be confirmed mere weeks before the election.

16 For a summary of MacKinnon's argument on this point, see Katharine T. Bartlett, "MacKinnon's Feminism: Power on Whose Terms?" *California Law Review* 75 (1987): 1559–1570.

17 "Reflections on Sex Equality Under Law," *The Yale Law Journal* 100, no. 5 (1991): 1321.

18 "Feminism, Marxism, Method, and the State," 650.

19 *The Portable Nietzsche*, trans. Walter R. Kaufmann (New York: Modern Library, 1977), 30.

20 Charlotte Alter, "The Failure of the Feminist Industrial Complex," *Time*, June 24, 2022, https://time.com/6190225/feminist-industrial-complex-roe-v-wade/.

21 According to Caroline Mala Corbin, "Christian Nationalism" is the belief that the United States is a Christian nation grounded in fundamentalistic Christian principles, that religious and national identity are co-determinate, and that "true Americans" are Christians and white; all others are aliens and a threat to God's protection of the community. Corbin describes the people who ascribe to this identity as hostile and intolerant toward others, leading to symbolic and actual discrimination and violence. "The Supreme Court's Facilitation of White Christian Nationalism," *Alabama Law Review* 71 (2019): 833–866.

This is the very antithesis of liberalism and reason. These people and their world view must be resisted to the utmost of our power.

22 And not just women. *Dobbs* portends even greater harm. We should take Justice Clarence Thomas at his word when he, in his concurring opinion, warns that "in future cases, we should reconsider all of this Court's substantive due process precedents, including *Griswold*, *Lawrence*, and *Obergefell* [. . .]. [W]e have a duty to 'correct the error' established in those precedents." *Dobbs*, 2301.

23 Thomas J. Main, *The Rise of Illiberalism* (Washington, DC: Brookings Institution Press, 2022).

24 A summary of these grievances can be found in Dorothy Roberts, "Reproductive Justice, Not Just Rights," *Dissent* 62, no. 4 (2015): 79–82. See Cinzia Arruzza, Tithi Bhattacharya, and Nancy Fraser, *Feminism for the 99%: A Manifesto* (New York: Verso, 2019), arguing that liberal feminism is "*equal opportunity domination*, one that asks ordinary people, in the name of feminism, to be grateful that it is a woman, not a man, who busts their union, orders a drone to kill their parent, or locks their child in a cage at the border" (2).

25 I acknowledge and honor that scholars of abortion have long argued that race is an important factor in considering the restriction of reproductive liberty. For elaboration of this point, see Melissa Murray, "Race-ing *Roe*: Reproductive Justice, Racial Justice, and the Battle for *Roe v. Wade*," *Harvard Law Review* 134, no. 6 (2021): 2025–2102; Khiara Bridges, *Reproducing Race: An Ethnography of Pregnancy as a Site of Racialization* (Berkeley, CA: University of California Press, 2011); and Marlene Gerber Fried, Elena Gutiérrez, Loretta Ross, and Jael Silliman, *Undivided Rights: Women of Color Organizing for Reproductive Justice* (Chicago, IL: Haymarket Books, 2016).

26 388 U.S. 1 (1967).

27 *Dobbs*, 2317.

28 *Women's Lives, Men's Laws* (Cambridge, MA: Harvard University Press, 2007), 70.

29 Rogers M. Smith, "'One United People:' Second-Class Female Citizenship and the American Quest for Community," *Yale Journal of Law and the Humanities* 1, no. 2 (1989): 229–293.

30 For a time, MacKinnon served as special gender advisor to the International Criminal Court. Her reflections on her international work are collected in *Are Women Human? And Other International Dialogues* (Cambridge, MA: Harvard University Press, 2006).

31 This is the major theme of my *In Defense of Partisan Criticism* (New York: Peter Lang, 2005), which is a social class critique of American legal history, as this current book is a gender-based analysis.

32 MacKinnon's call for an engaged female commitment to reassessing their status in the United States should not be seen as a disavowal of any woman's agency. Many people, women as well as men, are naïve regarding their experience of the present. How could we not be? Taking a critical approach to our lives is difficult and we receive so little encouragement. Moreover, being and thinking differently takes so much *effort*. On top of the inherent difficulties of such a stance, many people face significant other *discouragement*. In the United States, for instance, many of our citizens are disconnected from history. They are minimally or poorly educated, and too many Americans experience crushing, inescapable debt and hereditary poverty that consumes all their energy just to survive. Many of us do not know what it means to thrive. Additionally, Americans are often encased in the bias

and misinformation of our communities, chained by religion, drugs, and alcohol or other dogmatic scripts, and dulled intellectually and emotionally by the bombardments of our shallow consumerist culture. In this context, our lives assume a self-evident normalcy, a beingness and meanness defined by an existential worthlessness or resignation to accept the status quo inevitably and passively. Or worse, we embrace the active nihilism described and condemned by Nietzsche. Thus, we constantly need reminding that the present can only be understood through engaging with the past, and that we need to learn from the past, own it, accept it for what it was, and try to understand what it may mean to us today. Only then can we make informed decisions about how to describe the future we want and how to make the transition from surviving to thriving. Only with such an awareness do the problems with the present reveal themselves as an opportunity and motivation for intelligent growth and change.

33 Quoted in Stuart Jeffries, "Are Women Human?" [Interview with Catharine A. McKinnon], *The Guardian*, April 5, 2006, https://www.theguardian.com/world/2006/apr/12/gender.politicsphilosophyandsociety.

34 Efrat Tseelon, *The Masque of Femininity: The Presentation of Woman in Everyday Life* (Thousand Oaks, CA: Sage, 1995).

35 (New York: Dell Publishing, 1963), 351. Of course, by "American woman" Friedan meant "white middle-class women." See bell hooks, *Feminist Theory: From Margin to Center* (Boston: South End Press, 1984), 1. Also, I realize that Friedan has been deeply criticized for, among other things, promoting the "lavender menace," believing, as she did, that lesbian demands for quality would hurt heterosexual women. See Daniel Horowitz, *Betty Friedan and the Making of "The Feminine Mystique": The American Left, the Cold War, and Modern Feminism* (Amherst, MA: University of Massachusetts Press, 2000).

36 See Judith Rodin, L. Silbersein, and R. H. Striegel-Moore, "Women and Weight: A Normative Discontent," in *Nebraska Symposium on Motivation, 1984, Volume 32: Psychology and Gender*, ed. Theo B. Sonderegger (Lincoln: University of Nebraska Press, 1985), 267–307.

37 *The Metamorphosis* (New York: Modern Library, [1915]/1972).

38 In Terry Gross, *All I Did Was Ask: Conversations with Writers, Actors, Musicians, and Artists* (New York: Hyperion, 2004), 334.

39 See Gianna Melillo, "US Ranks Worst in Maternal Care, Mortality Compared With 10 Other Developed Nations," *American Journal of Managed Care* (December 3, 2020), https://www.ajmc.com/view/us-ranks-worst-in-maternal-care-mortality-compared-with-10-other-developed-nations; and Virginia Langmaid, "Study of Wealthy Nations Finds American Women Most Likely to Die of Preventable Causes, Pregnancy Complications," *CNN*, April 5, 2022, https://www.cnn.com/2022/04/05/health/us-women-health-care/index.html.

40 The text for the treaty can be found here: https://www.ohchr.org/en/instruments-mechanisms/instruments/convention-elimination-all-forms-discrimination-against-women.

41 See Katrina vanden Heuvel, "What's with the GOP's Absurd Fear of All Things U.N.," *The Washington Post*, December 11, 2012, https://www.washingtonpost.com/opinions/the-gops-absurd-fear-of-all-things-un/2012/12/10/c8b5a50a-42e2-11e2-8061-253 bccfc7532_story.html. Sadly, I recognize that, thanks to the hyper-politicization of the five permanent members of the Security Council, including the United States, the practice and experience of the UN often fails to live up to its great ideal.

42 Recall my disclaimer in footnote #5 of my Introduction contextualizing my use of apparent *ad hominem* descriptions.

43 *Women's Lives, Men's Laws*, 32.

44 "Forced Pregnancy: A Commentary on the Crime in International Criminal Law," *Amnesty International*, 2020, https://www.amnesty.org/en/wp-content/uploads/2021/05/IOR532711 2020ENGLISH.pdf.

45 Ibid., 8–9.

46 404 U.S. 71 (1971). *Reed* held, for the *first time*, that the Fourteenth Amendment protected women's claims for equal protection of the law. Many cases followed in expanding on this decision.

47 " 'The Spirit of Liberty,' I Am an American Day Address," *Digital Liberty*, May 2021, http://www.digitalhistory.uh.edu/disp_textbook.cfm?smtID=3&psid=1199.

48 The *Dobbs* Court majority knew full well the chaos and suffering they were unleashing on women in the United States and beyond. See Risa Kaufman, Rebecca Brown, Catalina Martínez Coral, Jihan Jacob, Martin Onyango, and Katrine Thomasen, "Global Impacts of *Dobbs v. Jackson Women's Health Organization* and Abortion Regression in the United States," *Sexual and Reproductive Health Matters* 30, no. 1 (2022): 1–10; Diana Greene Foster, Sarah E. Raifman, Jessica D. Gipson, Corinne H. Rocca, and M. Antonia Biggs, "Effects of Carrying an Unwanted Pregnancy to Term on Women's Existing Children," *The Journal of Pediatrics* 205 (2019): 183–189. As Justice Brennan notes, originalist-type readings lead to "a view that feigns self-effacing deference to the specific judgments of those who forged our original social compact. But in truth it is little more than arrogance cloaked as humility." Brennan, William J. Jr., "To the Text and Teaching Symposium," Georgetown University, Washington, DC, October 12, 1985. This arrogance, in the seat of what is supposed to be a clearheaded and impartial judiciary, reminds me of legal philosopher Lon L. Fuller's position that "[t]here is indeed no frustration greater than to be confronted by a theory which purports merely to describe, when it not only plainly prescribes, but owes its special prescriptive powers precisely to the fact that it disclaims prescriptive intention." "Positivism and Fidelity to Law-A Reply to Professor Hart," *Harvard Law Review* 71 (1957): 632. The cruel arrogance of the *Dobbs* majority is terrifying precisely because cold power, unchecked by a human sense of decency and compassion for the suffering of others, is the material of Orwellian nightmares. In this case, the nightmare more directly resembles that described in Margaret Atwood, *The Handmaid's Tale* (New York: Anchor Books, [1986]/1998).

49 "The Roots of our Partisan Divide," in *Imprimis: A 50th Anniversary Collection*, ed. Douglas A. Jeffrey (Hillsdale, MI: Hillsdale College Press, 2022), 22.

50 Ibid.

51 Cited in "Women: Trouble for ERA," *Time*, February 19, 1973, 25.

52 Taylor Caldwell, "They're Spoiling Eve's Great Con Game," *American Opinion*, September 1970, 8.

53 Susan E. Marshall, "Keep Us on the Pedestal: Women Against Feminism in Twentieth-Century America," in *Women: A Feminist Perspective*, ed. Jo Freeman (Mountain View, CA: Mayfield, 1995), 547.

54 *For Her Own Good: 150 Years of the Experts' Advice to Women* (New York: Anchor Books, 1978), 320.

55 409 U.S. 810 (1972).

56 *New State Ice Co. v. Liebmann*, 285 U.S. 262 (1932), 386.

57 "If the highly educated or the young are more likely to favor ERA or abortion, it is largely because many years of schooling and youth are associated with low levels of religious involvement." Jerome L. Himmelstein, "The Social Basis of Antifeminism: Religious Networks and Culture," *Journal for the Scientific Study of Religion* 25, no. 1 (1986): 7.

58 For a discussion of this in the context of the Civil Rights movement, see Mary L. Dudziak, "Desegregation as a Cold War Imperative." *Stanford Law Review* 41, no. 1 (1988): 61–120.

59 Throughout this book I refer to the American "South" with a disapproving tone. This is because I recognize, as does Stanford Levinson, that the South is a "distinctive region of our nation" presenting the "most exquisite difficulties in terms of establishing a truly coherent national identity." Further, "the cultural differences between North and South have been a staple of those who would analyze America at least since the nineteenth century." *Written in Stone: Public Monuments in Changing Societies* (Durham, NC: Duke University Press, 1998), 31–32.

60 Jack Beatty, *Age of Betrayal: The Triumph of Money in America, 1865–1900* (New York: Vintage, 2008).

61 "What's Wrong with 'Equal Rights' for Women?" *Iowa State University: Archives of Women's Political Communication*, January 1, 1972, https://awpc.cattcenter.iastate.edu/2016/02/02/whats-wrong-with-equal-rights-for-women-1972/#:~:text=This%20respect%20is%20part%20and,He%20created%20us%20this%20way.

62 *The Power of the Positive Woman* (New Rochelle, NY: Arlington House, 1977), 17.

63 Ibid., 18.

64 *Feminist Fantasies* (Dallas, TX: Spence Publishing Company, 2003), 28.

65 Donald Critchlow, *Phyllis Schlafly and Grassroots Conservatism: A Woman's Crusade* (Princeton, NJ: Princeton University Press, 2005), 42–43.

66 I concede that some conversative women may view their opposition to abortion as "pro-woman" aside from any religious context. For example, the unsupported claim that abortion "harms" women in some way or that it perpetuates the marginalization, exploitation, and abuse of women. Such a group is not a monolith, and the nuances of the argument can be found in Mary Ziegler, "Women's Rights on the Right: The History and Stakes of Modern Pro-Life Feminism, 1968 to the Present," *Berkeley Journal of Gender, Law & Justice* 28 (2013): 232–268. See also the essays, including from historical sources, collected in Mary Krane Derr, Linda Naranjo-Huebel, and Rachel MacNair, *Pro-Life Feminism: Yesterday and Today* (New York: Sulzburger & Graham Publishers, 1995).

67 "The American Woman: Then and Now," *The Equal Rights Amendment, Hearings Before the Subcommittee on Constitutional Amendments of the Committee on the Judiciary United States Senate* (1970), 668. Emphasis in original.

68 Timothy Walker, *Introduction to American Law* (Boston: Charles C. Little and James Brown), 222.

69 Ibid.

70 Ibid.

71 *Popular Misgovernment in the United States* (New York: Moffat, Yard, & Company, 1920).

72 570 U.S. 529.

· 3 ·

THE PROFOUND MISOGYNY OF THE COMMON LAW TRADITION WITHIN AND OUTSIDE OF COVERTURE

As I have been arguing, the *Dobbs* decision allowing (even encouraging) states to severely curtail or prohibit a woman's right to have an abortion is an excellent contemporary example of how the law is often used to reify social inequality, making a mockery of our purported ideals, hindering our efforts of achieving social justice in this society, and demanding our scholarly and civic response. *Dobbs* betrays our commitment to democracy,[1] the Rule of Law (i.e., what the *Dobbs* dissent characterized as the majority's rejection of *stare decisis* and the status of *Casey* as "precedent about precedent"),[2] as well as the law's belief in the dignity of the individual and his or her bodily integrity.[3] It lets down women and the men who partner with them, and the communities in which they live and express their lives,[4] while reifying unconscionable values from an unreasonable past that is best left far behind us. In this context *law is the problem*, not the solution, to our nation's failure to live up to its rhetorical commitment to freedom and equality, and judges must decide: to stand *for* or *against* total equality for women, and must step down from the bench if they stand against it. The fact that the *Dobbs* majority ruled as it did speak volumes to its own internalized misogyny.[5]

As I will demonstrate in this and in the following chapter, it is *undoubtedly* the case that, in the Common Law Tradition, women were considered second-class citizens (or worse), the property (or servant) of their husbands or fathers. This point was articulated well by Simone de Beauvoir: "By the time humankind reached the stage of written mythology and law, patriarchy was definitively established: it is males who write the codes. It is natural for them to give woman a subordinate situation."[6] Their identities, social value, and status as human beings were defined in contradistinction to their male counterparts. *He* sets the standards which *she* is obligated to follow. She exists to meet his needs. In surveying the development of the legal doctrine of "consortium," an influential Tort Hornbook[7] acknowledges that the "husband's interest in his relationship with his wife first received recognition as a matter of her services to him as a servant."[8] An early twentieth-century court exemplifies this view when it denied the right of a wife to recover for the loss of consortium due to her husband's injuries by a tortfeasor (i.e., the defendant in a tort lawsuit), stating:

> It is true that at common law the husband could maintain an action for the loss of the consortium of the wife, but within the legal meaning of consortium there was included not only affection, solace, comfort, companionship, and society incidental to the marital relation, but also the services of the wife. These services of the wife in the household, in the discharge of her domestic duties, in the care of the home, and in the education and rearing of the children belonged to the husband. They were of a practical and material value and capable of being estimated in money. If the wife for any reason was unable to perform them the loss was the husband's, not hers, and he was permitted to sue for the loss thereof.[9]

Most people today, who have not read the case law or studied legal history, have no real sense of what this meant, how totalitarian and awful society was (and still is in much of the world) toward women. We often wear rose-tinted glasses when we think about our past. We fail to see how (with few exceptions) utterly degraded and oppressed women were for the benefit of men and how that condition lasted for centuries. Given this knowledge, it should be obvious to all when, seen from the vantage point of today, how *outrageous* and unprofessional it is that the Supreme Court would countenance this brutal, soul-crushing history and give it a renewed salience as did the majority in *Dobbs v. Jackson Women's Health Organization*.[10] Because the Common Law Tradition's misogyny is still with us despite the best efforts of feminists to get rid of it, at least in a shadow but still corruptive form, this chapter engages with the historical record so that the impact of misogyny on society can be appreciated while we consider our collective response to *Dobbs*.

Coverture's Shadow in *Dobbs*[11]

Along with many of my readers (a presumption I feel confident in making), I have appreciated the world represented by *Roe* and *Casey* (at least in comparison to what came before it) and felt proud, more American, and wealthier as a citizen and human being because of it. Both cases (with all their faults) served as progressive social and cultural landmarks at the core of our citizenship. In other words, I value a nation that values its women and treats them with dignity and respect, and resent one that does not. I am shocked and saddened by the moral and social hole in our national fabric that is left by the demise of both cases and angered by the smug self-satisfaction of the Court in their dirty despicable work. I agree with President Barack Obama when he says that the "best judge of whether or not a country is going to develop is how it treats its women. If it's educating its girls, if women have equal rights, that country is going to move forward. But if women are oppressed and abused and illiterate, then they're going to fall behind."[12]

Most readers of this book are, if not feminists themselves of one sort or another, intelligent people with at least an interest in the history and cultural condition of women. They may have an inkling that something was terribly wrong in *Dobbs*. Granted, they do not like the *outcome* of *Dobbs*, stripping away a woman's constitutional right of reproductive freedom. There are many Supreme Court decisions that I do not like, but I nevertheless accept and understand the Court's reasoning for how it fits in with our larger legal context. I respect how other people have different views (but only to a point; I do not have to respect the viewpoints of Nazis or Klansmen, for example). I may have decided cases I disagree with differently, I tell myself, but so be it. Life goes on. *Dobbs*, however, is *different*. I not only dislike it, as others do, but I realize, as others may not, how unfounded legally it was and how it constitutes an unacceptable political *coup d'état* by—and I cannot help using this terrible judgmental and condemning word—the *enemy*. *Dobbs* represents yet another *low point* in American jurisprudence, along with *Johnson v. M'Intosh*,[13] *Prigg v. Pennsylvania*,[14] *Dred Scott v. Sandford*,[15] *Plessy v. Ferguson*,[16] and *Korematsu v. United States*[17] that must be repudiated (as these cases have been), the sooner the better. Democracy does have its enemies, personified in each of the above cases by the Supreme Court.

We may be irked, annoyed, even *outraged* by the ways in which the *Dobbs* Court came to its conclusion.[18] We suspect, although we may not be able to articulate why, that the *Dobbs* Court missed the forest for the trees. The Court's strategy of using the legal absence of protection for a woman's right to an abortion, while simultaneously ignoring all the ways in which this "absence" was part of an entrenched *affirmative* system of suppression and oppression of women as a class, cynically misdirects us from seeing the bigger picture. Instead of using this ugly and shameful past as an excuse for *not* changing (the *Dobbs*' reactive approach), we should use this past as evidence of the necessity (and inspiration) for granting women's *total* social and political equality. It is long past due.

Even intelligent readers may not often understand, viscerally that is, the *cutting* that history etched onto women's bodies, the slicing, the burning, the *pressing*.[19] Both Friedrich Nietzsche and Michel Foucault note the ways in which knowledge is a "knife" for cutting. They argue that knowing, punishment, and control are, throughout time, grisly rituals of induced pain on human bodies, a twisting, burning, molding, and disciplining of peoples' subjectivities.[20] This is another way, frequently unnoticed, by which women are created through the actions of men and the law's embedded violent masculinity. Man, the sovereign, demands his "pound of flesh" from *his* women. Man's claim to woman is among the oldest of property rights.[21] The obedience of women to his will is seldom enough: many men want to *consume* women.[22] This section provides that context for this legal bloodletting, spiritual and otherwise.

Women were utterly degraded by the Common Law Tradition, and we have come to recognize, for the most part, that such degradation is no longer desirable or appropriate and, thus, the authorities that the *Dobbs* Court relies on are simply incredulous, deserving not even a modicum of respect. Consequently, the *Dobbs* Court is disingenuous and manipulative for relying on them. Or, in the language I am using here, the legal authorities cited by the *Dobbs* Court are profoundly *anti-women* and, for that reason, should be rejected in the most strenuous terms possible. Recall, in *Casey*, the other precedent that the *Dobbs* Court callously overturned, the Justices were, unbelievably, in a position in which they had to hold unconstitutional the *husband's veto* over the wife's abortion, something in line with the Common Law Tradition's powers of the husband and the low status of the wife.

Consider what it means to grant power of that nature to a husband. In the late 1980s and early 1990s (as opposed to the 1880s or 1890s), some state legislatures (dominated by Christian, presumably white men) determined that it was a "good idea" that a woman's husband should be given such *sovereign*, life-changing power over his wife, a fellow citizen, nominally an equal under our secular laws. Such spousal veto power assumes an individual (the husband) who has the duty to *command* and another (the wife) who has a duty to *obey*. It reinforces, in the context of the family, the master/servant relationship between the sexes with the relative power differentials and legal effects. In rejecting this component of the legislation, the *Casey* Court noted:

> The husband's interest in the *life of the child* his wife is carrying does not permit the State to empower him with this troubling degree of authority over his wife. The contrary view leads to consequences reminiscent of the common law.[23]

It is interesting, from the point of view of this book, that this abortion-tolerant Court takes the position that the husband's interest here is that of the *child*. In effect, this is the same perspective of the *Dobbs* majority regarding the state's interest in rejecting a woman's constitutional right to an abortion. In contrast, what I argue below is that legal history suggests a *different* way of looking at understanding the husband's (or state's) interest, one that is suspicious of the Court's claim. Under this critical uncovering view, gleaned from the historical record, the husband's (or state's) interest is *less* in protecting the life of an unborn human being, and more about male or masculinist (and perhaps even sadist) *control* over women due to their entrenched second-class (or worse) status. As noted by the *Casey* court, this obscene power of a husband's sovereignty leads to *coverture*, the legal subordination of women to their husbands and other men in their lives. Imagine, the *Casey* Court continued:

> If a husband's interest in the potential life of the child outweighs a wife's liberty, the State could require a married woman to notify her husband before she uses a postfertilization contraceptive. Perhaps next in line would be a statute requiring pregnant married women to notify their husbands before engaging in conduct causing risks to the fetus. After all, if the husband's interest in the fetus' safety is a sufficient predicate for state regulation, the State could reasonably conclude that pregnant wives should notify their husbands before drinking alcohol or smoking. Perhaps married women should notify their husbands before using contraceptives or before undergoing any type of surgery that may have complications affecting the husband's interest in his wife's reproductive organs.[24]

This was *exactly* the situation of women in the Common Law Tradition, and a part of the United States today in the practice, under so-called "fetal protection" laws, of prosecuting women who are perceived of having insufficient "respect" to the health of their fetus (i.e., using alcohol, drugs, smoking, getting into accidents, being victimized, not wearing seatbelts, etc.).[25] Simply having a miscarriage may, in some states today, render a woman criminally suspect.[26]

A good overview of the claim that I am making regarding the inappropriateness of male domination over females, and downright ignored by the *Dobbs* Court, can be found in John Stuart Mill's *The Subjection of Women* (1869) when he summarized the relationship between women and men from the view of the mid-nineteenth century. This relationship "arose simply from the fact that, from the very earliest twilight of human society, every woman (owing to the value attached to her by men, combined with her inferiority in muscular strength) was found in a state of bondage to some man."[27] He goes on to explain:

> Laws and systems of polity always begin by recognizing the relations they find already existing between individuals. They convert what was a mere physical fact into a legal right, give it the sanction of society, and principally aim at the substitution of public and organized means of asserting and protecting these rights, instead of the irregular and lawless conflict of physical strength.[28]

In other words:

> Those who had already been compelled to obedience became in this manner legally bound to it. Slavery, from being a mere affair of force between the master and the slave, became regularized and a matter of compact among the masters, who, binding themselves to one another for common protection, guaranteed by their collective strength the private possessions of each, including his slaves.[29]

To say that women were, during the heyday of the Common Law Tradition and before, subservient to men would be no understatement. They were granted little agency or respect. While things have happily changed in some respects, the dependence of women on men still existed profoundly in Mill's time and existed through, at least, *Roe*, when the women's movement, utilizing a determined expressive purpose and strategic action, *forced* men to recognize their inherent autonomy and to respect their decisions. If men would not listen to them, the law, after *Roe*, would. And it did, at least for a while. Now, in some states, no one is compelled to listen to the urgent voice or pleas of a pregnant woman who wants or needs an abortion. Such a woman has been deemed an enemy of the state.

It is possible to read *Roe* differently, as some do, arguing (1) that *Roe* was more about facilitating consequence-free sexual access to women than it was about female equality; and (2) that the cultural moment of the 1960s and

1970s situating women's apparent empowerment was less about women's rights and freedoms and more about the rights women could be granted which would not threaten larger patriarchal and capitalist interests. These critics point to, among other things, the normalization and industrialization of pornography represented by the success of *Playboy* magazine and Hugh Hefner's support for legalized abortion, as well the idea that sexual liberation constituted a type of "rape," that many women were raped in the name of empowerment.[30] McKinnon's position on this issue is widely known. She argues that,

> under conditions of gender inequality, sexual liberation in this sense does not so much free women sexually as it frees male sexual aggression. The availability of abortion removes the one real consequence men could not easily ignore, and the one remaining legitimate reason that women have had for refusing sex besides the headache.[31]

As to the first point, it is one of the defining characteristics of liberalism that it is *not* radical, and we should not expect from it more than it can deliver. Rather, liberalism is cautious and hesitant in the types of change it supports. As it has become painfully clear, liberals often have big ideas but a weak stomach for substantive change and the sacrifices necessary to achieve them. Liberal reform is not revolutionary change and the more radical critics of the status quo are quick to point out the limited nature of liberalism's influence and its often fickle or insincere commitments. During the Civil Rights movement, both Martin Luther King Jr. and Malcolm X frequently articulated this point, chiding liberals by remarking in speeches that they almost preferred the white supremacist to the liberal in that they always knew what to expect from the white supremacist and were frequently disappointed by the seemingly friendly liberal. Finally, it is likely correct to say that liberalism has advanced women's rights only to the extent that a woman's interest aligns with liberal goals which can be limited, shortsighted, and compromised.[32]

As to the second point, the legalization and availability of abortion *does* increase sexual access to women by men. Nevertheless, I reject this cynical critique of abortion rights for the same reason I reject abortion restrictions: neither recognizes nor respects what the woman wants.

As Wendy Chapkis notes, "For a woman sex can be both an instrument to seduce male power *and* an interlude in the struggle with that power."[33] Moreover, women who are celibate, transexual, lesbian, or otherwise uninterested in vaginal intercourse may be profoundly pro-*Roe* for the reasons I am suggesting in this book: *Roe's* imperfect but important affirmation of a woman's autonomy, not just sexually, but in all aspects of her life. I see the essence of *Roe* as being when, for the first time, the Constitution backed women *as women* instead of seeing them only in their relationship to men. However imperfectly, *Roe* made real the power of a woman to say "no." Not just to childbirth, but to the demands of men generally. The predictable backlash against *Roe*, particularly in the church, must be seen in this context:

> Wives, submit yourselves to your own husbands as you do to the Lord. For the husband is the head of the wife as Christ is the head of the church, his body, of which he is the Savior. Now as the church submits to Christ, so also wives should submit to their husbands in everything.[34]

For giving power to women over men in this one important area, *Roe* was no minor moment in American legal history: for the first time, the Constitution recognized that the Rule of Law replaced the Rule of Might regarding women, creating the *semblance* of a more level playing field in the public sphere. This becomes clear when contemplating Mill's discussion of the historical "dependence" of women on men:

> But this dependence, as it exists at present, is not an original institution, taking a fresh start from considerations of justice and social expediency—it is the primitive state of slavery lasting on, through successive mitigations and modifications occasioned by the same causes which have softened the general manners, and brought all human relations more under the control of justice and the influence of humanity. It has not lost the taint of its brutal origin. No presumption in its favour, therefore, can be drawn from the fact of its existence. The only such presumption which it could be supposed to have, must be grounded on its having lasted till now, when so many other things which came down from the same odious source have been done away with. And this, indeed, is what makes it strange to ordinary ears, to hear it asserted that the inequality of rights between men and women has no other source than the law of the strongest.[35]

Unfortunately, few people outside of the legal profession have heard of the word "coverture" or the "merger" doctrine, but it was an important anchor in the legal and social lives of women for centuries, regulating with cold certitude nearly every aspect of a woman's day-to-day existence. As summarized by William Blackstone in 1769, upon marriage, husband and wife were one person, the wife having "merged" into that of her husband.[36]

In restating the rule that "an action at law may not be brought by a wife against her husband to recover money loaned by her to him," the Supreme Court of Pennsylvania embraced Blackstone's maxim of "merger" between husband and wife, precluding the possibility of a civil suit between them. This outcome, said the court, "is in exact accordance with the revealed will of God, was designed for the protection of the woman, and leads to that identification of sympathies and interests, which secures to families and neighbourhoods [sic] the blessings of harmony and good order."[37] Blackstone went as far as to write, without any apparent irony, that "even the disabilities which the wife lies under are for the most part intended for her protection and benefit: so great a favourite is the female sex of the laws of England."[38] Such "blessings" and "harmony" came at the *expense* of women because "merger" was no romantic sentiment or ideal, but the legal, political, and social *erasure* of the woman and a reinforcement of woman's second-class status generally.

Among other things, under coverture and other customs of the patriarchy in which they lived, women were prohibited from becoming educated or, if educated, practicing many professions such as being a doctor, lawyer, clergy, or barkeep.[39] Additionally, restrictive labor laws limited the number of hours a woman could work in certain occupations to protect the health of the "race" (i.e., the ability of the working-class women to reproduce the working-class labor pool).

Muller v. Oregon represents this trend.[40] The *Muller* Court, persuaded by Louis Brandeis' famous brief (light on legal argument but richly filled with sociological and empirical evidence of the poor condition of labor in this country)[41] in defense of the state law prohibiting women from working in laundries for more than 10 hours a day, was genuinely concerned with working mothers being too worn out or sick to nurse and raise children in safe and supportive environments, and the case presents an early and important victory for labor rights. However, as scholars have long pointed out, to achieve this laudable end, the Court and the law's supporters had to play up the notion of woman as "fetal containers" and "domestic servants," long assumptions in our nation's Common Law and religious traditions.[42]

Law and religion both demanded that women belonged in the home raising children. The problem, however, particularly when the Industrial Era was in full swing, was that working-class women needed employment outside of the home. These women had no choice and society needed to be ensured that such working women had enough stamina to survive, not only the rigors of industrial labor, but also what later became known as the "second shift,"[43] where working women, in addition to their paid labor, are held responsible for the lion's share of the child-raising, homemaking tasks, and uncompensated tasks of emotional labor. Harsh physical exertions and demanding working hours at manual labor, while acceptable for men who are "built" for it and are expected to excel in the marketplace on their own, must excuse women to protect their essential roles in the private sphere.[44] In *Muller*, the Court reasoned:

> It is impossible to close one's eyes to the fact that she still looks to her brother and depends upon him [. . .] that she is so constituted that she will rest upon and look to him for protection; that her physical structure and a proper discharge of her maternal functions—having in view not merely her own health, but the well-being of the race—justify legislation to protect her from the greed as well as the passion of man. The limitations which this statute places upon her contractual powers . . . are not imposed solely for her benefit, but also largely for the benefit of all [. . .]. The two sexes differ in structure of body, in the functions to be performed by each, in the amount of physical strength, in the capacity for long-continued labor, particularly when done standing, the influence of vigorous health upon the future well-being of the race, the self-reliance which enables one to assert full rights, and in the capacity to maintain the struggle for subsistence.[45]

For similar reasons, women (married or not) were prevented from competing in many sports; consider two examples. In *State v. Hunter*, the plaintiff, "a person of the feminine sex," was charged with the *crime* of "participating in wrestling competition and exhibition" in violation of a state statute, which the court upheld.[46] In *Lafler v. Athletic Board*, the court precluded a qualified female boxer from competition on the grounds that "[b]oxing has developed certain safety rules and procedures specifically designed for men."[47] Moreover, the court noted, "It is unrealistic to believe that women could enter the sport of boxing and operate under the same rules with no detrimental effect on the safety of the participants."[48]

While the *Lafler* court may, in some sense, be correct in mentioning the safety issue (boxing is a notoriously brutal and deadly sport),[49] it does not even consider how male sports such as boxing (or wrestling) were designed by men for men and that different rules and different protective equipment could be integrated into the sport, making it more inclusive to people of different body types. To take one example, "grunt perseverance" in *taking* a punch could be paired with some other skill set, perhaps one involving dexterity and the ability to *avoid* being hit. Even a sport as gender-neutral as running excluded women on the grounds that women were physiologically unfit for the event. This was challenged in 1967 by Kathrine Switzer who became the first (known) woman to run the Boston Marathon. Officials tried to physically prevent her from running and, when that failed, she was disqualified.[50]

Under the Common Law Tradition, women were denied having custody of their children on the demand by the husband (discussed below), inheriting property, managing community property,[51] and keeping their own domicile or their own names. As a late nineteenth-century court summarized the Common Law Tradition on this point noted:

> For several centuries, by the common law . . . a woman, upon her marriage, takes her husband's surname. That becomes her legal name, and she ceases to be known by her maiden name. By that name she must sue and be sued, make and take grants and execute all legal documents. Her maiden surname is absolutely lost, and she ceases to be known thereby.[52]

Another court, in upholding the Common Law Tradition rule, reasoned that

> so long as the husband is burdened with the responsibility of feeding and clothing the family, the wife, and children, that very responsibility ought to carry with it the authority to determine the location where his toil will earn its best reward for their benefit [. . .]. The burden of his responsibility is the secret of his authority.[53]

Or, as the Supreme Court noted in 1937, when it rejected a man's challenge to paying a poll tax that did not apply to women: "The laws of Georgia declare the husband to be the head of the family and the wife to be subject to him. To subject her to the levy would be to add to his burden."[54] Married women could not keep their own wages or acquire a credit card without their husband's approval.[55] In its rationale for why involuntary military service for men but not women was a legitimate government interest, one court observed, "Congress followed the teachings of history that if a nation is to survive, men must provide the first line of defense while women keep the home fires burning."[56] In sum, throughout much of history, a woman's identity was derivative—it came from the males in her life.

Political Franchise, Jury Duty, and Other Badges of Citizenship

Until 1920 with the passing of the Nineteenth Amendment, women had an uneven franchise in this country.[57] In an 1807 instance, New Jersey women had the franchise taken away from them after having had it for a number of years.[58] In his lyceum lecture of 1842, former President John Quincy Adams explained the reasoning behind the exclusion of women from the ballot box: namely, that the state presupposes the marital relationship in which "the will or vote of every family must be given by its head, the husband and father."[59] Consequently, Adams argues that women "can have no direct agency in the social compact which constitutes the body politic."[60] Another ex-President cast women's disenfranchisement in more overtly theistic terms. According to Grover Cleveland, "Sensitive and responsible women do not want to vote. The relative positions to be assumed by man and woman in the working out of our civilization were assigned long ago by a higher intelligence than ours."[61]

In some cases, a woman could be, under the Expatriation Act of 1907 (modified by the Cable Act in 1922 but not fully repealed until 1940), stripped of her U.S. citizenship if her husband was not a citizen.[62] In giving its blessing to this policy, the Court noted:

> The identity of husband and wife is an ancient principle of our jurisprudence. It was neither accidental nor arbitrary and worked in many instances for her protection. There has been, it is true, much relaxation of it but in its retention as in its origin it is determined by their intimate relation and unity of interests, and this relation and unity may make it of public concern in many instances to merge their identity, and give dominance to the husband. It has purpose, if not necessity, in purely domestic policy; it has greater purpose and, it may be, necessity, in international policy.[63]

The Court went on to explain that a woman's union with a foreigner could precipitate "international complications" which the federal government had the right to prevent.[64]

The more emotional and irrational sentiment underlying this legal disability was overtly stated in the educational context by J. L. McBrien, a state superintendent of public instruction, at an education conference. On a panel discussing "moral training" in the public schools, McBrien remarked:

> [E]very woman who abuses the freedom of American womanhood by unfaithfulness lends the powerful incitement of her personality to the slavery of the past and to the failure of the republic; that every woman who leaves the duty and decorum of her native land and prostitutes her American home to the scandals, the vices, the social immoralities and moral impurities of foreign cities, not only compasses her own shame, but mars the fame and name of all . . . daughters.[65]

In short, no rational woman would want to marry a foreigner. The act was tantamount to treason against body, soul, and state.

In *Bradwell v. Illinois* we see a similar attempt to define and control women when the majority found "the right to control and regulate the granting of license to practice law in the courts of a state" to be unimpaired by the

Fourteenth Amendment. Paralleling the *Dobbs* decision, this meant that it was a state's decision to grant this right or not based upon its views of the "proper" role of women. That role, then, was supplied by a notable concurrence, which read, "The natural and proper timidity and delicacy which belongs to the female sex evidently unfits it for many of the occupations of civil life [. . .]. The paramount destiny and mission of women are to fulfill the noble and benign offices of wife and mother. This is the law of the Creator."[66] The concurrence continued:

> Man is, or should be, woman's protector and defender. The natural and proper timidity and delicacy which belongs to the female sex evidently unfits it for many of the occupations of civil life. The Constitution of the family organization, which is founded in the divine ordinance as well as in the nature of things, indicates the domestic sphere as that which properly belongs to the domain and functions of womanhood. The harmony, not to say identity, of interest and views which belong, or should belong, to the family institution is repugnant to the idea of a woman adopting a distinct and independent career from that of her husband.[67]

Other courts and lawmakers felt similarly and pointed to the "dainty ears" of women as a reason for their political and civic exclusion. For instance, speaking against a bill allowing women to serve on juries in 1922, a legislator in the Maryland General Assembly warned: "Jury service is a revolting thing. You [Ladies] will be forced to hear horrible things, to listen to tales of vice and sagas of corruption. Your dainty ears will be filled with stories which will keep you awake at night and, in addition to that, it's no job for a woman."[68] In the same context, Judge Carroll T. Bond of the Supreme Bench of Baltimore City warned: "The appointment of women jurors would mean the entire reversal of our treatment of women. Those who sit on juries in criminal courts must face the unveiling of the utmost of human depravity."[69] This rationale was reiterated by another court:

> Criminal court trials often involve testimony of the foulest kind, and they sometimes require consideration of indecent conduct, the use of filthy and loathsome words, references to intimate sex relationships, and other elements that would prove humiliating, embarrassing and degrading to a lady.[70]

The legal doctrine that applied in these examples was called *propter defectum sexus*, a prohibition based on the "defect of sex."[71] As a court in 1944 explained, "[F]rom the earliest period in the history of the common law, grand and petit juries have consisted exclusively of men."[72] In striking down the practice of removing potential woman from juries via preemptory challenges, in 1994, the Supreme Court in *J. E. B. v. Alabama* reviewed:

> In this country, supporters of the exclusion of women from juries tended to couch their objections in terms of the ostensible need to protect women from the ugliness and depravity of trials. Women were thought to be too fragile and virginal to withstand the polluted courtroom atmosphere.[73]

A similar rationale was used to keep woman off of juries in another well-known case.[74] As the *Dobbs* dissent noted, just ten years before *Roe*, the Supreme Court in *Hoyt v. Florida* upheld a Florida law excusing all women from jury duty unless they volunteered because the Court found that women are "still regarded as the center of home and family life" and have "special responsibilities."[75] More closely echoing the nineteenth century's legal view of women being unfit for legal work, the Supreme Court of Mississippi, in the mid-twentieth century, said,

> The legislature has the right to exclude women [from jury service] so they may continue their service as mothers, wives, and homemakers and also to protect them (in some areas, they are still upon a pedestal) from the filth, obscenity, and noxious atmosphere that so often pervades a courtroom during a jury trial.[76]

Who knew that men could be so vile and disgusting? Women, of course, lived with men, but that lived experience did not mean that women had the right to *judge* men or to sit in judgment of *other* women charged for alleged crimes against *men*. This was the situation in *Hoyt* when a domestically abused wife was found guilty of murdering her husband by an all-male jury.

"A Jury of Her Peers," a short story published in 1916 by journalist Susan K. Glaspell dramatizes the inequality inherent in these types of situations. The story involves the murder of an abusive husband by his wife. (Using a rope, the wife strangled the husband while he slept.) The male investigators were summoned to the house to document the crime and collect evidence, searched in vain to discover a motive for the killing which they needed to secure the conviction of the wife. Along with them came two women (their wives) who, in an act of kindness, wanted to pick up a few things for the jailed wife (i.e., clothes and knitting supplies).

As the men conduct their investigation, they talk among themselves, belittling the women for their domesticity. In listening to the men go about their work, the women realize that the men *cannot* see the emotional abuse that the spouse-killing wife suffered at the hands of her husband. The women were able to discern the abuse from clues scattered through the clutter of the house—for example, the irregularity of a knitting pattern and the disarray of certain items in the kitchen. The women then solve the crime after they find the dead body of the wife's beloved canary whose song, they acknowledge, was her only joy in the world. Upon inspecting the bird, which was carefully wrapped in a small box, the women realize that the husband had *broken the bird's neck* in an act of spite against his wife, and that was the last straw, causing the wife to snap. The women, however, do not report their conclusion to the male investigators, as they clearly sympathized with the wife who was metaphorically smothered by her husband, who kept her lonely, isolated, and unhappy. These women, we realize, were scarcely better off than the defendant, fortunate only in having less abusive husbands but otherwise living the same life of stifling subordination and second-class status.[77]

Condemned or Controlled for Their Sexuality

Generally, women (married or not) were controlled by the law in a myriad fashion, including sexually. Writing in 2004, Thomas G. West states clearly the conservative belief that one's sexuality, far from being a private matter, has dire national security implications that society must regulate. He points with disdain to a famous (and somewhat nebulous) passage from the Supreme Court in *Casey* that declared: "the heart of liberty is the right to define one's own concept of existence, of meaning, of the universe, and of the mystery of human life" (note, this language was also attacked in *Dobbs*). West then draws out the implication of this view from the conservative world view:

> The Founders would have replied that we are precisely not free to define our own concept of existence and meaning. God and nature have established the "laws of nature and of nature's God," which have already defined it for us. Human beings, Jefferson wrote, are "inherently independent of all but moral law." If men defy that law, they are not free. They are slaves, at first to their own passions, eventually to political tyranny. For men who cannot govern their own passions cannot sustain a democratic government.[78]

While West is not singling out women here, society largely does. Society tends to be suspicious of sex, which means in practice that it is suspicious of women as sexual beings. For example, the federal Mann Act, passed in 1910, exemplifies the notion that independent women must be protected from sexual activity.[79] The Act assumes that women are naturally chaste and virtuous and cannot become a "whore" unless raped, seduced, drugged, or deserted. Eric Weiner explains the context for the Act: "[N]ew technologies such as the typewriter allowed women to support themselves for the first time, and many flocked to the cities. Suddenly, there were concerns about the country's moral underpinning."[80]

Likewise, the Muncy Act of 1913 required courts in Pennsylvania to assign women (but not men) an *indeterminate* sentence if convicted of a crime punishable for more than one year.[81] The law assumed that the inherent physical and psychological differences between the sexes, as well as the woman's potential role as a mother in nurturing and educating a child, justified the differential treatment (i.e., a *longer* period of incarceration) which was deemed "rehabilitational" to redeem the woman so as to serve her feminine function as a "good" mother.[82]

Even when the enhanced punishment went the other way and punished men more severely for acts of reciprocal responsibility, overt sexism lay at its roots. For example, as emphasized by a Hawaiian court upholding a differential punishment for adultery burdening the male, "There is in the law of nature as well as of civilized society a marked distinction between men and women and this distinction may well be taken into consideration by the legislature."[83] The difference, the court explained, was that

> the punishment of the woman, aside from any further punishment that might be prescribed by law, was already much more severe than that of the man, for in her case, besides the loss of her virtue and the ostracism attached to the wearer of the "scarlet letter," she ran the risk of becoming pregnant and forced to bear the burden of rearing an unwelcome intruder.[84]

This narrative appears decades later in a well-known Supreme Court statutory rape case "protecting" young women from sex by punishing the men (but not the women) who have consensual intercourse with her. Here, the Court reiterated the threat of pregnancy to the woman:

> We need not be medical doctors to discern that young men and young women are not similarly situated with respect to the problems and the risks of sexual intercourse. Only women may become pregnant, and they suffer disproportionately the profound physical, emotional, and psychological consequences of sexual activity. The statute at issue here protects women from sexual intercourse at an age when those consequences are particularly severe.[85]

While statutory rape laws tend to be gender-neutral these days, they are still deeply problematical, as they assume the irrationality and incompetence of younger women (and young men) who engage in otherwise healthy sexual activity, illustrating our society's irrationality (and severe repression) regarding sexuality, particularly in the case of women. Assuming that such women need "protection" from significantly older men who design to take advantage of her (an important concern, I understand, but also one that is questionable on agency grounds, as well as for the stereotyping of male behavior), such assumptions are clearly unwarranted with couples who are peers close in age. Even with modern so-called "Romeo and Juliet" qualifications, which reduce the severity of the crime and the punishment when both partners to the liaison are of a similar age and status, the state invasion of privacy is palpable and repugnant, its paternalism highly objectionable, and it leads to other terrible legal outcomes, for example, treating minors as sex offenders for consensual sexting.[86]

Moreover, "Romeo and Juliet" laws have been used to exclude same-sex couples from protection. In *State v. Limon*, for example, the Supreme Court of Kansas was faced with a same-sex couple who did *not* qualify for the reduction as the law was intended to protect *opposite*-sex couples, a clear example of legislative homophobia.[87] As a result, the defendant was sentenced to more than 17 years in prison for consensual oral sex with a younger male, close in age. If the "Romeo and Juliet" law had applied, as it would have had the consensual sexual encounter been between an opposite-sex couple, the maximum sentence would have been 15 months (also outrageous for harmless and even psychologically healthy behavior that millions of Americans, including those presumably under 18, regularly engage). But for the *Lawrence v. Texas* decision, which held irrational laws that discriminate against LGBT people solely on their sexuality,[88] decided *after* Limon's conviction but *before* his state Supreme Court appeal, Limon would have lost his case.

In other situations, society needed to be protected *from* women's sexuality. Soldiers, for example, during wartime, were seen as being particularly vulnerable to the advances of "immoral" women, putting them at risk for a sexually transmitted disease (STD), impeding their functionality as soldiers. As one publication warned: "Women who solicit soldiers for immoral purposes are usually disease spreaders and friends of the enemy."[89] Starting in World War I, the government grew concerned that soldiers in military training camps would be exposed to (and targeted by) the "presence of young girls in the neighborhood" due to the "lure of the uniform." It concluded that "Girls often lose their heads in a whirl of emotion brought about by these unusual conditions—and therein lies the problem."[90]

In this World War I context (then called the "Great War") of keeping men healthy and fit to fight, First Lieutenant Walter Clarke made a point to declare the male soldiers as the *innocent party* in consensual sexual relations who needed looking after by the government. These young men who, while as civilians, he claimed, lived upstanding and "wholesome" lives, were "entirely blameless" if they committed "an immoral act" with these flirty young women while in military service due to the "exceptional temptations which come to a man in uniform when on leave."[91] Clarke attributes any sexual transgression of the soldier to the fact that "he is living under conditions to which he is not accustomed. For this one lapse, he may be damaged and do damage out of all proportion to the seriousness of his offense. For such a man the government has a special responsibility."[92]

This "responsibility" became embodied in the Chamberlain-Kahn Act of 1918, a wartime public health program that came to be known as the "American Plan." The legislative intent was to fight the spread of STDs by targeting women and ignoring male responsibility for the spreading of venereal disease. It gave the Federal Government—which then encouraged (and funded) state governments to follow with their own legislation—the power to quarantine *any* woman suspected of having a STD. Women suspected to be prostitutes (or simply appearing to be attractive and found outside of their assumed "place") could be stopped, detained, forcibly inspected for evidence of disease, and sent to a rehabilitation center if they resisted, failed their examination, or registered a false positive.[93] Any evidence of venereal disease found during one of these exams could constitute proof of prostitution and be used against them. States then constructed facilities (detention centers) for the purpose of detaining and treating women with venereal disease; an estimated 30,000 women were detained and examined during the war.[94]

More generally, women could be harshly chastised (what today would constitute an assault) and beaten by their husbands.[95] They could be *institutionalized* on the word of their husbands with little to no recourse. Consider the experience of the nineteenth-century reformer, Elizabeth Packard, who, writing from personal experience, fought against a law that existed in 30 states at that time that allowed her to be institutionalized for over three years by her husband over a religious disagreement. According to the law,

> Married women and infants who, in the judgment of the medical superintendent . . . are evidently insane or distracted, may be entered or detained in the hospital on

> the request of the husband of the women, or the guardian of the infant, *without the evidence of insanity required* in other cases.[96]

Women could be raped by their husbands with impunity. According to Sir Matthew Hale, one classical common-law authority embraced by the *Dobbs* Court, "the husband cannot be guilty of a rape committed by himself upon his lawful wife for by their mutual matrimonial consent and contract the wife hath given up herself in this kind unto her husband which she cannot retract."[97] Under the "marital rape" doctrine, a married woman could not refuse sexual relations with her husband—the notion of "martial rape" was a legal oxymoron.[98] This began changing in the 1970s, but not until 1993 was it criminalized in all 50 states (although some distinctions between a married and unmarried defendant may still apply).

Women could be terrorized with impunity by the men in their lives who faced little to no accountability for their actions. In a particularly egregious case, the Supreme Court of Connecticut refused to grant a woman a divorce on the grounds of "intolerable cruelty" based on these facts:

> It appears, that the defendant insisted upon his marital rights [*i.e.*, coitus], against the wishes and remonstrances of his wife, when, in consequence of her ill health, it was indelicate, improper, unreasonable and injurious to her health to do so, and was calculated to endanger, and did in fact endanger her health.[99]

The court, however, sympathized with the husband: "We must believe from what is disclosed, that he knew [of his wife's poor health when he raped her], that such was her claim; but are we to allow nothing to the innocent opinions of a man mad with jealousy? Are we to allow nothing to the frailty of human nature, excited by passion?"[100] While divorce is easier today because of the liberalizing trend toward "no-fault" divorce since the 1970s, women continue to suffer extremely high levels of domestic violence. Globally, one in three women are victims of domestic violence[101] and there are low accountability rates for the men involved, as society refuses to see domestic violence as a systemic problem and enact policies to help reduce it.[102]

In a handful of states (Georgia, New Mexico, Texas, and Utah), a husband could *murder* his wife's lover with diminished responsibility or even be excused from legal liability entirely (in many other states, it was custom, not the law, that allowed husbands to do this). Under Article 1220 of the Penal Code of the State of Texas, for example, a homicide was considered "justifiable when committed by the husband upon one taken in the act of adultery with the wife, provided the killing take place before the parties to the act have separated."[103] This statute was in effect until 1973.[104] Georgia had a similar law in effect until 1977.[105] The logic for this legal rule (and cultural practice) was explained by an antebellum Georgia court:

> In what has society a deeper concern than in the protection of female purity, and the marriage relation? The wife cannot surrender herself to another. It is treason against the conjugal rights. Dirty dollars will not compensate for a breach of the nuptial vow. And if the wife is too weak to save herself, is it not the privilege of the jury to say whether the strong arm of the husband may not interpose, to shield and defend her from pollution?[106]

The threat to women then, and *now*, comes largely from *inside* the home, by lovers, boyfriends, and husbands. As Gloria Steinem observes, "The most dangerous situation for a woman is not an unknown man in the street, or even the enemy in wartime, but a husband or lover in the isolation of their home."[107] Or, as Murray A. Straus noted in 1977, which is still the case today, that "if one is truly concerned with the level of violence in America, the place to look is in the home rather than on the streets."[108] These men, who assault and rape their girlfriends and wives, constitute the *very people that impregnate them* and then want to control them by controlling the outcome of that pregnancy.[109] Reversing constitutional protection for abortion means that the state now stands *on the side of woman's abuser*, either husband, boyfriend, or a stranger who rapes or sexually takes advantage of her,[110] including economic or emotional coercion. Even kind, loving men can be manipulative of vulnerable woman under the trying circumstances of an unplanned or unwanted pregnancy, and that "privilege" can only be negated by allowing a woman the sole power to terminate her pregnancy.[111] If a woman cannot make this decision for herself, nothing else can possibly matter—she becomes an object to be manipulated by, and in the interest of, men.

Conclusion

For many women (and men), the past and the struggles that have brought us this far, are not seen as relevant to how we live our lives or how we think about ourselves. We fail to see how remnants of that past persist as a living force embodied in law and behavior permeating all that we do and are. We are encouraged to ignore this consciousness by all the superficial distractions of our environment, our mass-mediated and overly consumptive lives. It is sadly the case that an appreciation for the power of history (as well as *critical* history) is a luxury for us tenured white male academics who do not have to be concerned with the basic tasks of surviving the day, putting food on the table, and *not* getting sexually assaulted, luxuries that most women do not have.[112] For women experiencing life in the United States since the 1970s, when the constitutional landscape for women changed for the better, sexism, domestic violence, pay inequities, sexual harassment, etc. were, and continue to be, real issues to deal with, but they are not necessarily grounded in legal argument or an acknowledgment of past struggles and hard-won accomplishments. Rather, they are simply obstacles to overcome in trying to survive and get by in this society as a woman, which are even worse for women of color.[113]

The inequities of life's struggles are experienced individually, decontextualized from history and from the suffering of others. Struggling is something that women do as *women*, regardless of their other statuses as citizens, wives, lovers, homemakers, workers, members of religious communities, etc., and an appreciation of legal history does not seem relevant. As one early twentieth-century legal commentator pointed out, "Unjust as many of [the laws] appear it is probably that the idea of protesting against them seldom occurred to the women of that day. Many of them lived happy and contented lives, raised large families, and accepted their subordination as both natural and just."[114]

Undoubtedly women *did* protest to the extent they could, but the totality of the situation, as well as the human propensity to "put up with" hardships we cannot change, explains why woman have persevered for as long as they did under such deplorable conditions.[115] The fact that women like my mother might have, of necessity, embraced their chains and made the best they could with less-than-ideal circumstances, is still no argument for continuing to enslave them when we know better. And we know that most women want control over their bodies and their lives, even if they act in ways that seem—to men at least—counter to that end, as in the case of many Republican women.[116] As a result, some things pass as given, even if they have been forgotten or repressed by our busy, increasingly conservative-leaning judiciary and the society that relies on them to protect their rights. For example, Chief Justice John Roberts, part of the *Dobbs* majority, objected to the historical narrative I am sketching in this book. In his dissent in *Obergefell v. Hodges*, granting constitutional protection to same-sex marriages, he wrote, "If you had asked a person on the street how marriage was defined, no one would ever have said, 'Marriage is the union of a man and a woman, where the woman is subject to coverture.'"[117] But that just proves my point. People did not *think* about coverture, let alone judge it; they *lived it*: men to their benefit and women to their disadvantage and sorrow.

The legal and social subordination of women to men was, in many respects, being dismantled during the 1970s and the decades that followed. Much legal inequality, which governed the fundamental experience of women for centuries, had been going away. But how much did most women understand the totality of their past oppression and how it was presented as normative, or grounded in natural law theories of state paternal power? How many women, or men for that matter, see in that history more reason to fight for complete inclusion for us and our children? When do we say, "enough is enough!"? This sentiment lines up well with Seth Lerner's critical notion of "tradition," defined as "a continuous process in which we see the past through the present" which, in turn, "gives meaning to the past. It is our hindsight that discerns the patterns by which we make meaning out of disparate experiences. And in making meaning out of yesterday, we find purpose in today."[118]

It is easy to look to places like Saudi Arabia, Iran, or Afghanistan (or Alabama, Mississippi, or Texas) and congratulate us on our "progressiveness" when the ugly treatment of women (and LGBT individuals) in those nations and states are nakedly and unapologetically *chauvinistic, hateful, and murderous*. Outrage toward them, however justified, is not enough for us citizens in a democracy. We can be better. We can hold others to *our* standards when they imply a healthier, more well-rounded world, one accepting of difference and of the wisdom that comes from such recognition.[119]

While this is not the place for me to recount the litany and totality of the legal subordination of women in the United States, except in a few examples to help ground my various claims, I argue that, if women and men were more aware of the past and of the struggles for change, they would be less likely to accept the status quo as it currently stands. As Josephine Donovan warns, "Women will remain trapped in age-old patterns of enslavement and they will lose hard-won freedoms unless they learn and transmit their history."[120] Then they will see that the U.S. Supreme Court's *Dobbs* decision spits in their faces.[121] Strong words, I know, in an academic context, but nonetheless true. As Ruth Bader Ginsburg more diplomatically stated during her 1993 Supreme Court confirmation hearing before the Senate Judicial Committee, "The decision whether or not to bear a child is central to a woman's life, to her well-being and dignity. It is a decision she must make for herself. When government controls that decision for her, she is being treated as less than a fully adult human responsible for her own choices."[122]

Notes

1 At the time of the *Dobbs* decision, 64 percent of Americans opposed the overturning of *Roe*. See *Abortion Rights: NPR/PBS NewsHour/Marist National Poll*, NPR, May 2022, https://maristpoll.marist.edu/polls/npr-pbs-newshour-marist-national-poll-abortion-rights-may-2022/. That number has risen to 69 percent who approve of abortion being legal within the first three months of a pregnancy. See Lydia Saad, "Broader Support for Abortion Rights Continues Post-*Dobbs*," *Gallup*, June 14, 2023, https://news.gallup.com/poll/506759/broader-support-abortion-rights-continues-post-dobbs.aspx. It does not follow, however, to conclude that majority votes always achieve the correct ends; far from it, as the history of racism and homophobia demonstrate.

2 *Dobbs*, 2319.

3 The classic case is *McFall v. Shrimp*, 10 Pa. D. & C.3d 90 (1978), holding that an individual cannot be compelled by a court to aid another at their physical or mental expense, such as donating bone marrow to save the life of a sick person. Simply, there is no general "duty to rescue" others at one's personal expense. See, *Yania v. Bigan*, 397 Pa. 316 (1959). At the Supreme Court level, two important cases represent the right to protect one's body against government intrusion: *Winston v. Lee*, 470 U.S. 753 (1985) (prohibition against compelled surgical intrusion) and *Washington v. Harper*, 494 U.S. 210 (1990) (prohibition of involuntary use of antipsychotic medication).

4 Lauren Hoffman, Osub Ahmed, and Bela Salas-Betsch, "State Abortion Bans Will Harm Women and Families' Economic Security Across the U.S.," *Center for American Progress*, August 25, 2022, https://www.americanprogress.org/article/state-abortion-bans-will-harm-women-and-families-economic-security-across-the-us/.

5 In this context, it is fair to note that two of the justices in the *Dobbs* majority, Clarence Thomas and Brett M. Kavanaugh, have been credibly accused of serious sexual harassment, and that one, Amy Coney Barrett, has substantial connections to an extremist Christian sect with staunchly traditionalist (negative and highly pejorative) views of women as I have been criticizing here. Another, Samuel A. Alito Jr., is an outspoken champion of "religious liberty," by which he means that progressive social views that threaten religious *beliefs* (which are in fact protected by the First Amendment) and *practices* (which are unprotected under traditional First Amendment jurisprudence) need to be prevented by the courts. In other words, Alito wants to extend protections for discriminatory religious practices from civil rights objections by non-believers who want to be treated with respect and dignity in the public sphere. See Matt Ford, "Samuel Alito Believes That Christians Are Oppressed in America," *The New Republic*, August 2, 2022, https://newrepublic.com/article/167266/samuel-alito-religious-freedom-doctrine. "Religious freedom," for Alito, is freedom of religion (mainly *his*) to *impose* its beliefs on an unwilling society, a proposition we should *never* accept. Unfortunately, the Court has taken further steps down this road, with Alito authoring the Court's decision in 303 *Creative v. Elenis*, 143 S.Ct. 2298 (2023), allowing a First Amendment exception to public accommodations laws preventing discrimination based on sexual orientation.

6 *The Second Sex* (New York: Vintage, [1952]/1989), 104.

7 Hornbooks present overviews of an area of the common law that have percolated for centuries and are considered fundamental. They have historically been an important pedagogical tool for legal education. Popular hornbooks helped reify concepts across the profession and across generations. For a discussion of hornbook law, see https://www.law.cornell.edu/wex/hornbook_law.

8 *Prosser on Torts*, 3rd ed. (St. Paul: West Publishing Co., 1964), 895.

9 *Smith v. Nicholas Building Company*, 93 Ohio St. 101 (1915), 103.

10 142 S.Ct. 2228 (2022).

11 As discussed below, *coverture* is the not-so-ancient doctrine stipulating the legal subordination of women to their husbands and other men in their lives.

12 Diane Salvatore, from an interview with Barack and Michelle Obama, *Ladies' Home Journal*, September 2008.

13 21 U.S. 543 (1823), constitutionalizing the "doctrine of the sword" to justify the extermination of the Native Americans and the theft of their lands.

14 41 U.S. 539 (1842), upholding the Fugitive Slave Act of 1793, forcing free states to cooperate in the interstate rendition of escaped slaves found in their jurisdiction.

15 60 U.S. 393 (1857), excluding slaves and decedents of African slaves' protection from the constitution and the benefits of citizenship.

16 163 U.S. 537 (1896), establishing the "separate but equal" doctrine.

17 323 U.S. 214 (1944), upholding on racial grounds the rounding up and forced incarceration without trial of all members of a despised group.

18 The *Dobbs* majority provides four reasons for overturning precedent, including what it calls "legal error" by the *Roe* and *Casey* Courts, the difficulty in determining what constitutes an "undue burden" by a court on a woman's choice to have an abortion, the abortion right's purported "disruptive effect" on other areas of the law, and the absence of "concrete" reliance issues. I leave to others the in-depth critique of each of these, but argue, along with the *Dobbs* dissent, that the *only* reason why the *Dobbs* majority ruled the way they did was because they *wanted* to for ideological reasons, and they *could*: "The Court reverses course today for one reason and one reason only: because the composition of this Court has changed [. . .]. Today, the proclivities of individuals rule." Ibid., 2320.

19 "Pressing" was a common law legal form of torture in which stones or other weights were piled on a defendant who refused to enter a plea in a criminal proceeding. It was abolished in 1772 in England. Andrea McKenzie, "'This Death Some Strong and Stout Hearted Man Doth Choose': The Practice of *Peine Forte et Dure* in Seventeenth- and Eighteenth-Century England," *Law and History Review* 23, no. 2 (2005): 279–313.

20 See, Nietzsche, *On the Genealogy of Morals*, trans. Walter Kaufmann (New York: Vintage Books, [1887]/1989); and Foucault, "Nietzsche, Genealogy, History," in *Language, Counter-Memory, Practice: Selected Essays and Interviews* (Ithaca, NY: Cornell University, 1977), 139–164.

21 See generally, *Women and Property—Women as Property*, ed. Renée Hirschon (New York: Routledge, [1984]/2023).

22 Carole Adams, *The Sexual Politics of Meat: A Feminist-Vegetarian Critical Theory* (New York: Continuum, 1990).

23 *Casey*, 898. Italics added.

24 Ibid.

25 See Gabriela Weigel, Laurie Sobel, and Alina Salganicoff, "Criminalizing Pregnancy Loss and Jeopardizing Care: The Unintended Consequences of Abortion Restrictions and Fetal Harm Legislation," *Women's Health Issues* 30, no. 3 (2020): 143–146.

26 Aisha Sultan, "Could You Go to Prison for Having a Miscarriage?" *St. Louis Post Dispatch*, December 11, 2023, https://www.stltoday.com/news/local/column/aisha-sultan/sultan-could-you-go-to-prison-for-having-a-miscarriage/article_a5af41d0-9504-11ee-b4e8-33a37eee5d89.html.

27 (Arlington Heights, IL: Harlan Davidson, 1980), 5.

28 Ibid., 5–6.

29 Ibid.

30 Sheila Jeffreys, *Anticlimax: A Feminist Perspective on the Sexual Revolution* (Washington Square, NY: New York University Press, 1991); Whitney Strub, *Perversion for Profit: The Politics of Pornography and the Rise of the New Right* (New York: Columbia University Press, 2013); and Louise Perry, *The Case Against the Sexual Revolution* (Cambridge, UK: Polity, 2022).

31 *Toward a Feminist Theory of the State*, 190.

32 See generally, Allen J. Matusow, *The Unraveling of America: A History of Liberalism in the 1960s* (Athens, GA: The University of Georgia Press, [1984]/2009).

33 *Beauty Secrets: Women and the Politics of Appearance* (Boston: South End Press, 1986), 139.

34 Eph. 5:22–33 (NIV). For the classic nineteenth-century feminist response to Biblical sexism such as this, see Elizabeth Cady Stanton, *The Woman's Bible* (Amherst, NY: Prometheus Books, [1895]/1999).

35 *Subjection of Women*, 5–6.

36 *Commentaries on the Laws of England*, Book I (New York: Oxford University Press, [1775]/2016), 284–285. See also Edward Mansfield, *The Legal Rights, Liabilities and Duties of Women* (Salem, MA: Jewett and Co., 1845).

37 *Ritter v. Ritter*, 31 Pa. 396 (1858), 398. For a concise overview, see my, "Merger Doctrine," in *The Social History of American Families*, ed. Marilyn J. Coleman and Lawrence H. Ganong (Thousand Oaks, CA: Sage, 2014), 866–867.

38 *Commentaries on the Laws of England*, 287.

39 *Bradwell v. Illinois*, 83 U.S. 130 (1873) and *In re Goodell*, 39 Wis. 232 (1875) (lawyers); *Robinson's Case, 131 Mass*. 376 (1881), *Goesaert v. Cleary*, 335 U.S. 464 (1948), and *White v. Fleming*, 522 F.2d 730 (1975) (barkeeps). Elizabeth Blackwell, the first women to earn a M.D. in the United States recalls, in her autobiography, a dying friend pleading with her to study medicine, saying, "If I could have been treated by a lady doctor, my worst sufferings would have been spared me." *Pioneer Work in the Opening of the Medical Profession to Women* (London: Longsmans, Green, and Co., 1895), 27.

40 208 U.S. 412 (1908).

41 *Women in Industry: Decision of the United States Supreme Court in Curt Muller vs. State of Oregon: Upholding of the Oregon Hour Law for Women and Brief for the State of Oregon* (1908).

42 Lucinda J. Peach, "From Spiritual Descriptions to Legal Prescriptions: Religious Imagery of Woman as 'Fetal Container' in the Law," *Journal of Law and Religion* 10, no. 1 (1993): 73–93;

Ava Baron, "Protective Labor Legislation and the Cult of Domesticity," *Journal of Family Issues* 2, no. 1 (1981): 25–38.

43 Arlie Russell and Anne Machung, *The Second Shift: Working Parents and the Revolution at Home* (New York: Avon Books, 1990).

44 *Lochner v. New York*, 198 U.S. 45 (1905).

45 208 U.S. 412 (1908), 422.

46 208 Or. 282 (1956).

47 536 F. Supp. 104 (1982), 107.

48 Ibid.

49 "Statement on Boxing," *World Medical Association*, October 1983, revised October 2017, https://www.wma.net/policies-post/wma-statement-on-boxing/.

50 See Kathrine Switzer, *Marathon Woman: Running the Race to Revolutionize Women's Sports* (New York: Carroll & Graf, 2007).

51 It was not until 1979 that Louisiana, by Supreme Court decision, became the last state to treat spouses equally to manage community property. See *Kirchberg v. Feenstra*, 450 U.S. 455 (1981).

52 *Chapman v. Phoenix National Bank*, 85 N.Y. 437 (1881), 449.

53 *In re Bushbey*, 112 N.Y.S. 262 (1908), 264.

54 *Breedlove v. Suttles*, 58 S.Ct. 205 (1937), 207.

55 This was remedied by Equal Credit Opportunity Act of 1974.

56 *United States v. St. Clair*, 291 F. Supp. 122 (S.D.N.Y. 1968), 125.

57 *Minor v. Happersett*, 88 U.S. 162 (1875).

58 For the politics of this disenfranchisement, see Campbell Curry-Ledbetter, "Women's Suffrage in New Jersey 1776–1807: A Political Weapon," *George Town Journal of Gender and the Law* 21 (2019): 705–723.

59 John Quincy Adams, "The Social Compact, Exemplified in the Constitution of the Commonwealth of Massachusetts (preface, 8)," transcript of speech delivered at the Franklin Lyceum, Providence, RI, November 25, 1842, https://archive.org/details/socialcompactexe00adam/page/n9/mode/2up.

60 Ibid.

61 "Would Woman Suffrage Be Unwise?" *The Ladies Home Journal* 22 (1905): 6–7.

62 A contemporary, Rose Bres reviews the noteworthy case of Inez Milholland Boissevain, one of the few females practicing law and a suffragist leader who lost both her citizenship *and* her right to practice law because of her marriage to man with a Belgian nationality. *Maids, Wives, and Widows: The Law of the Land and of the Various States As It Affects Women* (New York: E.P. Dutton & Company, 1918), 50. For an overview of the Expatriation Act and efforts to amend it, see Meg Hacker, "When Saying 'I Do' Meant Giving up Your U.S. Citizenship," *Prologue* (2014): 56–61. For a detailed study, see Candice Lewish Bredbenner, *A Nationality of Her Own: Women, Marriage, and the Law of Citizenship* (Berkeley: University of California Press, 1998).

63 *MacKenzie v. Hare*, 239 U.S. 299 (1915), 311.

64 Ibid., 312.

65 "Moral Training Thru the Agency of the Public School" (lecture, National Education Association, Journal of the Proceedings and Addresses of the Forty-Fifth Annual Meeting, Los Angeles, CA, July 8–12, 1907).

66 *Bradwell v. Illinois*, 141.
67 Ibid.
68 Cited in Dennis M. Sweeney, "Commentary: June 1 Marks Anniversary of Having Women on Maryland Juries," *The Daily Record*, May 21, 2010, https://thedailyrecord.com/2010/05/31/june-1-marks-anniversary-of-having-women-on-maryland-juries/.
69 Ibid.
70 *Bailey v. State*, 215 Ark. 53 (1949), 61.
71 See my co-authored (with Candice Nunag Tardio) chapter, "*Propter Defectum Sexus* and the Stalled Gender Revolution," in *Women and Inequality in the 21st Century*, ed. Brittany C. Slatton and Carla D. Brailey (New York: Routledge, 2019), 24–39.
72 *State v. Emery*, 224 N.C. 581 (1944), 584.
73 511 U.S. 127 (1994), 132.
74 *Taylor v. Louisiana*, 419 U.S. 522 (1975).
75 368 U.S. 57 (1961), 62.
76 *State v. Hall*, 187 So. 2d 861 (1966), 863.
77 Susan K. Glaspell, *Her America: "A Jury of Her Peers" and Other Stories* (Iowa City: University of Iowa Press (2010), 81–102. The film adaption of Glaspell's story directed by Sally Heckel is powerful, visually reinforcing the skewed power dynamics and profound inequality of the male/female social relationship (New York, NY: Women Make Movies, 2005).
78 "The Liberal Assault on Freedom of Speech," in *Imprimis: 50th Anniversary Collection*, ed. Douglas A. Jeffrey (Hillsdale, MI: Hillsdale College Press, 2022), 220.
79 See Jessica Rae Pliley, "Any Other Immoral Purpose: The Mann Act, Policing Women, and the American State, 1900–1941" (PhD diss., Ohio State University, 2010) for a study of how the "any other immoral purpose" clause of the Act was used to criminalize (perceived) promiscuity, encouraging the draconian policing of women's sexuality.
80 Eric Weiner, "The Long, Colorful History of the Mann Act," March 11, 2008, in *National Public Radio's All Things Considered*, https://www.npr.org/transcripts/88104308.
81 Like much of the rest of ameliorative changes in the law we have been discussing, it was not until the late 1960s and early 1970s that the practice of sex-based sentencing began to change. See, for example, *Commonwealth v. Daniel*, 430 Pa. 642 (1968) and *United States ex rel. Robinson v. York*, 281 F. Supp. 8 (D. Conn. 1968).
82 See Gail Armstrong, "Females Under the Law—'Protected But Unequal,'" *Crime & Delinquency* 23, no. 2 (1977): 109–120.
83 *Territory v. Armstrong*, 28 Haw. 88 (1924), 97.
84 Ibid.
85 *Michael M. v. Superior Court*, 450 U.S. 464 (1981), 471.
86 Amy Adele Hasinoff, *Sexting Panic: Rethinking Criminalization, Privacy, and Consent* (Urbana, IL: University of Illinois Press, 2015).
87 280 Kan. 275 (2005).
88 539 U.S. 558 (2003).
89 American Social Hygiene Association, *Keeping Fit to Fight* (1917), 4.
90 War Department, *Committee on Protective Work for Girls* (1917), 3.
91 "Social Reasons for Medical Prophylaxis," *Social Hygiene* 5, no. 1 (January 1919): 46.

92 Ibid. How often at the time of sentencing have we heard judges regretting the punishment of male sex offenders using similar language, before offering a lighter sentence—the case of Brock Turner, who had raped an unconscious woman in the street outside of a college party, being a recent example. See Matt Hamilton, "Brock Turner to be Released from Jail After Serving Half of Six-Month Sentence in Stanford Sexual Assault Case," *Los Angeles Times*, August 30, 2016, https://www.latimes.com/local/lanow/la-me-ln-brock-turner-release-jail-20160829-snap-story.html. In another extreme case, a judge gave an *18 month sentence* to a man who *murdered* his wife after finding her in bed with another man. Said the judge at the sentencing hearing, "I seriously wonder how many men married five, four years would have the strength to walk away without inflicting some corporal punishment." *The New York Times*, October 19, 1994, https://www.nytimes.com/1994/10/19/us/punishment-is-18-months-for-killing-cheating-wife.html.

93 Martha Falconer, "The Part of the Reformatory Institution in the Elimination of Prostitution," *Social Hygiene* 5, no. 1 (January 1919): 160–166; William Thomas, *The Unadjusted Girl* (Boston: Little, Brown, and Company, 1923).

94 See Scott Wasserman Stern, "The Long American Campaign against Venereal Disease and Its Carriers," *Harvard Journal of Law and Gender* 38 (2015): 373–436.

95 *Bradley v. State*, 1 Miss. 156 (1824), 157 upholding the husband's power of "moderate correction" of his wife on the grounds that he is "answerable for her misbehaviour."

96 Packard, *Modern Persecution, or Married Woman's Liabilities* vol. II (1874), 216, italics added. This phenomenon is discussed in Phyllis Chesler's "Women of the Asylum: First-Person Accounts of Women Hospitalized in American Psychiatric Institutions 1840–1945," in *Patriarchy: Notes of an Expert Witness* (Monroe, ME: Common Courage Press, 1994), 15–33.

97 *Pleas of the Crown* (London, [1736]/1847), 629.

98 Maria Pracher, "The Marital Rape Exemption: A Violation of a Woman's Right of Privacy," *Golden Gate University Law Review* 11, no. 3 (1981): 717–757.

99 *Shaw v. Shaw*, 17, Conn. 189, 195 (1845).

100 Ibid.

101 According to the World Health Organization, "Across their lifetime, 1 in 3 women, around 736 million, are subjected to physical or sexual violence by an intimate partner or sexual violence from a non-partner." "Devastatingly Pervasive: 1 in 3 Women Globally Experience Violence," *WHO News Release*, March 9, 2021, https://www.who.int/news/item/09-03-2021-devastatingly-pervasive-1-in-3-women-globally-experience-violence.

102 Alisha Haridasani Gupta, "Is the Legal System an Effective Solution to Domestic Violence?" *The New York Times*, December 15, 2020, https://www.nytimes.com/2020/12/15/us/domestic-violence-fka-twigs-shia-labeouf.html#:~:text=LaBeouf%20told%20The%20New%20York,or%20a%20conviction%2C%20said%20Ms.A scholarly but dated discussion appears in Caroline Forell and Donna Matthews, *A Law of her Own: The Reasonable Woman as a Measure of Man* (New York: New York University Press, 2000).

103 *Price v. State*, 18 Tex. Ct. App. 474 (1885). This protection applied only to the man. When a woman tried to evoke this in her defense of shooting her husband's lover, it was denied in *Reed v. State*, 123 Tex.Crim. 348 (1933). For context, see William M. Ravkind, "Comment, Justifiable Homicide in Texas," *Southwestern Law Journal* 13 (1959): 508–524.

104 *Shaw v. State*, 510 S.W. 2d 926 (1974).

105 *Burger v. State*, 238 Ga. 171 (1977).

106 *Briggs v. State*, 29 Ga. 723 (1860), 729.

107 *Revolution from Within: A Book of Self-Esteem* (Boston: Little, Brown and Company, 1992), 261.

108 "Sexual Inequality, Cultural Norms, and Wife-Beating," in *Women into Wives: The Legal and Economic Impact of Marriage*, ed. James Robert Chapman and Margaret Gates (Beverly Hills, CA: Sage, 1977), 543. As Betty Friedan noted in a 1968 speech, "Perhaps the least understood fact of American political life is the enormous buried violence of women in this country today." "Our Revolution is Unique," reprinted in Kenneth M. Dolbeare and Michael S. Cummings, *American Political Thought*, 5th ed. (Washington, DC: CQ Press, 2004), 452.

109 United Nations Office on Drugs and Crime, "Global Study on Homicide" (Vienna, 2018).

110 See Nayanika Guha, "In Multiple States, Rapists Can Sue Their Victims for Parental Custody," *Prism*, March 22, 2022, https://www.who.int/news/item/09-03-2021-devastatingly-pervasive-1-in-3-women-globally-experience-violence. Guha reports that nearly 3 million women in the United States have experienced a rape-induced pregnancy in their lifetimes. Few rapes lead to convictions and non-convicted rapists can have standing (i.e., the legal right) to sue the women he attacked for shared parental rights; Michaela Haas, "When Your Rapist Demands Custody," *Mother Jones*, September/October 2019, 30–32.

111 Recall Abigail Adams' warning to her husband, John Adams while at the Constitutional Convention in March 1776: "Do not put such unlimited power into the hands of the Husbands. Remember all Men would be tyrants if they could." "Abigail Adams to John Adams, 31 March 1776," Founders Online, accessed January 1, 2024, https://founders.archives.gov/documents/Adams/04-01-02-0241. To which he responded, "Depend upon it, we know better than to repeal our masculine systems." "Letter from John Adams to Abigail Adams, 14 April 1776" [electronic edition], Adams Family Papers: An Electronic Archive, Massachusetts Historical Society, accessed January 1, 2024, http://www.masshist.org/digitaladams/.

112 I am not suggesting that academic women are free of these problems. Being a woman (and being a mother as well) has its own inequities in academia, regardless of the status that comes with that position. Moreover, not all people in higher education benefit equally from that status as the academic hierarchy is gendered. For essays that engage the inequality in higher education between women and men, see *Mama PhD: Women Write about Motherhood and Academic Life*, ed. Elrena Evans and Carolina Grant (New Brunswick, NJ: Princeton University Press, 2008) and *Surviving Sexism in Academia: Strategies for Feminist Leadership*, ed. Kirsti Cole and Holly Hassel (New York: Routledge, 2017).

113 See the path-breaking black-feminist anthology *All the Women Are White, All the Blacks Are Men, But Some of Us Are Brave*, ed. Akasha Gloria Hull, Patricia Bell-Scott, and Barbara Smith (Old Westbury, NY: The Feminist Press, 1982).

114 Ruth A. Gallaher, *Legal and Political Status of Women in Iowa* (Iowa City: State Historical Society of Iowa, 1918), 12.

115 The psychological theory of "Learned Helplessness," first articulated in 1967, is one way to explain this phenomenon. See Steven F. Maier and Martin E. P. Seligman, "Learned Helplessness at Fifty: Insights from Neuroscience," *Psychological Review* 123, no. 4 (2016): 349–367.

116 Sam Zaleski, "More Republican Women Than You Think Have Had Abortions. Here's How I Know," *Politico*, July 31, 2022, https://www.politico.com/news/magazine/2022/07/31/republican-women-have-abortions-too-00048632. It is not just republican *women*; see Arwa Mahdawi, "A Republican Theme on Abortions: 'It's OK for Me, Evil for Thee,'" *The Guardian*, August 25, 2018, https://www.theguardian.com/world/2018/aug/25/a-republican-theme-on-abortions-its-ok-for-me-evil-for-thee.

117 576 U.S. 644 (2015), 692.

118 *Tradition* (New York: Oxford University Press, 2016), ix.

119 A reader of this book commented that feminists and other critics complaining about such things are often accused of "cultural imperialism." I experienced this directly. At Duke University where I earned my JD, and at the University of Maryland in a "job talk," I defended the (then new) U.S. policy of recognizing foreign women fleeing their nations to avoid being subjected to female genital mutilation as eligible for political asylum. In both settings I was attacked as endorsing "cultural imperialism," imposing my western liberal views on other cultures. I rejected that view on the grounds that the condemnation of cruelty is not only a "western" value. This episode, and my defense of the U.S. policy against this charge, as well as my preference for liberal against illiberal views, is recounted in my chapter, "Hierarchy Is Not Harmony: A View of the Traditional Chinese Family," in *Chinese Communication Studies: Contexts and Comparisons*, ed. Xing Lu, Wenshan Jia and D. Ray Heisey (Westport, CT: Greenwood Press, 2002), 119–133.

120 *Feminist Theory: The Intellectual Traditions*, 3rd ed. (New York: Continuum, 2000), 15.

121 For example, when the *Dobbs* majority portrays that the common law was "anti-abortion" or "pro-life" a knowledgeable person should wince. Not only is the Common Law Tradition anti-women, but its only concern with women *as women* dealt with reduction to their ovaries and whatever services they could provide to men. If this is not an example of "invidiously discriminatory animus" toward women as required by the Court for judicial cognizance in *Bray v. Alexandria Women's Health Clinic*, 506 U.S. 263 (1993), discussed in Chapter 5, I do not know what can be, and the Court's inability to recognize it as such shows the ineffectiveness and disgrace of the Common Law Tradition as well as the poverty of the "originalist" school of constitutional interpretation which guided the Court's analysis in this case.

122 *Nomination of Ruth Bader Ginsburg to be Associate Justice of the Supreme Court of the United States, Hearings Before the Committee on the Judiciary, United States Senate*, 103rd Cong. 207 (1993). Ironically, Justice Ginsberg, the individual most responsible for the legal revolution in women's rights, refused—near the end of her illustrious career when, in poor health and clearly dying—to resign from the court when, at a time a few years earlier, Congress would have been able to replace her with someone committed to not only *Roe* but to everything which *Roe* stood for. Jim Geraghty, "Ruth Bader Ginsburg's Unexpected Legacy," *National Review*, June 24, 2022, https://www.nationalreview.com/corner/ruth-bader-ginsburgs-unexpected-legacy/.

· 4 ·

CHRISTIANITY, AND THE *PATRIA POTESTAS* POWER OF THE HUSBAND/FATHER/STATE IN THE COMMON LAW TRADITION

This chapter continues the historical narrative begun in the previous one. Both chart how the historical—and some would say, current—social and legal limitations on a woman's dignity and agency were grounded in patriarchy, an ideological construct that provided reasons and values for why women were (or should be) subordinate to men. As we have seen, and will continue to explore, men were for religious and/or biological reasons believed to be responsible for their households and leaders for society. Suffragist Elizabeth Cady Stanton sums up the Biblical position on woman thusly:

> The Bible teaches that woman brought sin and death into the world, that she precipitated the fall of the race, that she was arraigned before the judgment seat of Heaven, tried, condemned and sentenced. Marriage for her was to be a condition of bondage, maternity a period of suffering and anguish, and in silence and subjection, she was to play the role of a dependent on man's bounty for all her material wants, and for all the information she might desire on the vital questions of the hour, she was commanded to ask her husband at home.[1]

Or, to quote an influential antebellum southern fundamentalist preacher in his pro-slavery book, the husband "has authority, from God, to rule over you [the wife]. You are under service to him. You are bound to obey him *in all things*. Your service is very . . . often involuntary from the first, and, if voluntary at first, becomes hopeless necessity afterwards."[2]

In more secular terms, there was, it was argued, a natural hierarchy at work, one in which women were represented by proxy (i.e., through male relatives). The values that flowed from patriarchy had everyday effects on property ownership, custody of children, political participation and so on. Feminist scholar Susan Brownmiller argues that laws proscribing rape can be understood within this context, writing that "[t]he nature of the unpardonable crime [of rape] was not that it was an act of violence against a young girl's body, but that it was a crime against her father's honor and estate. The heinous act that could not be forgiven was the theft of a father's daughter's virginity, the ruination of her pristine state and, thus, her fair price on the marriage market."[3]

While we today use the metaphor "market" to denote the availability of an individual for partnership, the "market" was much more literal then: daughters were *actual commodities* to be bartered, sold, or exchanged. We think today of marriage being a union between two people, grounded in love. This was far from the case historically, as marriage was more about property and lineage issues or social power, and still is today in many parts of the world. People married partners they did not even know and persevered as best they could in the very likely event that the two individuals could not stand each other.[4] Too much was at stake to ground relationships in things as fickle as "love." According to Bertrand Russell, the notion of romantic love as being the reason for getting married did not gain traction until the French Revolution.[5]

To the extent that the majority in *Dobbs v. Jackson Women's Health Organization*[6] relies on the Common Law Tradition for legal and moral support, it is an expression of religious bias, being the legal embodiment of the male white Christian perspective within a monarchical and intolerant society. We must remember that England, the society that birthed the Common Law Tradition we think so highly of, also grew into the world's most successful imperial/colonial power since Roman soldiers walked this earth.[7] We must not fetishize English "liberty" or its Rule of Law. It is a myth to think that England, because it was so powerful for so long (at great cost to its colonized peoples), is worthy of our admiration and emulation. We should have other standards for respect and self-respect.

English (and European) imperialism/colonialism should not be romanticized or sugarcoated. Nor should it be downplayed or forgotten as we are apt to do. Empires or colonial powers may be many things, but they are not bastions of the "democracy," "freedom," or other "benevolent" gifts we uncritically attribute to the Common Law Tradition (or to Christianity and to our own government, for that matter). Empires, particularly of the European variety, are ruthless, heartless, and cruel hierarchies grounded in racism, violence, degradation, and exploitation (rape, plunder, and genocide) that exemplify the patriarchal ideal in excess (e.g., in Nazism), resulting in the "*thingification*" of people for reproduction of colonial interests (and literal colonial bodies) and the glory of the masculinist state/race.[8] While I recognize that no country, religion, or legal tradition is perfect and that, with the exception of the Nazis, few are all bad all the time, I argue that *no* country, religion, or legal tradition can be *respectable* if it does not at least treat women justly and see them as full-fledged human beings on grounds equal to men in all aspects of life. Imperial/colonial logic and law, at least in the American tradition, are ideally (although not necessarily in practice) in contradistinction to this principle.

Sir Matthew Hale, the seventeenth-century judge and legal scholar cited with respect by the *Dobbs* Court for his authoritative view on abortion prohibitions, was an "authority" for other things as well. For example, Hale was the "authority" on marital rape (he approved). He was an "authority" on witches and presided over at least two trials in which women were condemned to death as "witches."[9] While the *Dobbs* majority conveniently overlooks these facts, other legal scholars have, for centuries, acknowledged them and used them to criticize Hale. In his 1830 legal treatise, Thomas Cooper, after reviewing Hale's views on religion, women, and witchcraft, wrote: "I have no respect for Sir Matthew Hale; he was a weak and bigoted man, deeply dyed with the legal servility of the times."[10] Cooper rightly condemned Hale's "bigoted stupidity."[11] Why could not the *Dobbs* Court do this and, in particular, call out and condemn the "legal servility of the times" rather than *countenance* it? It seems like an easy thing to do, as I am doing here.[12]

Hale was also authority for the proposition that "Christianity is parcel of the laws of England,"[13] a view which becomes embedded problematically in U.S. courts centuries later. As summarized by influential Supreme Court Justice Joseph Story in 1829:

> One of the beautiful boasts of our municipal jurisprudence is, that Christianity is a part of the common law, from which it seeks the sanction of its rights, and by which it endeavors to regulate its doctrines [. . .]. [T]he boast is as true as it is beautiful. There has never been a period, in which the common law did not recognize Christianity as lying at its foundations.[14]

As recently as 1913, the Texas Supreme Court wrote that marriage "was not originated by human law."[15] Rather, it said, marriage was ordained by God as revealed in the Bible and that "[a]ll of the duties and obligations that have existed at any time between husband and wife existed between those husbands and wives before civil government was formed."[16] In other words, all the limitations found in the Common Law Tradition of coverture and related gendered distinctions are divinely inspired and immutable. They are not for us to question or call into consideration. Or, as a Hawaiian court articulated in more secular terms, "We are fully aware that the trend of recent legislation has been to put women in all respects on equal footing with those of the opposite sex but, granting all this, the distinction between the sexes remains. Men and women remain men and women forever."[17]

Contra Justice Story, "true" is not necessarily "beautiful," nor do the religious foundations of a past intolerant society necessarily govern the way we should think about relationships today (they should not).[18] Post the "Age of Enlightenment," which took place in the seventeenth and eighteenth centuries in Europe, religion and law have become distinct. This is widely seen as a positive development, allowing for the blossoming of technological, moral, and social progress, the hallmarks of the "modernism" to which we owe our freedoms and social, political, and scientific achievements. If anything, law is supposed to protect us *from* the religion of others, just as much as it should *protect* religious believers from persecution for their beliefs. A secular society does not preclude private, personal religious belief. It does, however (at the very least) prevent letting religious or quasi-religious state interests define a woman's relationship with her fetus.

As I argue in my next chapter, the agency responsible for fixing the definition of the growing fetus within a woman's womb is the *woman* (however we want to define her), whose history and life experiences situate that understanding, and whose body is appropriated to the production, care, and responsibility of it. To quote two salient abortion rights slogans, "Keep Your Rosaries Off My Ovaries" and "If I Wanted the Government in my Uterus, I'd Fuck a Senator." To this, sadly, I must add, "I Can't Believe We're Still Protesting This Shit." We may be exhausted ("bone-tired" and deeply disappointed), but we have to protest with whatever energy or means we can muster. The stakes are too high to give up. In the words of Nicole Walter, who writes of her abortion: "My life would not have been my own. I would be a prisoner subject to a body's whims—and not *my* body's whims, but the whims of a teenage boy."[19] Her case was extreme, but no different from that of other young women who must navigate the uncertain and awkward social life of being a teenager in a society with a discernable rape culture (i.e., a society in which sexual assault/abuse is normalized and even celebrated, and victims are made to feel like the harms they suffered were their own fault).[20] How can any thinking person countenance such conditions?

The *Dobbs* majority, however, disagrees with my argument. In this sense, they are no better than Hugh L. Hodge, a mid-nineteenth-century medical doctor and lecturer at the University of Pennsylvania, who, after lamenting educated women who pursue abortions, exhorted his fellow physicians to "grasp the conscience of his weak and erring patient, and let her know in language not to be misunderstood, that she is responsible to her Creator for the life of the being within her."[21] Thus, when it comes to a female's bodily autonomy, I turn not to Hale, Story, or even William Blackstone for authority, but instead turn toward people such as Catharine A. McKinnon, Gloria Steinem, or Ruth Bader Ginsburg (three extraordinary feminists and citizens), who understood the positionality of women before the law and how that has been impacted by the intersections between religion and patriarchy, and between desire and felt necessity. They had no illusions about the Common Law Tradition and its caustic and inhumane treatment of women, so why does the *Dobbs* majority fall short? Perhaps because of their own extreme Christian beliefs, articulated overtly or thinly in their decision?

To be clear, I agree completely that the religious beliefs and "spiritual" commitments of judges and justices should not matter. Like any of us, our religious or other moral beliefs are often very important, dear to our hearts, and define our world view. This is human and makes us the interesting creatures that we are. Richard Rorty defines these beliefs as a person's "final vocabulary," the individual "bricks" in the foundations of our idiosyncratic moral makeup. They are the cornerstones of the "poetry" which is our lives.[22] We want our leaders, including our judges and justices, to have rich inner lives: religious, spiritual, or however they want to define it. Additionally, we want them to have an appreciation for the diversity of different viewpoints and positions that exist in the world, which hopefully is nurtured by the dynamic intellectualism that could result in a rich inner moral vocabulary. Judges with rich inner moral vocabularies are a boon to the practice of law.

The key, however, is the word *inner*. Those same religious commitments or moral imaginations of justices (colorful or dark) *do matter* to the extent that they express them in the law that all of us are obliged to follow. After all, we hire these people to be jurists, not theologians, and it's *our* Constitution, not that of the Vatican or any other church or religious institution. Moreover, the Court works for the American people, not just for the "faithful." As radical as it might sound, we all deserve *equal protection under the law*. If members of the Court cannot separate their religion from their professional identity as jurists when they write their decisions, they should not serve as justices. They know this. They have been told again and again that they lack a judicial ethics and yet they resist, out of arrogance unbefitting of their office, all calls for accountability on this and related ethical issues.[23]

Why this recalcitrance? Being exceptionally bright people, the conservative members of the Supreme Court should go back to teaching law school at private institutions, where they will be free to practice their faith as legal scholars. Academic discourse, not legal opinions, is the place for the partisan endorsement of one's values, secular or otherwise (as I am exemplifying here, being partisan and polemical in my writing but not in the classroom where I welcome, embrace, and help *all* my students, not just the ones I agree with politically or religiously). Law and its agents are necessarily *secular*. They must be. To co-mingle law and religion is to breed popular dissent, encouraging people to question their political allegiance to the state. For example, many people would fight to defend a *secular* state, as many, including religious people, have done and continue to do in our 20-plus years-long "war on terror" against primarily Muslim nations. Many of those people, however, would be loath to defend a state that enacted, with a similar fundamentalism as our enemies, the religious values that we loathe. Neither ISIS nor the Taliban, nor the government of Iran (nor Saudi Arabia, a nation *not* our enemy but one just as terrible in terms to their treatment of women and gay people) trusts women to make decisions for themselves. After *Dobbs*, how are we any different?

As a Jewish American, I have no allegiance (and a great contempt) for any Catholic, Jewish, or Muslim state. Religious states or state religions of whatever kind are anathema to modern, cosmopolitan, and pluralistic ways of thinking and being, which is what we need to move humanity forward.[24] As Stephen Eric Bronner notes:

> The cosmopolitan sensibility presumes a certain capacity for empathy on the part of all individuals beyond the constraints imposed by their race, gender, or "situation." It assumes the existence of cultural differences and, from a critical standpoint, it celebrates the friction between the particular and the universal.[25]

Theocracies, in sum, belong to the immature period of human political thought, as do religions. Individuals can be religious if they want (it can be a sign of intellectual vitality, although it is often a hindrance to such vitality); states, however, should never be. Lest my comments appear unnecessarily harsh or biased against Christianity or any other religion, I point to a recent passage by former President Jimmy Carter, a leader I admire greatly and whose profound lifelong commitments to Christianity are beyond reproach. Here, Carter explains why he severed his ties to the Southern Baptist Convention, a notoriously sexist and homophobic organization:

> At its most repugnant, the belief that women must be subjugated to the wishes of men excuses slavery, violence, forced prostitution, genital mutilation and national laws that omit rape as a crime. But it also costs millions of girls and women control over their own bodies and lives, and continues to deny them fair access to education, health, employment and influence within their own communities [. . .]. The truth is that male religious leaders have had—and still have—an option to interpret holy teachings either to exalt or subjugate women. They have, for their own selfish ends, overwhelmingly chosen the latter.[26]

Surely, as committed, practicing self-identifying Christians, the *Dobbs* majority is aware of the historical legacy of their faith when it concerns women, as President Carter does by repudiating the Southern Baptist Convention. How could they not? That history is everywhere around us, evident within the church (in the Bible itself) as well as outside it, and, as I am demonstrating in this book, layered into the Common Law Tradition. A person can certainly be religious without appreciating this foundational history, but one would be a hypocrite if she or he does not allow that knowledge to modify their beliefs, taking into consideration the *consequences* of that history and its contemporary implications. A religion that does not understand its past is in no position to dictate the terms of the present. The same goes for judicial reasoning. Politicians in a democracy are notoriously shortsighted. Further, there is no requirement or expectation that they be intelligent and educated people. That is not the case with judges and justices who we hire, in part, to see the bigger picture and to understand the hopes and failures of our legal history.[27]

The modern theorist most responsible for developing an ideological critique of the "pathology of patriarchy" in religion is Mary Daly, in works like *The Church and the Second Sex*,[28] and *Beyond God the Father*.[29] As Daly notes, "If God is male, then male is God. The divine patriarch castrates women [an awkward yet accurate metaphor] as long as he is allowed to live on in the human imagination."[30] In other words, while women strive for relevance and respect in religion, they are still doing so in terms of the masculine. One, however, does not need social theory to discern the misogynistic roots of Christianity (or Judaism and Islam). Christianity has long condemned women *for being women*. For example, church father Clement of Alexandria wrote, "Every woman should be filled with shame by the thought that she is a woman."[31] This was part of a tradition among early Christian leaders to attribute to women the "original sin" of causing the "fall" and of being the evil temptress of men.[32]

In his treatise "On the Dress of Women," for example, church father Tertullian considered women to be the "Devil's gateway" for Eve's role in causing Adam's expulsion from the Garden of Eden. According to Tertullian, every woman is guilty of that original transgression against God. She should be

> walking about as Eve mourning and repentant, in order that by every garb of penitence she might the more fully expiate that which she derives from Eve—the ignominy, I mean, of the first sin, and the odium (attaching to her as the cause) of human perdition [. . .]. And do you not know that you are (each) an Eve? *The sentence of God on this sex of yours lives in this age: the guilt must of necessity live too*.[33]

As a "deserter of the divine law" women became the eternal desecrators responsible for all the evils existing in the world:

> And do you not know that you are Eve? God's sentence hangs still over all your sex and His punishment weighs down upon you. You are the devil's gateway; you are she who first violated the forbidden tree and broke the law of God. It was you who coaxed your way around him whom the devil had not the force to attack. With what ease you shattered that image of God: Man! Because of the death you merited, even the Son of God had to die [. . .]. Woman, you are the gate to hell.[34]

Hating sex, yet presumably being drawn to it as normal humans, sex became sublimated as woman hatred. Religious men (being men) desired women sexually, felt "guilty" for those longings, resented this one power women had over them, and despised women for it. Anti-*sex* became anti-*women* as women became reduced to their sexual functions and punished for their being desired sexually by men. In words attributed to Saint Augustine, "Women should not be enlightened or educated in any way. They should, in fact, be segregated as they are the cause of hideous and involuntary erections in holy men."[35] Moreover, Augustine writes, "What is the difference whether it is in a wife or a mother, it is still Eve the temptress that we must beware of in any woman [. . .]. I fail to see what use woman can be to man, if one excludes the function of bearing children."[36] Or, according to theologian Martin Luther, "A woman is never truly her own master; God formed her body to belong to a man, to have and to rear children. Let them bear children till they die of it, that is what they are for."[37]

Given the respect the Christian world has for these "saints" and theological Titans, it does not take the proverbial "rocket scientist" to see how this early Christian antagonism toward women and sex pollutes the Western mind. By "offering" temptations to men, women were seen as agents of the devil.[38] As Saint Anthony claimed, "When you look upon a woman consider that you face not a human being, but the Devil himself. The woman's voice is the hiss of the snake."[39] Then, as now, religious doctrine was used to justify the dehumanization of women, to deprive them of civil, human, economic, and political rights. Is it too much of a stretch to realize that the same dehumanization extends to wanting to deny them the right to have an abortion?

As Carter makes clear, however, the difference is not whether a person is Christian (or Jewish or Muslim). It is what *choices* that person makes and their political implications for people not of that faith. Religious or not, the woman involved in the question of abortion is not an abstraction—she is an agent in history, one not legally beholden to the outrageous prejudices and practices of the past. The fetus, however, while a potential human being, *is* an abstraction, a cluster of cells no different than that of any other mammalian fetus. The fetus has no history, no community, no property, no personality, no sense of self or identity, and no connections besides being in some metaphorical sense "parasitical" on its host.[40] The fetus is a potential subject, what I labeled a "child-in-waiting;" it is an important one, worthy of serious consideration and contemplation, but it is only a *potentiality*, not an actual human being in the same way as the woman who is carrying it. It is our history and our memories that make us who we are: our experiences, our hopes, desires, passions, and fears. It is these that make us unique and special, not our DNA marking our membership in a species. If mere membership in a species were enough to make us members of a moral community, we would not have racism, sexism, homophobia, nationalism, and religious wars. Let's end these horrors (racism, sexism, etc.) and *then* talk about ending abortion. My guess is that, once we end those social scourges and sexual repression more generally, the need for a woman to have an abortion would be much less felt.

On the other hand, it is dehumanizing that abortion opponents treat pregnant woman—our mothers, daughters, wives, and friends—as objects to be bantered about in political or legal rhetoric for base political pandering, reducing them to their status as state-regulated incubators. It is infantilizing for a woman to be told what she can and cannot do about her reproductive choices. Rather, she is a flesh and blood person different from everyone else able to be pregnant. Anti-abortion activists do not speak for all women. No one can. Not all women react the same to the news/condition of pregnancy, nor should they. But that is what *choice* means: every woman for *herself* based on *her* circumstances, needs, hopes, and desires. There is simply no room for politics here.

As indicated earlier, I grant that abortion is the destruction of potential life. But unlike the *Dobbs* Court, the balancing of interests that needs to be done to make the decision to terminate a pregnancy is an *individual* one, not one the state gets to make categorically. Only in this way does the abortion decision become democratic (not to mention humane): every woman chooses for herself based upon her situation, what she needs, wants, and on her understanding of herself, something no court can do, which, ironically, is one of the points the *Dobbs* majority made in condemning *Casey*. For example, they complain that *Casey* calls

> on courts to examine a law's effect on women, but a regulation may have a very different impact on different women for a variety of reasons, including their places of residence, financial resources, family situations, work and personal obligations, knowledge about fetal development and abortion, psychological and emotional disposition and condition, and the firmness of their desire to obtain abortions.[41]

Of course, the *Dobbs* Court's response is *not* to liberalize abortion laws on the grounds that it is difficult to second-guess a women's needs, but to go to the other extreme. In the name of "democracy," the Court frees the very states that have *created* and *justified* the injustice toward woman to be the police of their own actions toward women. This sounds like the mean-spiritedness and Machiavellianism of the Supreme Court in its post-reconstruction litigation of the Civil War Amendments, holding (among other things) that the Fourteenth Amendment does *not* empower Congress to supplement the police power of the states to regulate the actions of private persons to prevent racial segregation and apartheid. That was the sole responsibility of the states, which were, in fact, the main *agents* of segregation and repression (as they are today with their often racist, sexist and homophobic/transphobic legislation) who institutionalized the practice in the first place.[42] Consequently, the Fourteenth Amendment meant little until the second half of the twentieth century, when the proverbial foxes, knives in hand, were charged with guarding the forlorn henhouse and its much-beleaguered denizens.

The problem, I argue, is that this agency of women has seldom been recognized in the Common Law Tradition, as well as in our constitutional tradition, and that the states have strategically used this to the disadvantage of women. This only began to change with the women's rights movement and the emergence of a class of women who asserted their autonomy and dignity against the forces that long denied it. These women demanded state respect for their most intimate decisions and subjectivities and power over their lives as co-equal citizens in our Republic. This woman was largely the creation of the post-1960s revolution in women's rights (i.e., Second Wave feminism), of which *Roe* was the pinnacle.

It would be a serious mistake to read *Dobbs* as simply a decision about abortion. It is more than that. Without *Roe*, at least, as a foundation and immutable right grounded in the respect society has for women as individuals equal to men in *all* legal, political, and social respects, many of the terrifying practices and utter brutalities of the Common Law Tradition threaten to return. In fact, they never really went away; they just became submerged, papered over, and less overtly sanctioned by legislators as they were in the past. With *Roe*, many (but not all) women had a potent tool to fight back. Not anymore. Perhaps I am being hyperbolic, but I sound no different than the *Dobbs* dissent, which I think is as accurate in its reasoning as the majority was flawed; a whole host of repressive legislation has been approved in advance by the *Dobbs* majority, with much more to come after. For all the changes in the status of women since the 1970s, *echoes* of Common Law Tradition attitudes remain in the law and were on full display in the *Dobbs* decision. "Echo," however, may not be a strong enough word. A bellowing bullhorn might be a better metaphor.

Most crucially, as any critical reader of *Dobbs* would notice, there is almost *no* discussion about women *at all*: her interest and agency were erased as if it were *rational* to ignore her interest (which is, in fact, what the *Dobbs* Court held). It was as if, in talking about abortion, women somehow had nothing to do with it: they had no interest in the issue. *Roe* itself was portrayed by the Court as "anti-baby" not "pro-women." Furthermore, the *Dobbs* Court had the gall to write that women do *not* need the rights of *Roe*, that society has changed such that *Roe*, in addition to "the profound wrongness of the decision,"[43] is anachronistic. Women are free! Just like there is (supposedly) no systemic racism in society,[44] the *Dobbs* Court believes that women's equality, dignity, and freedom is compatible with a forced pregnancy and forced parenthood: a shameful Orwellian oxymoron if ever there was one.

The Common Law Tradition and the *Patria Potestas* Power

What the court ignores from their review of history is that anti-abortion is *not* "pro-baby." The Common Law Tradition was never "pro-baby." Rather, it was pro- "*Patria Potestas*," the absolute and despotic power of the father and husband.[45] The father was, in the private sphere, what the state was to the public: sovereign, authoritarian, and unaccountable. Attorney John Proffatt calls it "the despotic, we may say the unlimited, power given to the head of a family over the lives and fortunes of its members."[46] The *Patria Potestas* power "gave the father a right to be sole judge in his own family . . . he could sell his daughter, give her to a husband of his own selection, and divorce her at pleasure."[47] Proffatt goes on to note that "this authority which the father exercised was transferred in marriage to the husband, whose power over the life and fortune of his wife then became absolute."[48] His wards, his wife, and his children lived and thrived at his unquestioned and unreviewable whims. Legally, socially, and epistemically, father knows best.

Consider the following string of cases and explanation concerning the father's power over his children, and the complete *negation* of the mother or child's interests. In a famous early nineteenth-century case, a wife alleged that her husband was intolerable and moved out of the family home, taking the couple's eight-month-old daughter with her. The husband had the child returned from her mother and the mother sued for the daughter's release into her custody. The court denied the mother's request, holding that a married father is entitled to custody of his children while he is still married to their mother, even if the children are very young: "the law is clear that the custody of a child, of whatever age, belongs to the father."[49]

In *Rex v. Greenhill* (1836), a blameless mother was forced by the court to hand over three daughters under 6 years old to an abusive and cruel husband. The father took the children and placed them in charge of the women he was cohabitating illegally. Indeed, the common-law rule was that all power over the child belonged to the father. As English women's rights activist and author Caroline Norton (speaking from experience) summarized:

> The custody of legitimate children is held to be the right of the Father *from the hour of their birth*: to the utter exclusion of the Mother, whose separate claim has no legal existence, and is not recognized by the Courts. No circumstance can modify or alter this admitted right of the father: though he should be living in open adultery, and his wife be legally separated from him on that account.[50]

I added the italics in the above quote to illustrate a central point I am trying to make. The father's right was one *over the mother*, *not an interest in protecting the life* of his child, as the law allowed the father to remove a nursing child from its mother in an era where there was no baby formula. Without a wet nurse or substitute nurturer, the child would starve to death:

> Should it so happen that at the time of separation, or afterwards, the children being in the mother's possession, she should refuse to deliver them up, the father's right extends to forcibly seizing them; *even should they be infants at the breast*. Or he may obtain, on application, a writ of habeas corpus, ordering the mother to produce the child in Court, to be delivered over to him; and should this order be disobeyed, he can cause a writ of attachment to issue against her; or, in other words, cause her to be imprisoned for contempt of court.[51]

As Norton goes on to explain:

> The fact of the wife being innocent and the husband guilty, or of the separation being an unwilling one on her part, does not alter his claim: the law has no power to order that a woman shall even have occasional access to her children, though she could prove that she was driven by violence from her husband's house, and that he had deserted her for a mistress. The Father's right is absolute and paramount and can no more be affected by the mother's claim, than if she had no existence.[52]

A significant change in the English Common Law Tradition occurred with Justice Talfourd's Act in 1839 which ameliorated the situation somewhat by qualifying the parental rights of the father. Before then, the mother's claim was not recognized at all.[53] Now there was recognized a right, which U.S. courts imperfectly followed, as evident by an 1842 case in which the court sided with the mother in such a dispute, prompting this from the dissent:

> We are informed by the first elementary books we read, that the authority of the father is superior to that of the mother. It is the doctrine of all civilized nations. It is according to the revealed law, and the law of nature, and it prevails even with the wandering savage, who has received none of the lights of civilization.[54]

An 1869 scholarly treatise helps to explain this attitude from the courts toward women which *continued* to work toward the detriment of women, despite the modest legal reforms:

> Man is the natural bread-winner. Woman lives by the bread which man has earned. Ergo, it is fit and right that the man who wins should have absolute disposal, not only of his winnings, but of every other small morsel or fraction of earnings or property she may possess. It is a fair return to him for his labour in the joint interest of both. He supports her, pays any debts she has incurred before or after marriage, and provides for the children which are hers as well as his. For all this, it is but just he should receive whatever she has to give. The woman's case is that of a pauper who enters a workhouse. The ratepayers are bound to support him; but if he have any savings they must be given up to the board. He cannot both claim support and keep independent property.[55]

Also consider the explanation of a California court at the end of the nineteenth century dealing with a case concerning the tort of "criminal conversation," which, in the Common Law Tradition, was a suit brought by a husband for monetary damages from his wife's consensual lover in the case of adultery which does not end in divorce (which would make the legal cause-of-action "alienation of affections"). The legal theory is that a husband has a property right to his wife's "services." Thus, the wife's lover is liable to the husband for interfering with the husband's "property":

> The foundation of the husband's right of action is the wrong done him by the defendant in violating his personal rights. The husband has the right to the conjugal fellowship of his wife, to her society, her aid, and her fidelity in every conjugal relation. Any act of another by which he is deprived of this right constitutes a personal wrong, for which the law gives him a redress in damages. Her sexual intercourse with another is an invasion of his rights, and it is immaterial whether this invasion is accomplished by force or by the consent of the wife.[56]

The court reasons here that:

> As the right belongs to the husband, it is no defense to his action for redress that its violation was by the consent or procurement of the wife, for she is not competent to give such consent [. . .]. The wrong to the husband consists in the carnal intercourse with his wife by another, and it is immaterial whether this intercourse is accomplished by persuasion or by force. His right of action is established upon proof of the intercourse, and the means by which this intercourse was effected are but incidents to increase or mitigate his damages.[57]

A mid-twentieth-century case sums up the lingering effect of such thinking:

> The plaintiff is the master of his household. He is the managing head, with control and power to preserve the family relation, to protect its members and to guide their conduct. He has the obligation and responsibility of supporting, maintaining, and protecting the family, and the correlative right, to exclude intruders and unwanted visitors from the home despite the whims of the wife.[58]

As I have been demonstrating, the Common Law Tradition's rights of the husband made him the financial and dictatorial head of the family, entitling him to the control of his wife and children; their property and all family property belonged to the husband to do with how he wanted. In other words, a husband was entitled to services of his wife and children and their wages, should they work, as well as to values of service for even *nonpaid* labor. For example, in an early nineteenth-century case, a father successfully sued a neighbor for the services of his teenage daughter after the daughter, who was abused at home by the father, left the father to find shelter elsewhere. She lived with a kindly neighbor for three and half years who took her in. As a result of his successful lawsuit, the father recovered from the neighbor the value of the services (cleaning, cooking, etc.) that the daughter provided to the neighbor for her upkeep.[59] In some cases, the father had the power to kill the illicit lover of his daughter.[60]

Sexist Views in Medicine and Philosophy's Alignment with the Views of the Common Law Tradition

As I have been describing, the Common Law Tradition was profoundly anti-women. If it was not an outright hatred of women, it was a fear of female agency, sexuality, and independence that has been resurrected legally today by the *Dobbs* majority. This feeling goes back to the beginning of our nation, if not before. As expressed by Thomas Jefferson, in a letter where he describes his vision of "pure democracy," he specifically recognizes that it would *exclude* from the deliberative process infants, slaves, and "women who, to prevent depravation of morals, and ambiguity of issue, could not mix promiscuously in the public meetings of men."[61] Note the familiar trope: women, merely by being women, *cause* men to misbehave, frustrating other men's property relationship with their wives and ownership of their children. The problem, then as is now, is framed as woman's *nature* and not men's *behavior*. A modern recognition of how wrong these assumptions are can be found in the growing recognition that it is not enough to teach our daughters how not to get raped; rather, more needs to be done to teach our sons not to rape.[62]

For the purposes of this book, there are two areas in which clear echoes of the Common Law Tradition's contempt for women were evident, mocking any integrity in which the *Dobbs* Court seeks to ground its decision. The two areas are interrelated. First, there is a hatred, fear, distrust, contempt, and disregard of women, particularly independent or successful women (Hillary Clinton or Nancy Pelosi, for example), who compete with men and *win* because they believe in themselves and in their abilities and are undeterred by the misogyny they encounter. That is, women who define themselves on their own terms and fight like hell to protect them. These proud, forceful, and unrepentant women are the product of the twentieth century and not the seventeenth century. Such women firmly reject the crippling limitations of the past and work to make things better for the next generation.

Second, the Common Law Tradition and the popular culture that supported it maintained that women were nothing more than "baby machines" and thus, structured society to limit women to that function. In other words, law and society conspired to reduce women to their uteruses. Doctors, lawyers, religious leaders, etc., feared women and saw their value only as mothers and supporters for their husbands. In the medical context, for example, physician James Compton Burnett warned in his medical treatise of the "defrauded womb":

> During the past twenty years the number of cases in which married women prevent conception is steadily on the increase; their many dodges in attaining this end need not be dwelt upon, but the almost uniform results are following: The breasts shrivel, and in extreme cases almost disappear: the erstwhile fine bust, the shapely breasts shrink into shocking ugliness. The great female characteristics diminish, and the individual is apt to become hairy in the face and elsewhere, while the rotundity of limb is a thing of the past: the limbs are often scraggy and thin, or, if obese, flabby and old.[63]

Such woman, notes Burnett, becomes "irritable and cross and miserable."[64] This, however, is not the worst part of the condition:

> The uterus is the greatest sufferer all: it has been cheated, and resents the wrong done to it with terrible vigor: it becomes enlarged, hard and gristly, and is not infrequently the seat of tumors of various kinds. And no woman with such a womb is, or can be, other than miserable and discontented.[65]

The book *Sex in Education*, published in 1873 (with 17 subsequent printings) by Harvard Medical School professor Edward H. Clarke, argues that having a college education contributes to sterility and long-term negative health consequences among young women, making them miserable, insufferable, and undesirable as wives.[66] Clarke was writing in a period in which women were demanding suffrage, employment opportunities, and increased access to education. Clarke claimed that women who engaged in sustained vigorous mental activity risked atrophy of the uterus and ovaries, leading to sterility, insanity, and, in some cases, death. Clarke was a powerful member of the medical community, and his argument was taken seriously and widely debated in the United States and in England. American psychologist G. Stanley Hall advised similarly:

> Reproduction requires a far larger proportion of body and function in females. Now the leaders of the new education for girls recommend training them for self-support, assuming that if wifehood and motherhood come those who have received such a training can best take care of themselves. This assumption is radically wrong and vicious, and should be reversed. Every girl should be educated primarily to become a wife and mother, and, if this is done widely and broadly, the small minority who remain single will with this training be best able to care for themselves.[67]

Englishman Henry Maudsley popularized similar arguments in England, warning women not to "rebel . . . against the tyranny of their organization" by neglecting the "physiological functions of their nature."[68] As Maudsley goes on to explain, "a proper regard to the physical nature of women means attention given, in their training, to their peculiar functions and to their foreordained work as mothers and nurses of children."[69] Yet another doctor warned,

> Visit the female colleges and you will be impressed with the large numbers of pale-faced girls whose roseate blushes of youth have been chased away by nervous exhaustion born of the shadows of midnight toil; bright eyes have been dulled by brain-fag, and sweet temper transformed into irritability, crossness, and hysteria, while the womanhood of the land is deteriorating physically and filling our hospitals with invalids.[70]

He concluded, "She may be highly cultured and accomplished, and shine in society, but her future husband will discover too late that he has married a large outfit of headaches, backaches, and spine-aches, instead of a woman fitted to take up the duties of life."[71] Such authorities reduced women to their ovaries which, they claimed, made women weak and dependent. Their *telos* as women—their reason for existence—was reproduction. Anything that frustrated that function caused physical, psychological, or spiritual pain, undermining a woman's health, sanity, and desirability in the eyes of men.

Philosophers and reformers picked up on this idea of education being detrimental to a woman's moral and physical stamina. For example, in 1897, clergyman and social reformer Charles Parkhurst warned,

> [W]hatever certain adventurous women may think about it, it is sufficiently clear that nature has certain pretty decided opinions of its own on the matter and that nature has so wrought its opinions into the tissue of woman's physical constitution and function that any feminine attempt to mutiny against wifehood, motherhood, and domestic "limitations" is a hopeless and rather imbecile attempt to escape the inevitable.[72]

A generation later, English philosopher Ernest Belfort Bax underscored this point, writing:

> It cannot be denied by any sane person familiar with the barest elements of physiology that the whole female organism is subservient to the functions of child-bearing and lactation, which explains the inferior development of those organs and faculties which are not specially connected with this supreme of end Woman.[73]

More recent examples of this view are not difficult to find; perhaps, the most poetic can be found in George Gilder's influential conservative screed, *Wealth and Poverty*. Gilder argues that "[b]ecause female sexuality, as it evolved over the millennia, is psychologically rooted in the bearing and nurturing of children, women have long horizons within their very bodies, glimpses of eternity within their wombs."[74] In short, society, until recently, reflected the view that a woman who does not value or want to have children will be at odds with her body and is a threat to society.[75]

In this context, can we not say that preventing a woman from having an abortion is the supreme expression of the belief that no sane woman would want to have an abortion or to be anything other than a mother, and that abortion in the name of a woman's "freedom" is a crime against womanhood? In *Gonzales v. Carhart* the U.S. Supreme Court, upholding a federal abortion prohibition, betrays this bias when writing,

> Respect for human life finds an ultimate expression in the bond of love the mother has for her child [and that] it seems unexceptionable to conclude some women come to regret their choice to abort the infant life they once created and sustained. Severe depression and loss of esteem can follow.[76]

The Court's observation here is erroneous in several ways. In fact, not many women regret their "choice" to have an abortion. According to one recent study, 95 percent of women, 5 years after having an abortion, report they made the correct decision.[77] It also ignores the fact that some women, for whatever reasons, cannot bond with their infants or even love them. Some women are incapable of being good mothers and that does not in itself make them bad people. My point is that the Court is falsely concluding that because a woman is *capable* of bearing a child, that she will necessarily experience the condition as an "ultimate" love or as the embodiment of her essence. Many women do not feel this way. For some women, pregnancy is just something that *happens to them.* To these women, a pregnancy is not "destiny" or "love" but a biological inconvenience that must be managed in some way. They may "fake it" and nevertheless be good providers or they may struggle and be terrible parents but see their child through its teenage years into adulthood. Or they may give up and succumb to the unhappiness associated with being burdened by an unwanted child. Such women, who do not feel as the Court assumes they feel, are often treated as monsters by society when, in fact, they are merely constituted differently, as all individuals are unique. These women are being held to a standard they never accepted or agreed to.

Moreover, such stereotypical writing belittles men who may have a "respect" for human life and profound spiritual or emotional connections with their children, as well as the fact that "respect" for human life is *not* biological (not something we have because we are *homo sapiens*)—it is cultural and political, it must be nurtured. It is also very selective even today among anti-abortion/pro-death penalty advocates as well as people who support or even celebrate U.S. military interventions abroad, which are profoundly murderous and destructive.[78] Politically, philosophically, and morally, the exalted "respect for human life" is less a general one, and more a self-serving interest in a *specific* class of life. In other words, instead of asking, in the abstract, that we respect something called "human life," we instead look at *whose* life we actually and selectively respect. For example, the systemic and routine police violence toward Black people in this country underpins the necessity for a movement such as "Black Lives Matter" to raise consciousness among white Americans to the problem of how our society devalues the lives of Black women and men (as well as poor people, generally).

Contribution of the American Medical Association to the Degradation of Women[79]

As discussed earlier, women were reduced by law, philosophy, and medicine to their ovaries which were pitted against their brains and their freedom.[80] Their ovaries, dedicated singularly to the difficult and often dangerous task of begetting children, were seen as making them weak, unable to perform any other function, and in need of male authority and guidance in all other aspects of their lives. Their telos as women was *reproduction*, and women were perceived and treated as walking wombs. Potential motherhood determined everything they could do, precluding education, political activity, professional work, and any other sort of commitments that took their primary attention away from their home and family responsibilities. Men of knowledge said as much, religion supported it, and the "experience" of women (as perceived by their male physicians) reinforced it. It follows that abortion—the voluntary termination of a pregnancy by a woman—was unnatural and, therefore, wrong.

Regarding abortion, women's bodily autonomy, and medical authority, I frame this section by juxtaposing it with contemporary issues in the unfortunate fight over abortion rights today. Though the contemporary debate about abortion stems from the response of fanatical Christians and reactionaries to the *Roe* decision, the debate about abortion in the United States is, in fact, far older and is part of the ideological battle that educated men had in establishing their expertise against the knowledge claims of women when it came to their sexual health and bodily autonomy.

Modern abortion politics did not start with religious moralizing about the "sanctity of fetal life," but rather began with, and is contextualized by, an ideology that asserted women to be subordinate to men and slave to their reproductive capacities. These beliefs precipitated a pseudo-scientific ideology that served to substantiate and justify women's subordinate status by use of *medical* reasoning why women are inexorably tethered to their reproductive faculties, with, as we have seen, dire consequences should they go against their "nature." With this line of argument, the mid-nineteenth century started to see the heavy hand of male doctors asserting their authority through the subordination of women medically, particularly when it came to the issue of reproductive freedom. According to the American Medical Association (AMA) in 1871, if a woman has an abortion, "She sinks into old age like a withered tree, stripped of its foliage; with the stain of blood upon her soul, she dies without the hand of affection to smooth her pillow."[81]

It is important to note that, at this time, the AMA was working to professionalize its almost exclusively male membership and was on the offensive against "traditional" medicine, often dominated by women. Attacking such women (and subject-knowledge) served as a foil in the AMA's effort to bring "respectability" to the field. An important strategy for doing this was by medicalizing women and advocating for the criminalization of abortion.[82] Notably, the AMA's attempt at professionalization came at the expense of not only women's historical practice of medicine (i.e., midwifery) but also at the expense of *actual* women's bodies.

Take, for example, Dr. James Marion Sims, a recognized medical pioneer in the mid-nineteenth century, considered the "father of modern gynecology." Though Sims' research and surgical practices remain relevant, debate continues over his methods.[83] Sims started his career as a "plantation physician." His job was to "protect" the profitably of female slaves by ensuring their availability for breeding purposes. Such women were susceptible to *vesicovaginal fistulas*, a result of their poor nutrition, overwork, and frequent forced pregnancies to increase the owner's stock of slaves. A female slave who suffered from this condition was unable to have additional children or contribute meaningfully to the economy of the plantation and thus remained a financial burden on her owner. Sims eventually established a clinic to treat such women where he would operate on them without the use of anesthetics.[84]

As these gruesome origins of modern gynecology suggest, interest in women's reproductive health was not of the moralistic concern frequently cited in the present debate about abortion. On the contrary, during a time when women's bodies were medicalized and brutally researched for the sake of medical status and the protection of private property, it was widely held in the medical community that women's reproductive health was considered "repugnant."[85] Doctors' repulsion toward women's bodies and health was informed by Victorian culture and sensibilities of modesty and prudence in the United States and Europe at the time. Within the purview of this cultural constraint, doctors were trained to look directly into the eyes of clothed women patients while performing pelvic exams. This way, doctors could spare themselves the embarrassing and vile contact with a woman's naked body.[86] Moreover, many young (male) students learning to become doctors in the mid-nineteenth century had little experience with live births; instead (finding female bodies so abhorrent), students were taught about labor and birth with dummies.[87] In short, obstetrics and gynecology were not brought about with the sole intention of saving women's lives or supporting women in finding and maintaining optimal health. If anything, there was a concerted *dis*interest and disgust in women's health and bodies. Then, as now, medicine has a distinctly masculinist bias.[88]

As discussed, the medicalization of women's bodies and reproductive health exemplify the misogyny I have been discussing throughout this book.[89] Doctors' disgust with women's bodies makes it obvious that their endeavors to regulate women's healthcare were vested in blatant self-interest. In other words, because of the misogynistic practices and beliefs of doctors in the late nineteenth and throughout much of the twentieth centuries, it is plain to see that their interest in obstetrics or gynecology was for uncompassionate control of women and their health, and cultivation of their own endeavors toward power and prestige. In this case, misogyny operates in a self-fortifying way: informing the practices of doctors that go on to use social power and status to further curate institutionalized misogyny in the form of laws that diminish women's bodily autonomy and are informed by the fear and mistrust of women.

Not only were women being used to enhance the AMA's professional position socially and politically, but the results of the professional medical field also worked directly to disadvantage women and their bodily autonomy. For example, Kristin Luker describes the movement among doctors to use the abortion issue to increase their professional status. She explains,

> The most visible interest group agitating for more restrictive abortion laws was comprised of elite or "regular" physicians, who actively petitioned state legislatures to pass anti-abortion laws and undertook through popular writings a campaign to change public opinion on abortion.[90]

In this they were largely successful as anti-abortion laws started being enacted. Luker concludes that "scholarship on the nineteenth-century abortion debate has been hard-pressed to find any other group of anti-abortion activists as central and visible as physicians."[91]

While the abortion issue obviously has other dimensions than the efforts of the AMA to become respectable, it is important to realize that the motivation to outlaw abortion was *not* solely grounded in fundamentalist Christian theology as it is now, but in the desire of educated men to use the vehicle of science to elevate their own credentials in the eyes of the public at the expense of women. Those on the front lines of the battle to keep abortion safe and available for women ought to keep this point firmly in mind as the autonomy of women has been the subject of many different threats. Again and again, and in a myriad of ways, the bodies and minds of women became the terrain of masculinist manipulations in mankind's continued war on women.

Similarities as well as differences between the rhetoric of physicians and religious interests in the long-standing dispute around abortion are important for drawing a parallel, not between moralizing about women's faculties or the value of life, but rather the seemingly ubiquitous tendency to err on the side of distrust or suspicion of women. What the anti-abortion medical groups of the past and the pro-life religious groups of the present have in common is this: *they do not trust women to make decisions about their bodies.*

Conclusion

In this and the previous chapters, we have seen that women's intellectual pretensions or aspirations were quickly squashed by men as women were largely shut out of the marketplace of ideas—women suffered an enforced ignorance that weighed heavily upon most of them. Many went crazy or developed weird psychosomatic diseases which, in turn, as evidence of their "inferiority," was used to justify further repression against them. Women were to serve men obediently and silently—unseen and unheard, like children. Husbands were lords over both and the family was beholden to the dictates of father/husband, who was sovereign. A woman who aspired to the status of an intellectual or a thinker was derided as a *bluestocking*, a pejorative term levied against any women expressing intellectual interests or literary tastes. This was a negative term because it was considered ungraceful and perverted for woman to aspire to learning—such pursuits were unhealthy and made them unsuitable for marriage. Such women frequently found themselves shunned and often became derided as "old maids." In other words, and in some historical circumstances, such women were defined as "witches" and deemed a threat to morality and the social order.

In the next chapter, I develop my argument that the state does *not* have a rational interest in telling women what they can or cannot do with their own bodies when it comes to reproduction and that reproductive freedom is an inalienable right for all women. The state cannot privilege a fetus over the interests, desires, and decisions of a grown woman without impermissibly burdening the woman, of reducing her to a second-class citizen; this is morally indefensible. Without the right to an abortion, all women, even anti-abortion women, are harmed as women, as a class, and are reduced to an unequal status with men.

Notes

1 *The Woman's Bible* (Amherst, NY: Prometheus Books, [1895]/1999), 7.
2 Fred A. Ross, *Slavery Ordained of God* (Philadelphia: J.B. Lippincott & Co., 1859), 55.
3 "Under Law, Rape Was at First a Crime Only Against a Father's Property, But That Has Changed," *The New York Times*, October 1, 1975, 45. Brownmiller's classic study of rape is *Against Our Will: Men, Women, and Rape* (New York: Penguin Books, 1975).
4 Even today, for the woman, it can be too much. See Fraidy Reiss, "At 19, I Was Forced to Marry a Stranger and Was Sexually Assaulted Every Month for 12 Years." Notes Reiss, "I love my daughters, but I did not consent to having them." *Huffpost Personal*, January 9, 2024, https://www.huffpost.com/entry/fraidy-reiss-forced-marriage_n_6592d981e4b0bf73e176edb9.
5 *Marriage & Morals* (New York: Liveright Publishing, 1957), 74–75. In law school I took a two-course sequence in ancient and contemporary Chinese law. My instructor, Jonathan Ocko, told the class how he witnessed a divorce proceeding in China. Two old ladies from the community served as mediators. One of them asked the wife why she wanted to get divorced from her husband. "I don't love him," the wife replied. In response, the old ladies said, "So what? We didn't love our husbands for the first 30 years."
6 142 S.Ct. 2228 (2022).
7 Caroline Elkins, *Legacy of Violence: A History of the British Empire* (New York: Alfred A. Knopf, 2022).
8 Aimé Césaire writes in his powerful indictment of European colonialism that it is "responsible before the human community for the highest heap of corpses in history." *Discourse on Colonialism* (New York: Monthly Review Press, [1955]/2000), 45.
9 G. Geis, "Lord Hale, Witches, and Rape," *British Journal of Law and Society* 5, no. 1 (1978): 26–44.
10 *Law of Libel and the Liberty of the Press* (New York: G.F. Hopkins & Son, 1830), 119–120.
11 Ibid.
12 Maybe it is because criticism, as I see it, requires a level of knowledge not expected from those committed to upholding the status quo, or to those, say, participating in charity and reactionary assistance to communities, however defined. Charity (or judicial fidelity to constitutional abstractions) does not require understanding of the structures and mechanisms of inequality, nor do charitable acts threaten or destabilize social institutions—in fact, they often serve to prolong them. In other words, the *Dobbs* majority violates the integrity of our judicial institutions under the guise of what the majority called "correcting constitutional decisions that, on reconsideration, are found to be mistaken." *Dobbs*, 2265, quoting *Thornburgh v. American College of Obstetricians and Gynecologists*, 476 U.S. 747 (1986) (Justice White, dissent). This distinction between "charity" and "justice" is cogently discussed in Phillip K. Tompkins, "Communication, Charity, Social Justice, and the Abolition of Homelessness," in *Social Justice and Communication Scholarship*, ed. Omar Swartz (New York: Routledge, 2012), 53–75.
13 *Taylor's Case*, 86 Eng. Rep. 189 (K.B. 1676). For an overview of the literature on this point, see, Stuart Banner, "When Christianity Was Part of the Common Law," *Law and History Review* 16, no. 1 (1998): 27–62.

14 "Value and Importance of Legal Studies: A Discourse Pronounced Upon the Inauguration of the Author, As Dane Professor of Law in Harvard University," in *The Miscellaneous Writings of Joseph Story* (Cambridge, MA: Houghton and Haywood), 517.
15 *Grigsby v. Reib*, 105 Tex. 597 (1913), 607.
16 Ibid.
17 *Territory v. Armstrong*, 28 Haw. 88 (1924), 95.
18 The United States is unique, for the most part, among the nations of the world for the simple reason that we have *no* official religion, no presumptive or normative theological center, no faith history that is "owned" by any one specific group who stand out as the "real" people of this country. In spite of what many Americans across the political spectrum may believe, we are *not* a "Christian" nation, nor have we ever been, although the majority of the people who live in the United States are Christians of one sort or another. This group, however, is far from monolithic, and few assumptions can be made regarding commonalities between different communities identifying as "Christian." Further, these Christians live alongside Buddhists, Jews, Muslims, Hindus, and atheists who are also not monolithic in their beliefs, and others who subscribe to dozens of different religions, theologies, moral philosophies, or world views.
19 "My Abortion at 11 Wasn't a Choice. It Was My Life." *The New York Times*, August 18, 2022, https://www.nytimes.com/2022/08/18/opinion/abortion-pregnancy-child-roe.html.
20 Kate Harding, *Asking for It: The Alarming Rise of Rape Culture—And What We Can Do About It* (Boston: Da Capo Lifelong Books, 2015).
21 *On Criminal Abortion; Lecture Introductory to the Course on Obstetrics, and Diseases of Women and Children* (Philadelphia, PA: T.K. and P.G. Collins, 1854–1855), 19.
22 *Contingency, Irony, and Solidarity* (New York: Cambridge University Press, 1989).
23 Kimberly Strawbridge Robinson, "Congress Can't Force Ethics Code on Supreme Court, Alito Says," *Bloomberg Law*, July 28, 2023, https://news.bloomberglaw.com/us-law-week/congress-cant-force-ethics-code-on-supreme-court-alito-says. See also *PBS News Hour*, season 49, "Amid Ethics Issues, Supreme Court Justices Say No Fix Needed," written and reported by Jessica Gresko, aired April 26, 2024, on Rocky Mtn PBS, https://www.pbs.org/newshour/politics/amid-ethics-issues-supreme-court-justices-say-no-fix-needed.
24 For the claim that contemporary societies that do not have a Western secular-state model lag behind western states on a variety of measures, see Bernard Lewis, *What Went Wrong? Western Impact and Middle Eastern Response* (New York: Oxford University Press, 2002).
25 *Ideas in Action: Political Tradition in the Twentieth Century* (Lanham, MD: Rowman & Littlefield, 1999), 333.
26 Jimmy Carter, "Losing My Religion for Equality," *The Age*, July 15, 2009, https://www.theage.com.au/politics/federal/losing-my-religion-for-equality-20090714-dk0v.html.
27 Popular democracy, unchecked by humanist principles, is dangerous and often self-destructive. An independent, honest, and fair judiciary is an important corrective. In *National Federation of Independent Businesses v. Sebelius*, Chief Justice Roberts exemplifies, *heroically*, the position I am advocating. As expected, Roberts *could* have struck down the Affordable Care Act, a controversial but necessary piece of legislation enacted to deal with our nation's chronic health care crisis but chose *not* to because doing so would be catastrophic for the nation. To protect this law, but also to adequately address the substantial Constitutional concerns involved, he wrote a decision that denied the expansive

federal powers he felt dangerous for federalism yet *upheld* the law by reading it narrowly (and unconvincingly, I might add) as a permissible "tax." In so doing, Justice Roberts singlehandedly saved the nation a colossal amount of carnage and despair while modeling responsible national leadership. He did this while also pointing out, "It is not our job to protect the people from the consequences of their political choices." 567 U.S. 519 (2012), 538. Yes, but sometimes that is precisely what the Court needs to do.

28 *The Church and the Second Sex* (Boston: Beacon Press, 1986).

29 *Beyond God the Father* (Boston: Beacon Press, 1993).

30 Ibid., 19.

31 Cited in Helen Ellerbe, *The Dark Side of Christian History* (San Rafael, CA: Morningstar Books, 1995), 114.

32 Jewish Orthodox men are instructed via prayer ("*Shelo Asani Isha*") to thank God everyday "for not making" them a woman.

33 Cited in Joseph E. Early, *Because of Eve: Historical and Theological Survey of the Subjugation of Women in the Christian Tradition* (Irvine, CA: Universal Publishers, 2022), 74.

34 Ibid.

35 Cited in Christopher Reyes, *In His Name*, vol. 4 (Bloomington, IL: Trafford Publishing, 2014), 368.

36 Cited in Karen Armstrong, *The Gospel According to Woman: Christianity's Creation of the Sex War in the West* (Garden City, NY: Anchor Press, 1986), 68.

37 Quoted in Lisa Isherwood and Dorothea McEwan, *Introducing Feminist Theology* (Sheffield, UK: Sheffield Academic Press, 1993), 50.

38 Sharon L. Coggan, *Sacred Disobedience: A Jungian Analysis of the Saga of Pan and the Devil* (Maryland: Lexington Books, 2020).

39 Cited in Barbara G. Walker, *Restoring the Goddess: Equal Rites for Modern Women* (New York: Prometheus Books, 2000), 37.

40 Murray Rothbard, *For a New Liberty: The Libertarian Manifesto*, 2nd ed. (Auburn, Alabama: Ludwig von Mises Institute, [1973]/2006), 132.

41 *Dobbs*, 2273.

42 See *The Slaughter-House Cases*, 83 U.S. 36 (1873); *United States v. Cruikshank*, 92 U.S. 542 (1876); *The Civil Rights Cases*, 109 U.S. 3 (1883); and *Plessy v. Ferguson*, 163 U.S. 537 (1896).

43 *Dobbs*, 2272.

44 In fact, such racism is pervasive. See Michelle Alexander, *The New Jim Crow: Mass Incarceration in the Age of Colorblindness* (New York: New Press, 2010).

45 For a review of this doctrine, see John Crook, "*Patria potestas*," *The Classical Quarterly* 17, no. 1 (1967): 113–122.

46 *Woman Before the Law* (New York: G.P. Putnam's Sons, 1874), 18.

47 Ibid.

48 Ibid.

49 *King v. DeManneville*, 102 Eng. Rep. 1054 (1804).

50 *The Separation of the Mother and Child By the Law of "Custody of Infants" Considered* (London: Roake and Varty, 1838), 2.

51 Ibid., italics in original.

52 Ibid., 3.

53 See Lelia Robinson, *The Law of Husband and Wife* (Boston: Lee and Shepard, 1889), 46–47.

54 *Foster v. Alston*, 7 Miss. (6 Howard) 406 (1842), 463.
55 Frances Cobbe, *Criminals, Idiots, Women, and Minors. Is the Classification Sound? A Discussion on the Laws Concerning the Property of Married Woman* (Manchester, UK: A. Ireland and Co., 1869), 7.
56 *Bedan v. Turney*, 99 Cal. 649 (1893), 653.
57 Ibid.
58 *Chapman v. Mitchell*, 23 N.J. Misc. 358 (1945), 360.
59 *Benson v. Remington*, 2 Mass. 113 (1806).
60 *Miller v. State*, 9 Ga. App. 599 (1911).
61 "Thomas Jefferson to Samuel Kercheval, September 5, 1816," https://founders.archives.gov/documents/Jefferson/03-10-02-0255.
62 See Jennifer Shore, "Rape Culture in America," *Focus for Health Foundation* (December 9, 2019), https://www.focusforhealth.org/rape-culture-in-america/.
63 *Organ Diseases of Women* (Philadelphia, PA: Boericke & Tafel, 1897), 21–22.
64 Ibid., 23.
65 Ibid.
66 *Sex in Education* (Cambridge, MA: Houghton, Mifflin, 1873).
67 "The Ideal School as Based on Child Study," *The Review of Education* 7, no. 3 (1901): 93.
68 *Sex in Mind and in Education* (Syracuse, NY: C.W. Bardeen, 1884), 7.
69 Ibid., 14.
70 William Edgar Darnall, "The Pubescent Schoolgirl," *American Gynecological and Obstetrical Journal* 18 (1901): 490.
71 Ibid.
72 *Talks to Young Women* (New York: Curtis Publishing, 1897), 25.
73 *The Fraud of Feminism* (London: Grant Richards, 1913), 32.
74 *Wealth and Poverty* (Regnery Gateway: New York, [1981]/2012), 105.
75 I do not mean to suggest that contemporary women who chose to remain childless are entirely free from social pressure. Robert T. Muller, "Childfree Women Are Still Subjected to Stigma," *Psychology Today*, March 11, 2022, https://www.psychologytoday.com/us/blog/talking-about-trauma/202203/childfree-women-are-still-subjected-stigma.
76 550 U.S. 124 (2007), 159.
77 Corinne H. Rocca, Goleen Samari, Diana G. Foster, Heather Gould, and Katrina Kimport, "Emotions and Decision Rightness over Five Years Following an Abortion: An Examination of Decision Difficulty and Abortion Stigma," *Social Science & Medicine* 248 (2020): 2.
78 The paradigmatic case is, of course, Vietnam and the war in Southeast Asia, generally. U.S. military action in Central and South America throughout the twentieth century are also significant for the wanton death toll and the immoral justifications for the military involvement. More recently, Neta C. Crawford of the Watson Institution at Brown University estimates that post 9/11, as many as half a million people have been killed in Iraq, Afghanistan, and Pakistan as a result of the "War on Terror." This does not include "indirect" deaths from starvation, lack of medicine, and the resulting poverty that comes from having one's country destroyed. See "Human Cost of the Post-9/11 Wars: Lethality and the Need for Transparency," Watson Institute at Brown University, November 2018, https://watson.brown.edu/costsofwar/files/cow/imce/papers/2018/Human%20Costs%2C%20Nov%208%202018 %20CoW.pdf.

79 I acknowledge Candace Nunag Tardio, my former graduate student, for her help on this section concerning the AMA. We wrote this section together as part of our work, resulting in two co-authored book chapters, and we never used this material which I have integrated here.

80 For a chapter length discussion of this phenomenon, see my (co-written with Nunag Tardio), "Gender, Education and Careerism: The Recurring 'Conflict' Between Ovaries and Brains in the 19th and Early 20th Centuries," in *Emerging Strategies for Public Education Reform*, ed. Marquis C. Grant (Hershey, PA: IGI Global, 2021), 235–252.

81 Cited in Nadine Taub and Elizabeth M. Schneider, "Women's Subordination and the Role of Law," in *The Politics of Law*, 2nd ed., ed. David Kairys (New York: Pantheon, 1990), 160.

82 James C. Mohr, *Abortion in America: The Origins and Evolution of National Policy, 1800–1900* (New York: Oxford University Press, 1978).

83 Sarah Spettel and Mark Donald White, "The Portrayal of J. Marion Sims' Controversial Surgical Legacy," *The Journal of Urology* 185 (2011): 2426.

84 L.L. Wall, "The Medical Ethics of Dr. J. Marion Sims: A Fresh Look at the Historical Record," *Journal of Medical Ethics* 32, no. 6 (2006): 346–350.

85 Durrenda Ojanuga, "The Medical Ethics of the 'Father of Gynecology,' Dr. J. Marion Sims," *Journal of Medical Ethics* 19, no. 1 (1993): 28.

86 Judith Walzer Leavitt, *Brought to Bed: Childbearing in America, 1750 to 1950* (New York: Oxford University Press, 1986), 40–42.

87 Ojanuga, "The Medical Ethics of the 'Father of Gynecology,'" 28–31.

88 Edward Shorter, *Women's Bodies: A Social History of Women's Encounter with Health, Ill-Health and Medicine* (New York: Routledge, 2017).

89 In this section I have been arguing that, historically at least, the profession of medicine contributed to the subjection of women. I note here the *irony* that *Roe* fundamentally located the right to abortion within physician authority (although there are female physicians who, presumably, have different attitudes to the male authorities I have been discussing). This granting of authority to physicians has contributed to the inequal access to abortion care. See Katie L. Gibson, "The Rhetoric of *Roe v. Wade*: When the (Male) Doctor Knows Best," *Southern Communication Journal* 73, no. 4 (2008): 312–331; and Katrina Kimport, Tracy A. Weitz, and Lori Freedman, "The Stratified Legitimacy of Abortions," *Journal of Health and Social Behavior* 57, no. 4 (2016): 503–516.

90 *Abortion and the Politics of Motherhood* (Berkeley: University of California Press, 1984), 16.

91 Ibid., 20.

· 5 ·

ABORTION RESTRICTIONS ARE ANTI-WOMEN

In the previous chapters, I explored the judicial philosophy of "originalism" from the point of view of its assumptions, derived from an uncritical utilization and veneration of the Common Law Tradition, that reify a past that was intolerable to the interest and lives of women (and others as well, i.e., Black and LGBT people). I also examined feminism's critique of the law and the tension between liberal and radical feminism as it struggles to rectify the inequalities of the Common Law Tradition that persist in today's world. I presented a detailed review of that past to warrant my view, as I will elaborate upon in this chapter, that anti-abortion stances that *ignore* the woman's interest, in the context of a history in which women's interests have been disregarded by religious and political traditions, are fundamentally and inexcusably *anti-women*, and that constitutes both a constitutional and moral violation in our society. Such degradation of women is unworthy of any society, such as our own, that aspires (at least in its public rhetoric) to the highest ideals of justice and equality. As the dissent in *Dobbs v. Jackson Women's Health Organization* notes,

> As of today, a State can always force a woman to give birth, prohibiting even the earliest abortions. A State can thus transform what, when freely undertaken, is a wonder into what, when forced, may be a nightmare [...]. At the least, they will incur the

> cost of losing control of their lives. The Constitution will, today's majority holds, provide no shield, despite its guarantees of liberty and equality for all.[1]

I have also conceded that abortion restrictions/regulations which do not preclude a woman's choice may be permissible, however. For example, I accept in principle abortion-related health care regulations for medical-safety purposes as permitted under *Planned Parenthood of Southeastern Pennsylvania v. Casey*[2] when they are not a *pretext* for denying a woman's request for an abortion, as they often are.[3] My argument is that the state does *not* have a rational interest in telling women what they can or cannot do with their own bodies when it comes to reproduction, and that reproductive freedom is an inalienable right for all women. While it appears that the abortion issue presents a conflict between two separate interests (the woman, on the one hand, and her fetus, on the other), that is, I argue, a false binary (at least until later in the pregnancy), created as leverage to have power over a woman. There is, as a practical matter, *only the woman*. Abortion is about the woman and her interest in unmolested bodily integrity and an unwanted fetus is, by definition, such a violation. *Listen to her, she does not want it.* State prohibitions on a woman's agency to look after herself, therefore, become a form of government-sanctioned rape, a violation of the highest order that renders a woman powerless and is thus far *worse* than the abortion procedure itself. The state cannot privilege a fetus over the interest, desires, and decisions of a grown woman without impermissibly burdening and demeaning the value of the woman. I cannot think of any example where a man is placed in a similar situation. In fact, part of what I have been suggesting is that, if men *were* in a similar situation, the law and social attitudes, most likely, would be different, reflecting the male interest.[4]

Woman do *not* "have eternity in their wombs" (to cite Gilder from the previous chapter), that state or religious guardians must protect from an unappreciative or irrational potential mother who rejects it. Instead, pregnant women have *decisions* about their wombs with profound lifelong implications that must be processed and determined within a relatively short period of time, and often in difficult contexts, with no clear "good" options. For many women, an unwanted pregnancy is a *dilemma* in the true sense of the word, and they are the ones who must live with their decision to terminate or not, regardless of what other people think, and with or without their support and help. In our humanity, how could we not support such a woman during this most consequential time in her life? It is cruel to shun, judge, criticize, or condemn such a woman or otherwise make her life any more difficult than it may be. Whether a woman chooses to have an abortion or continue her pregnancy to term is *no one else's business*. Providing state sanction for abortion objectors' idiosyncratic opinions, cloaked as they may be in "sincere religious belief," reifies pre-existing state biases and further reifies historical wrongs, making it difficult for all women to thrive now and in the future.

This much is clear. A state's anti-abortion stances are profoundly anti-women, no matter what its legislatures claim, and much of what they say is incredulous. They are not "helping" the women, they are not "educating" the women, they are not "protecting" the woman from herself. Indeed, women, as documented in this book, need to be *suspicious* of the state in terms of its ability (or desire) to protect their interests. The state is not their "guardian" and is not their "father." Considering the Constitution's chronic infidelity to women (as noted by McKinnon in Chapter 2), any obligation women have to the state should be qualified and tentative, based on tangible results (e.g., meaningful protections against domestic violence and sexual assault, subsidized child-care, and low-cost higher education opportunities to help combat poverty and allow for increased chances for social mobility). When women are no longer beaten by the men in their lives, sexually abused as part of "male privilege," or are the "face" of poverty along with their children and locked into disheartening low-wage jobs, then, and only then, can we talk about the state being an "ally" of women. Until that time, the state is the *problem*.

Women (but not only women) should give allegiance and respect to the state only to the extent that they receive it in kind. Abortion prohibitions are the antithesis of such respect. They are the ultimate "slap in the face" to a woman's subjectivity, her self-ownership, and her sense of "being." Nothing says "you don't matter, you are but a thing to be used" like forcing a woman to carry an unwanted pregnancy to term. Mere promises of pro-woman policies, encomiums to the "fairer sex," and "sleight of hand" changes that take as much (or more) as they give, are insufficient: women need to *know* and to *experience* what equal citizenship feels like, one that does not belittle their choices or reject the integrity of their lives. That's the essence of any healthy relationship, one grounded in a mutuality of respect and a position of equality. Without respect from the state, women (or any racial or sexual minority group) owe the state no respect in return. This is not a new notion. It is basic to the Workers' Rights movements of the late nineteenth and early twentieth centuries, and to the Civil Rights movement and LGBT Rights movement later in the twentieth and early twenty-first centuries. No one owes the state anything if the state does not treat them as full-fledged members of the political community. When the state picks and chooses the people it likes (as it does now in places where Republican legislators are dominant), those excluded have the moral right to turn their backs upon the state. In our democracy, however, those excluded can fight for inclusion because they love the larger community and believe that, in time, they will be welcomed as equal members. But how long must women wait?

The sovereign father of patriarchy must be thrust down from his throne and integrated with the feminine (i.e., he must lose his white-straight-male-Christian-middle-class privilege). Men also would benefit from this rethinking of the sovereign. When the state is viewed as "sovereign" and as "all powerful," it holds itself above all of its citizens: female and male, black and white, poor and rich. It then personifies a distinct demographic and wages a repressive war on all difference, turning disfavored citizens into outcasts or victims. In many respects, we still have a king, a patriarch, a stern sovereign-father, in the way we allow states to reproduce ancient misogynist—not to mention racist and homophobic—sentiments. This king must die so that the rest of us can live as twenty-first-century women and men.

Of course, the state, not as sovereign but as an expression of the intelligent collective will of the people may, in its largesse and generosity, express its interest in childbirth (children are beautiful, and for those of us who want them, they are of great importance in our lives) and back it up with resources and support. There is no reason why, in America, the state cannot make decisions for the good of its citizens, including its mothers and children, and actively help families as they commonly do throughout Europe. Sadly, this remains to be seen, particularly in the states most eager to limit a woman's reproductive freedom.[5] The state, however, is not "pro-life" because it is not, has never been, and *cannot* be such. As part of its fundamental sovereignty and basic operation, all states routinely kill or "let die" in a variety of circumstances, either directly or through policies that have that effect. Politics is always a violence of one type or another. Michel Foucault's idea of "bio-power" and Giorgio Agamben's notions of *homo sacer*, the "state of exception," and "bare life" illustrate this idea.[6] They all involve the operations of power that secure and defend the nation-state as it permeates and circulates its control within civil society. It refers to the techniques of "subjugation of bodies and the control of populations."[7] In other words, power over life emerged as a replacement for the decline of sovereign power in the traditional sense: "the ancient right to take life or let live was replaced by a power to foster life or disallow it to the point of death."[8] In their vanity, states often "play god" with the lives of their citizens and with the planet, while protesting profusely that it is blasphemy to do so.

Moreover, the state is nothing but the political embodiment of those in power, no matter how unrepresentative they are of the population, which means we have to pay attention, as political power does *not* equal popular support. And while our nation is demographically diverse, our leaders tend to not be of the *demos*. In the context of this book, we are dealing with mostly financially well-off white Christian straight men, who tend toward authoritarianism and irrationalism, often with the discernable traits of racism, sexism, antisemitism, and homophobia they need to get elected and to stay in power.[9] To say the state is "pro-life," therefore, is a rhetorical ploy and is often irrational to the extent that it is a "code" for religious values or other anti-women ideology, neither of which have a place in law or in contemporary society. While politics, unfortunately, is often steeped in such biases, the purpose of the Constitution (idealistically) is to keep political persecution *away* from harming individuals, and courts are tasked to protect our liberties against majoritarian overreach. The Supreme Court has failed us here just as it has failed Black Americans for generations.[10] Again, I ask: when will we be able to hold the law accountable for its past failures and direct the law's power toward creating a more equal society?

In the previous two chapters I developed my argument with empirical/historical evidence of the law's intolerance for women's freedoms and bodily autonomy. However, I still need to review and engage the Supreme Court's rejection, generally, of my proposition that abortion restrictions that preclude a woman's choice to have an abortion are anti-women and, if not irrational, highly suspect as a respectable state interest.

The Court's Contrary Position Reviewed and Rejected

The *Dobbs* Court's preemptive objection to this argument I am making consisted of it categorically restating its *earlier* conclusion that "the goal of preventing abortion does not constitute invidiously discriminatory animus against women."[11] It went on to explain that "laws regulating or prohibiting abortion are not subject to heightened scrutiny."[12] As indicated by the Court,

> the regulation of a medical procedure that only one sex can undergo does not trigger heightened constitutional scrutiny unless the regulation is a mere pretext designed to effect an invidious discrimination against members of one sex or the other.[13]

Instead, "they are governed by the same standard of review as other health and safety measures."[14] In other words, there is, according to the Court, nothing special or unique about pregnancy per se and how it may affect a woman's health and life. It is the equivalent of having an appendectomy.

On the other hand, the Dobbs majority *does* think that pregnancy is *different* from other medical procedures and from other claims to privacy, but in a way that prejudices women: "abortion is different in that it kills an unborn human being."[15] The authority the Court references for this contradictory prejudicial attitude is *Bray v. Alexandria Women's Health Clinic.*[16] In *Bray*, regional abortion clinics sued to prevent anti-abortion protesters (so-called "Operation Rescue" supporters) from blocking clinic entrances to prevent women from accessing reproductive health services, arguing that the protesters were acting to deny women their constitutional right to an abortion. Operation Rescue is a well-known and controversial evangelical Christian organization which experienced different iterations over the years, with splinter groups during its troubled history, but it has always had the goal of creating an "abortion-free" America. Of course, what they mean by "abortion-free" is an America where all abortions are *illegal* and women are made criminals, as abortion cannot be eradicated. It can only be safe (or not) for the woman who needs one.

The purpose of Operation Rescue is to prevent women, through violence or civil disobedience, from experiencing their right to have an abortion under *Roe* and its progeny.[17] That much is clear. Moreover, this was *exactly* what the protesters were doing in *Bray*, combining to frustrate a women's right to exercise her bodily autonomy, telling her what she can and cannot do with her life. Without any doubt, the protesters "conspired" to prevent women from doing what they were legally able to do, disregarding their agency and freedom. One would think that the Court would protect women from such activities and defend their constitutional rights and human subjectivity, but one would be wrong.

The Supreme Court disagreed with the clinics, holding absurdly that the anti-abortion protesters who were blocking entrances to abortion facilities were *not* motivated by a malevolent or benign purpose against *women* per se. That was the context in which the Court rejected the claim that "opposition to abortion reflects an animus against women in general."[18] For the *Bray* court, "animus" is not legally significant unless it "focuses upon women *by reason of their sex*."[19] The example the Court gives is "the purpose of 'saving' women *because they are women* from a combative, aggressive profession such as the practice of law."[20] This is, of course, a reference to *Bradwell v. Illinois*,[21] the infamous Supreme Court case that rejected the claim by a woman that she had a Fourteenth Amendment right under the Constitution's Privileges or Immunities Clause to be an attorney.

In fact, the Court emphasized, the protesters could care less about the women and that is why the protesters prevailed. Simply, the presence of women at the abortion facility was immaterial to the protesters, according to the Court's convoluted reasoning, rendering the women's subjectivities invisible or irrelevant. This, I argue, is *precisely* the problem, which the Court could not see, and which men often do not see. People (or institutions) often do not care about women as women, but only as a *means* to some other ends, which has long been the Biblical, conservative, or *Playboy* view. Woman matter only to the extent that they matter to men. As stated by the Court, the protesters were *not thinking about women at all* much less being antagonistic toward them. As the Court explained, the protesters defined their actions as "rescues" and "not with reference to women, but as physical intervention 'between abortionists and the innocent victims,'" and that "all [petitioners] share a deep commitment to the goals of stopping the practice of abortion and reversing its legalization."[22] Women, it seems, have nothing to do with this. They become objectified bodies without an interest or point of view. They have been rendered legally irrelevant.

Thus, in the Court's view, this legally cognizable explanation for the defendants' behavior was somehow not anti-woman at all, and no "conspiracy" to deny women their constitutional rights could be sustained. The issue, for the protesters, according to the Court, was between "unborn human beings" and unethical doctors who wanted to murder them. The pregnant women were simply that, walking pregnancies containing endangered babies that needed protection. Because the protesters ignored the women and what she thought was best for her, the Court felt it appropriate to ignore them as well and to accept the terms set by the illegal protesters as legally determinative of what the Court should allow. This is unconscionable. When the law allows defendants to subjectively define the terms of their actions, we should be concerned.[23] The protesters, in this case, were the "bad guys," defendants in a criminal case who broke the law and were using their constitutionally protected religious *beliefs* to shield their illegal and harmful *actions*. Their pretextual "love" for the fetus was a thinly covered, if not hatred of its mother, a profound disdain of *her*. Unborn fetuses do not have an interest or a voice independent of its mother. To elevate the fetus above that of the mother is to reduce her to an object, a thing. It is to love the abstract and to hate the particular.

The *Bray* Court proceeds to offer the following bizarre analogy that highlights its negation of the women in that case:

> Some activities may be such an irrational object of disfavor that, if they are targeted, and if they also happen to be engaged in exclusively or predominantly by a particular class of people, an intent to disfavor that class can readily be presumed. A tax on wearing yarmulkes is a tax on Jews.[24]

In contrast, explained the Court, opposition to

> abortion cannot possibly be considered such an irrational surrogate for opposition to (or paternalism towards) women. Whatever one thinks of abortion, it cannot be denied that there are common and respectable reasons for opposing it, other than hatred of, or condescension toward (or indeed *any view at all concerning*), *women as a class*—as is evident from the fact that men and women are on both sides of the issue, just as men and women are on both sides of petitioners' unlawful demonstrations.[25]

Of course, people can be passionately anti-abortion for a variety of "good-faith" reasons, and no one ever denied that there may be reasons for some people to oppose abortion, as is their right. *Roe*, itself, was criticized on this point for not recognizing these interests, and *Casey* was, for better or for worse, an attempt to strike a "more appropriate" balance between the various interests (e.g., religious or "health" objections, no matter how contrary to scientific evidence), leading critics to suggest that, after *Casey* and before *Dobbs*, *Roe* was dying of a "thousand cuts" due to the Court's tolerance of Targeted Regulation of Abortion Providers (TRAP) Laws made possible by *Casey*.[26]

Still, it cannot be denied that many people oppose abortion for reasons that are immensely personal and important for them, and that should be respected. Everyone is entitled to their personal views for which they do not have to answer to anyone. Further, no one says that abortion is *harmless*; I certainly am not. The purpose of abortion is to *terminate* a fetus, as the *Bray* court recognized using emotive rather than medical language. For the woman, however, abortion is a safe procedure if done by trained medical staff in an atmosphere dignified and protected by law. Additionally, few argue, as a matter of principle, that all women should have abortions just because they *can*, or to use abortion as the preferred form of birth control, or that the abortion procedure is as inconsequential as going to the dentist for a root canal. Far from it. Abortion rights activists and the women they serve understand that the purpose of abortion is to *terminate* a pregnancy by destroying a fertilized egg (preventing, ultimately, the development and birth of a human being). There is no mystery here. Nothing about abortion is morally inconsequential.

The "destruction" of a fetus is, of course, a form of "violence," no one disputes that. We, however, do violence *all the time* in a variety of circumstances, including eating and drinking, creating medicine, feeding our pets, and removing flora and fauna from what we deem to be inconvenient places. When we approve of the violence, we call it something else, or have others do the killing for us (butchers, slaughterhouses, military drones, etc.). So, the question is not: is something "violence;" but, did we need to do what we just did, and for what reasons? Were they "good" reasons, warranted by other, equally important values, interests, goals, or objectives? Finally, if asked, how do we *justify* our actions to others if not to ourselves? There are no abstract "right" answers to these questions, only people struggling to live their lives as best they can in generally difficult situations. What matters are the social policies that either *help* or *hinder* people as they struggle to manage their own lives. Policies and their impact matter because they can be judged in ways that politics, religion, or ideology cannot.

Abortion rights activists understand all this, and, given the calculus I just described, they simply argue that those interests that others assert ("protecting fetal life"), important as they are to those who articulate them (and reasonable in-and-of itself), do *not* justify sacrificing a woman to achieve those ends. If we must choose between the mother and her fetus, all the weight comes down on the side of the mother. The First Amendment confirms that the life and agency of a woman is more important than someone else's abstract theology, no matter how sincerely and closely felt. Recall the important belief/action distinction originally articulated in *Reynolds v. United States* when the Court, in denying Reynolds' right to engage in polygamy, said that, while Congress could not outlaw a *belief* in the correctness of polygamy, it could outlaw its *practice*.[27] To permit Reynolds' exemption on religious grounds to a valid law of general applicability, noted the Court, "would be to make the professed doctrines of religious belief superior to the law of the land, and, in effect, to permit every citizen to become a law unto himself."[28] More than 100 years later, the Supreme Court reaffirmed this point of *Reynolds* against the religious liberty claims of two members of the Native American Church who unsuccessfully argued for the right to ceremoniously ingest peyote.[29]

While Christians and other religious objectors to abortion can certainly pray for our souls and live their lives upon the principles they hold "dear and true," they must leave the rest of us alone to live our lives on our own terms as free adult women and men. We owe religious observers and their world view *nothing*. Their faith cannot be *our* law. Their faith is theirs, and it is protected, no matter how much they whine that Christianity is persecuted in the United States.[30] What the rest of us need are protections from their *actions*, the forced imposition of their backward religious values on our lives. The closed and intellectually small worlds of these religious people are the result of their freedoms, and that is fine for them if that makes them happy. We, however, make *other* choices while recognizing that minority or even mainstream religious communities have rights to their beliefs. Therefore, let there be legal abortion and let the Christians protest as loud and as publicly as they want while, I hope, work to create a world in which every child is wanted, loved, and supported. If Christianity is such a beneficence to our society, let's see it enacted in helpful social policy that is progressive and inclusive. That is the best solution I can think of, and it is the world that was once *Roe* and *Casey*.

The hatred of minorities (or of other powerless people) often turns to violence against them, further degrading society, institutionalizing systems of oppression, and providing cultural nausea in the form of secondhand hatred which gnaws at our national psyche. While many people acknowledge this point generally, they fail to recognize that the *oppression of women* has been of such a magnitude and so ingrained that it is not much different than the oppression of other groups more easily acknowledged as targets (Jews and Black people, for example): irrational, systemic, deadly to body and mind, and corrosive of society's great goals of justice and equality for all. Denying someone the ability to wear a religious item is as unacceptable as is forcing a woman to harbor a fetus she perceives to be against her interest. Why does not Court not see this?

The *Bray* Court points to a series of cases that buttress their view. For example, the Court pointed out that, in *Geduldig v. Aiello*, it rejected a claim that a state disability insurance system that denied coverage to certain disabilities resulting from pregnancy discriminated on the basis of sex in violation of the Equal Protection Clause of the Fourteenth Amendment.[31] "While it is true," they said, "that only women can become pregnant, it does not follow that every legislative classification concerning pregnancy is a sex-based classification."[32] Two additional Supreme Court cases dealt specifically with the disfavoring of abortion and established conclusively that it is not *ipso facto* sex discrimination. In *Maher v. Roe*[33] and *Harris v. McRae*,[34] the Court held that the constitutional test applicable to government abortion-funding restrictions is not the heightened-scrutiny standard that case law demands for sex-based discrimination, but the ordinary rationality standard:

> Whether one agrees or disagrees with the goal of preventing abortion, that goal in itself . . . does not remotely qualify for such harsh description, and for such derogatory association with racism. To the contrary, we have said that "a value judgment favoring childbirth over abortion" is proper and reasonable enough to be implemented by the allocation of public funds, and Congress itself has, with our approval, discriminated against abortion in its provision of financial support for medical procedures. This is not the stuff out of which . . . "invidiously discriminatory animus" is created.[35]

Since the court is so interested in "invidiously discriminatory animus," why do they not honestly study legal history and professional culture more generally as I have provided in this book? Why not face and admit the sorry ways in which women have been "screwed" by the law for centuries and do something about it? If it is not asking too much, why not acknowledge the many ways in which our "glorious" constitutional identity and legal culture is built on the lie of "freedom and justice for all," or the fact that American civilization is itself dependent upon that lie?[36] How can we expect more from our political system, or from ourselves, if we do not acknowledge and correct this fact? In the end, if the Supreme Court cannot stand for justice, then what good is it?[37]

Who Should Define the Fetus?

My position is bold, but it is, I believe, in line with the *Dobbs* dissent, in emphasizing the *singular importance* of a woman's bodily integrity and agency in her decision as to whether to bear and birth a child.[38] Regardless of one's views on the issue of abortion or other interests that may be implied, nothing is more fundamental than a women's agency over her own body. There can be no compromise on this point. No one has the authority, reason, warrant, insight, or right to compel a woman to bring an unwanted child to term. Forced maternity, with all the bodily and social harms that may derive therefrom—the likely poverty and the hijacking of a woman's aspirations, as well as all the hurt and disadvantage that flow from the condition of an unwanted pregnancy, and all the sacrifices involved including lifelong ones—is far crueler than any "cruelty" people may attribute to the abortion itself.[39] Imperfect a nation as we are, we are not Iran, Saudi Arabia, or Afghanistan. Nor do we want a Christianized version of them, as is threatening to emerge in some regions of the nation.[40]

I realize that many people in this country identify as "Christian," but that is too vague a term to differentiate among a wide swath of individuals. There are many different types, branches, and theologies of that religion, and as many ways to be a "Christian" as anything else. There are also many other religions co-existing with Christianity in the United States, as well as atheists, and that means there is no one Christian "center" or religious status quo for all the nation to rally behind. This was the great point of *West Virginia State Board of Education v. Barnette*,[41] the famous "flag salute" case. The case, however, was more than about flags. It is about there being no ideological center, theistic or otherwise, defining who we are as a nation. Christians, Buddhists, atheists, feminists, socialists, libertarians, Republicans, LGBT people, and the entire smorgasbord of American cultural identities, all have an equal stake and say in this country. Instead of always fighting, we need to learn how to get along. This is far from being a platitude. Our continuing existence as a nation and a species depends upon it. This means that we need an *extension* of liberalism, not a *retraction* of it, if we are to live up to our nation's highest ideals. The right to an abortion is a fundamental part of this liberalism and needs to be appreciated as such. In fact, there can be no liberalism *without* it.

This beautiful, fantastic idea of religious and cultural pluralism is more or less unique to the United States. Imperfect as it has been expressed over our nation's history, it was baked into this country from the start. As I noted in the Introduction to this book, the poetic profusion of religiosity is all well and good. Following the teachings of William James and John Dewey, religious discourse, rich and diverse in our nation, is often a positive good. In recent years, however, a more militant, muscular, intolerant, and reactionary form of Christianity has emerged:

> ("We believe in Jesus! Not pluralism" reads one church sign), emboldened in significant part by the backlash of the *Roe* decision itself and the political opportunities it provided for conservative aggrandizement. There is no good way to characterize this new religious expression. "Christian Nationalism" is one attempt.

Another way can be found in reference to the so-called "Christian Taliban." This highly pejorative term is used by critics of the radical right and Christian conservatives. It is a crude attempt to associate the traditionalist views of some conservative Christians with the extremist intolerance found in Afghanistan's ruling Taliban government, a group we fought against and lost to during nearly 20 years of bloody war. First Amendment scholar Martin Margulies was the first to use the term "Christian Taliban" to describe the theocratic discourses that surrounded support for the Bush Administration after 9/11.[42] Some politicians clearly lean toward this condition, at least in their rhetorical posturing.[43]

On an important level, however, there is no comparison. In their five years in power before the United States invasion of Afghanistan after the September 11, 2001, terrorist attacks on the United States, the Taliban, inspired by an extreme form of Islamic identity, brutally stripped women of all civil and political rights and made them prisoners in their homes, subject to the near total power of a father or a husband. Now that the Taliban have returned to power following the U.S. withdrawal from Afghanistan in August 2021, it has reversed the substantial gains made by Afghani women under the U.S. occupation in terms of career, education, and basic freedoms.[44]

In any society that views itself as committed to "freedom" and equality of the sexes (which is what we purport to be and what Afghanistan is *not* under either the U.S. occupation or the Taliban), no other conclusion than reproductive freedom for women must be secure is logically possible without adding a premise grounded in misogynistic assumptions as found throughout the law about women's functions, roles in society, or "maternal instinct." And while it is outside the scope of this book, I take note that such misogynistic assumptions align with homophobia, racism, MAGA Republicanism, and many other types of social diseases and political disasters that hurt us as a nation. As Caron E. Gentry argues, "Antisemitism, racism, pro-life beliefs, and extreme Christian ideology have long been acknowledged to be a feature in far-right terrorist violence in the United States" and "is the underpinning element of misogyny."[45] I repeat, when it comes to pregnancy and the different rights and interests involved, the most important and overarching interest at issue is the one that belongs to the *woman involved*. Even against a fetus.

Again, I accept the argument that abortion is the ending of a potential human life (i.e., the fetus is genetically set to become a person) and thus, at some point, the interest of the fetus becomes salient, and that there is no easy way to determine when that is. The woman's interest and the fetus' interest are not, however, equally salient, and the necessity for action (one way or another) is acute. For me, I therefore conclude that what matters most is the bodily autonomy of the woman, even if it means the deliberate termination of her pregnancy:

> Many feminists . . . attempt to deny the depth of the choice to abort by claiming that a zygote is nothing but a clump of cells or that, while a fetus may be a potential person, it is not morally significant. I think this is an error. The choice to abort a fetus is morally significant. To legitimize the choice we need not deny its moral import [. . .]. As a moral agent, a mother who makes such a choice is making a choice about what is possible.[46]

A fetus can be, at some point, an "unborn baby," of course, or a "child-in-waiting," but no one knows what that point is; these are, after all, categories we are imposing on nature which does not moralize human social practices. While a fetus (defined as that part of prenatal development following the embryotic stage after conception) is clearly *not* an "unborn baby" or a "child-in-waiting" at conception (it consists of only one cell), I recognize that it *can be* after viability: a court-created, arbitrary, but defendable distinction.[47] This means that the tripartite framework of *Roe*, or something like it, makes. As the *Casey* court noted,

> The viability line also has, as a practical matter, an element of fairness. In some broad sense it might be said that a woman who fails to act before viability has consented to the State's intervention on behalf of the developing child.[48]

This may be the best distinction we can have. Nothing in this area of law is going to be perfect. The difficulty of drawing (and fudging) lines, however, is not an excuse for eviscerating the need for lines. The democratic debate has been since *Roe*, and should continue to be, *where* to draw the line: a little here, a little there, keeping in mind a range of relevant contingencies and interests, including pro-life interests where relevant. The *Dobbs* majority, for ideological reasons, rejects this as an unprincipled and unworkable standard, but that seems incorrect. As the dissent points out, there are all sorts of ways courts, and the law, can balance the varying interests involved in the abortion decision post-viability or at some other point. Time and again, the Court has pointed out that the longer a woman waits to have an abortion, the weightier the interests of the state in forcing the continuation of the pregnancy. All else being equal, that seems reasonable as a pragmatic give-and-take solution between the two extremes of no abortion for any reason, on the one hand, and abortion on the day before vaginal or Caesarean birth, on the other. I realize this will not make all people happy, but it is far better than what the *Dobbs* Court offered.

Additionally, the fetus can be many other things. Seen from the point of view of its pregnant carrier, the fetus can be a "blessing," a burden, a health threat, or a condition of psychological harm. A pregnant woman may be overjoyed, scared, apprehensive, terrified, alone, or supported; these are all real and valuable feelings and emotions, part of our shared humanity. But they are hers and hers alone to struggle with and make sense of. We can help support her, and I hope we do, but we must follow her lead and allow her to meet her needs as she sees them. She knows what she needs. They are hers. Only *she* knows if she wants to become a mother, whether she has the necessary desire, constitution, emotional stamina, and resources. Only she knows what an aborted fetus means to *her*, something to mourn, repent, forget, or simply accept.

A pregnant woman contemplating terminating her pregnancy can consult with a priest, rabbi, boyfriend, girlfriend, parents, husband, or friends, if she likes, but all must defer to her and not take advantage of her fear and vulnerability. She must not be subject to emotional or psychological manipulation or abuse. The mighty state can try to persuade her of its desires all it wants, but it stands powerless (at least morally) to coerce the woman's choice. While the state can and apparently *will* engage in such physical coercion now that *Roe* is gone, the state is violating its powers and the trust of the American people. It is acting like the Taliban in Afghanistan or the mullahs in Iran, governments we rightly condemn (although not strongly enough) for their human rights abuses against women and LGBT people. Specifically, the state is violating the rights and dignity of each individual woman it coerces into carrying and delivering an unwanted child. All Americans should be outraged by this. Comparisons to nations such as China in this respect should give us pause. We condemn China for *forced abortions* against Uyghurs or for population control as barbaric and totalitarian.[49] But it is no different, from the perspective of the pregnant woman and her allies, to force her into giving birth, and our nation is likewise acting immorally now that we allow it to occur. This is far from hyperbole. As noted by the *Dobbs* dissent:

> *Roe* and *Casey* were from the beginning, and are even more now, embedded in core constitutional concepts of individual freedom, and of the equal rights of citizens to decide on the shape of their lives. Those legal concepts, one might even say, have gone far toward defining *what it means to be an American*. For in this nation, we do

> not believe that a government controlling all private choices is compatible with a free people.[50]

Moreover, if I may play loose with common law principles (the *Dobbs* majority does) and be deliberately shocking, I can declare that, from the point of view of a pregnant woman, an unwanted fetus is a *trespasser*. This is a libertarian view known as *evictionism*. I am not a libertarian, and I am critical of libertarianism generally, but I recognize the salience of John Locke's famous doctrine:

> [E]very Man has a Property in his own Person. This no Body has any Right to but himself. The Labour of his Body, and the Work of his Hands, we may say, are properly his. The great and chief end therefore, of Mens uniting into Commonwealths, and putting themselves under Government, is the Preservation of their Property.[51]

When landlords evict tenants who do not pay their rent or otherwise waste the owner's property, it is the sheriff who comes to remove them by *force* if necessary. In the debate over abortion, this view was expressed by economist Murray Rothbard:

> If we are to treat the fetus as having the same rights as humans, then let us ask: What *human* has the right to remain, unbidden, as an unwanted parasite within some other human being's body? This is the nub of the issue: the absolute right of every person and hence every woman, to the ownership of her own body. What the mother is doing in an abortion is causing an unwanted entity within her body to be ejected from it: If the fetus dies, this does not repute the point that no being has a right to live, unbidden, as a parasite within or upon some person's body.[52]

My point is that the fetus can be *many things*, including being an "unborn human being" destined to being loved, nurtured, and supported throughout her or his long life in the United States. But that is not its essence or, absent its abortion, its necessary outcome.[53] While we want all children to be wanted, cared for, nurtured, and loved, the fact of the matter is that such positive attention does not necessarily follow merely *being alive*. Our society, as democratic or religious as it may (or may not) be, often fails to provide basic needs for its citizens, filling its prisons, homeless shelters, mental institutions, morgues, and cemeteries with used up, discarded, unloved, and broken people. Many of these "broken people" started out as broken *children*, born into a world of poverty, racism, pollution, inadequate medical care, and social indifference. While we insist that we *do care* about our children we may not, in practice, do so. Moreover, we clearly do not care about *other* people's children.

Anti-abortion activists like to shriek, "all life is sacred," when, in fact, our society does not practice that principle, nor has it ever. Both state and church are grounded in histories of blood, pain, and terror. Moreover, they both like to judge, punish, segregate, and blame people for their own predicaments. What sociologist Philip Slater famously wrote in the 1970s, in the context of the Vietnam War, seems equally applicable today, considering our decades-long wars in Afghanistan and Iraq, as well as our continuing police and structural violence against Black and poor people:

> Americans have always been genocidal: witness our systematic extermination of the Indian, the casual killing of blacks during and after slavery, and our willingness to drop the atomic bomb on a large civilian populace [. . .]. We have long had a disturbing tendency to see non-whites—particularly Orientals—as nonhuman [. . .]. We maintained that every human life was a thing of value. Yet we engaged in the mass slaughter of innocent persons by the most barbarous means possible and showed few qualms about it.[54]

Within this context, a fetus can be many different things, depending upon who is looking at it and what they *want from it*. Anti-abortion Christians, for example, may (their protestations to the contrary) see in the fetus, not a human being per se, but an expression and affirmation of their faith or as a weapon for controlling women or for "punishing" the mother for "sinning," while a woman who chooses an abortion sees in the fetus an impediment to achieving something she needs in her life, or as a frightful attachment to an abusive and dangerous man. What the fetus is *not*, however, is *one thing only* as defined by the state. The state may *say* it has a view, but that view is not inclusive or representative of all members of the community. Rather, the state's view is, by default, "male," "white," "Christian," and "militaristic"—recall, for example, how, during the Napoleonic Wars and the nationalist wars (1803–1815) which followed on the European continent, large populations throughout Europe were bred to be "cannon fodder" for national pride, a position that lasted at least until the end of World War I.[55] Such a view of the state, along with the traditional prerogatives of that community, persists at some level,[56] regardless of how many women participate in the political process.

As the *Dobbs* majority correctly points out, participation of women in politics and in the voting booth is far from trivial: "Women are not without electoral or political power."[57] Women tend to register and vote in a "consistently higher" manner than men, it is true, and, that, in the 2020 election in Mississippi (the state where *Dobbs* occurred), women consisted of 55.5 percent of the voting population.[58] Indeed, I happily concede that women are included in the political process in ways greater than they have ever been, which is something to celebrate. Nevertheless, as I have indicated, because the other identities women have (i.e., religious, political, social class, racial) are so powerful, and are continually reinforced socially, women are often unable to approach social issues in terms of their collective gender interests. For example, a woman's religious identity may trump her gender consciousness, as religious indoctrination is often reinforced socially by other anti-feminist messages and education (as Mills suggests).

Men do not have this problem as *men*, for their lives take place in a masculinist world where everything aligns with their world view. They experience much less cognitive dissonance simply being alive and existing in this world as do women. Men may be abused and discriminated against in all other sorts of ways, but they always benefit from being *male* in a patriarchal society. In other words, men have cultural resources and capital (indeed, the entire world of "masculinity") backing them up; thus, the victimization of women is more difficult to combat through ideological awareness, something that feminism of all stripes has struggled with from the beginning.

To define the fetus in one way, as a "forlorn baby" needing to be "rescued" from its "confused" and "irrational" mother, is to force a view onto the world that is at odds with history and law, and with the lives of people and the community in which they live. It is, literally, a violence to the world of a woman, even if other people do not see it that way. It is a profound affront to all that she is, all that she hopes, desires, and dreams. It is a raw act of state power backed by antiquated religious and sexist biases and an obsolete sense of state paternalism. As stated by the Supreme Court of Nebraska early in the twentieth century, "Women and children have always, to a certain extent, been wards of the state."[59] Such a state is not worthy of our respect and is undeserving of our allegiance. Such a state needs to either change or be rejected. I vote for change.

Notes

1 142 S.Ct. 2228 (2022), 2319.

2 505 U.S. 833 (1992).

3 I realize that this argument can be "flipped." I read *Casey* as a positive decision, even though it was a compromise that left many feminists dissatisfied. *Casey*, and *Roe* before it, can be seen as deeply problematic in who they *harmed*. In fact, both decisions resulted in mandatory pregnancy upon some women, which is precisely the outcome I abhor. See Diana Greene Foster, *The Turnaway Study: Ten Years, a Thousand Women, and the*

Consequences of Having—or Being Denied—an Abortion (New York: Simon and Schuster, 2020). As I criticize *Dobbs* relegating more people to being denied wanted abortions, I admit that *Roe* and *Casey* had that effect as well. See Rachel K. Jones and Doris W. Chiu, "Characteristics of Abortion Patients in Protected and Restricted States Accessing Clinic-Based Care 12 Months Prior to the Elimination of the Federal Constitutional Right to Abortion in the United States," *Perspectives on Sexual and Reproductive Health* 55, no. 2 (2023): 80–85; and Rachel K. Jones, Lori F. Fohwirth, and Anne M. Moore, "'I Would Want to Give My Child, Like, Everything in the World': How Issues of Motherhood Influence Women Who Have Abortions," *Journal of Family Issues* 29, no. 1 (2008): 79–99. In short, all the abortion cases I am discussing in this book (which are admittedly few), and all of those that I am *not* discussing, are far more complicated in their nuances than I can capture. Nevertheless, I maintain, there is a world of difference between a case such as *Dobbs* and cases such as *Roe* and *Casey* in terms of access to abortion and, more importantly, in cultural impact on a woman's status as a human being. As I have hopefully made clear throughout this book, my intent is not to track what the law of abortion is or is not, but to consider what we take, collectively, a woman to be in our society. The fact that abortion remains legal in many states after *Dobbs* does little to detract from my claim that *Dobbs* hurts all women in the United States for its perpetuation of a profoundly sexist attitude as embodied in the Common Law Tradition and religion.

4 For a well-known satirical take on this point, see Gloria Steinem, "If Men Could Menstruate," *Women's Reproductive Health* 6, no. 3 ([1978]/2019): 151–152.

5 Rachel Treisman, "States with the Toughest Abortion Laws Have the Weakest Maternal Supports, Data Shows," August 18, 2022, in *National Public Radio's Special Series: Reproductive Rights in America*, https://www.npr.org/2022/08/18/1111344810/abortion-ban-states-social-safety-net-health-outcomes; Zoe Han, "States That Restrict Access to Abortion Have Higher Rates of Maternal and Infant Mortality, Study Finds," *Market Watch*, December 16, 2022, https://www.marketwatch.com/story/states-that-restrict-access-to-abortion-have-higher-rates-of-maternal-and-infant-mortality-study-finds-11671202629?siteid=; and David W. Chen, "15 States Shut Out Food Aid for 8 Million Children," *The New York Times*, January 12, 2024, https://www.nytimes.com/2024/01/12/us/school-lunches-assistance-republicans.html?searchResultPosition=1.

6 *Homo Sacer: Sovereign Power and Bare Life*, trans. Daniel Heller-Roazen (Stanford, CA: Stanford University Press, 1998); *State of Exception*, trans. Kevin Attell (Chicago: University of Chicago Press, 2005).

7 Foucault, *Security, Territory, Population: Lectures at the Collège de France 1977–1978* (New York, NY: Picador, 2009), 140.

8 Foucault, *The Foucault Reader* (New York: Pantheon Books, 1984), 261.

9 Matthieu Van Pachterbeke, Christopher Freyer, and Vassilis Saroglou, "When Authoritarianism Meets Religion: Sacrificing Others in the Name of Abstract Deontology," *European Journal of Social Psychology* 41, no. 7 (2011): 898–903.

10 See Derrick A. Bell, *Race, Racism, and American Law*, 4th ed. (New York: Aspen Law, 2000).

11 *Dobbs*, 2246.

12 Ibid., 2245.

13 Ibid., 2246.

14 Ibid.

15 Ibid., 2236.
16 506 U.S. 263 (1993).
17 Bernard Nathanson, "Operation Rescue: Domestic Terrorism or Legitimate Civil Rights Protest?" *The Hastings Center Report* 19, no. 6 (1989): 28–32.
18 *Bray v. Alexandria*, 269.
19 Ibid., 270.
20 Ibid.
21 83 U.S. 130 (1873).
22 *Bray v. Alexandria*, 270.
23 So-called "stand your ground" laws do this, with disastrous outcomes, particularly for women and people of color. See Katheryn Russell-Brown, "Go Ahead and Shoot-The Law Might Have Your Back," in *Deadly Injustice: Trayvon Martin, Race, and the Criminal Justice System*, ed. Devon Johnson, Amy Farrell, and Patricia Y. Warren (New York University Press, 2015), 115–145.
24 *Bray v. Alexandria*, 270.
25 Ibid., italics added.
26 Serena Mayeri, "How Abortion Rights Will Die a Death by 1,000 Cuts," *The New York Times*, August 30, 2018, https://www.nytimes.com/2018/08/30/opinion/brett-kavanaugh-abortion-rights-roe-casey.html.
27 98 U.S. 145 (1879).
28 Ibid., 167.
29 *Employment Division, Department of Human Resources of Oregon v. Smith*, 494 U.S. 872 (1990). *Smith*, of course, became central to a major front in the Culture Wars. Although *Smith* was written by Justice Scalia, and even though it simply reaffirmed more than 100 years of constitutional precedence and was grounded in sound social policy as well as "common sense," there was significant public backlash against the decision. Congress soon after passed the misnamed "Religious Freedom Restoration Act," which effectively negated *Smith* by supplying statutory relief to people whose religious *practices* (as opposed to *beliefs*) were burdened by generally application laws for the social good (e.g., environmental rules or land-use laws).
30 Alan Noble, "The Evangelical Persecution Complex," *The Atlantic*, August 4, 2014, https://www.theatlantic.com/national/archive/2014/08/the-evangelical-persecution-complex/375506/.
31 417 U.S. 484 (1974).
32 Ibid., 496, footnote.
33 432 U.S. 464 (1977).
34 448 U.S. 297 (1980).
35 *Bray*, 274.
36 See, for example, *Johnson v. M'Intosh*, 21 U.S. (7 Wheat.) 543 (1823).
37 Both Justices Sonia Sotomayor and Elena Kagan have expressed publicly their concerns about where the Court is heading with *Dobbs* and other similar cases. Sotomayor went so far as to say that the *Dobbs* decision left her with a "sense of despair" and that she was both "shell-shocked" and "deeply sad." Karen Loan, "Sotomayor Felt 'Shell-Shocked' After U.S. Supreme Court's Abortion Decision," *Reuters*, January 4, 2023, https://www.yahoo.com/news/sotomayor-felt-shell-shocked-u-213826007.html. While I appreciate Sotomayor's

reaction, the egregiousness of the *Dobbs'* decision demands *more*; namely, a sustained and strategic public *disruption*, acts of brave civil disobedience at all levels of society, including conscientious Justices. Sometimes speaking out, even bitterly and with intent to frustrate the operation of state power, is better than remaining silent. These are not normal times. There are times in which even family members get to the point where they no longer talk to each other because someone did something "unforgivable." *This may be one of those times.*

38 Again, to be clear, this is my position; it did not exist in the legal doctrines of either *Roe* or *Casey*. I celebrate *Roe* and *Casey* for what they did, not what they did *not* do. I mourn the passing of both cases while, at the same time, desire to move *beyond* them in the interest of a richer and more comprehensive reproductive freedom for women.

39 Cases such as the Mississippi child who was raped and unable to secure an abortion, will once again become common. Kelly Rissman, "Thirteen-Year-Old Girl Is Forced to Give Birth Under Mississippi Abortion Ban," *Independent* (UK), August 14, 2023, https://www.independent.co.uk/news/world/americas/teen-girl-mississippi-abortion-ban-b2392968.html.

40 Stella Rouse and Shibley Telhami, "Most Republicans Support Declaring the United States a Christian Nation," *Politico*, September 21, 2022, https://www.politico.com/news/magazine/2022/09/21/most-republicans-support-declaring-the-united-states-a-christian-nation-00057736.

41 319 U.S. 624 (1943).

42 "Lawyer Calls Bush a 'Christian Taliban' Panel Examines the Blurring Line Between Church, State," *The Stamford Advocate*, January 21, 2005.

43 See Adela Suliman and Timothy Bella, "GOP Rep. Boebert: 'I'm Tired of This Separation of Church and State Junk,'" *The New York Times*, June 28, 2022, https://www.washingtonpost.com/politics/2022/06/28/lauren-boebert-church-state-colorado/.

44 Rahim Faiez, "UN: Afghanistan is World's Most Repressive Country for Women," *Associated Press*, March 8, 2023, https://apnews.com/article/taliban-afganistan-women-rights-united-Nations-591c39436d53f83e5a0c423c5e06891c.

45 "Misogynistic Terrorism: It Has Always Been Here," *Critical Studies on Terrorism* 15, no. 1 (2022): 209.

46 Sarah Lucia Hoagland, *Lesbian Ethics: Toward New Value* (Palo Alto, CA: Institute of Lesbian Studies, 1990), 97.

47 I recognize that *Roe* and *Casey* were also vulnerable on the "viability question." See Alan Zaitchik, "Viability and the Morality of Abortion," *Philosophy & Public Affairs* 10, no. 1 (1981): 18–26.

48 *Planned Parenthood v. Casey*, 870.

49 Jing-Bao Nie, "The Problem of Coerced Abortion in China and Related Ethical Issues," *Cambridge Quarterly of Healthcare Ethics* 8, no. 4 (1999): 463–475; and Gregory K. Pike, "Coerced Abortion-The Neglected Face of Reproductive Coercion," *The New Bioethics* 29, no. 2 (2022): 85–107.

50 142 S.Ct. 2228 (2022), 2320, italics added.

51 *Two Treatises of Government, a Critical Edition* (Cambridge, UK: Cambridge University Press, [1689]/1963), 305–306.

52 *For a New Liberty: The Libertarian Manifesto*, 2nd ed. (Auburn, Alabama: Ludwig von Mises Institute, 2006/1973), 132. Modern writers have developed Rothbard's idea. See Walter

E. Block, "Evictionism and Libertarianism," *The Journal of Medicine and* Philosophy 39, no. 3 (2014): 248–257.

53 Christina J. Cross, Paula Fomby, and Bethany Letiecq, "Interlinking Structural Racism and Heteropatriarchy: Rethinking Family Structure's effects on Child Outcomes in a Racialized, Unequal Society," *Journal of Family Theory & Review* 14, no. 3 (2022): 482–501.

54 *The Pursuit of Loneliness* (Boston: Beacon Press, 1970), 39.

55 Matti Häyry, "*Roe v. Wade* and the Predatory State Interest in Protecting Future Cannon Fodder," *Cambridge Quarterly of Healthcare Ethics* (2022): 1–9.

56 Lauren Berland reports seeing anti-abortion bumper stickers that read, "Support Our Future Troops!" and asks, "What kinds of anxiety and theory of personhood are expressed by such slogans? How can we make sense of recent alliances between imperialism and pro-life patriotism?" *The Queen of America Goes to Washington City: Essays on Sex and Citizenship* (Durham, NC: Duke University Press, 1997), 101.

57 *Dobbs*, 2277.

58 Ibid.

59 *Wenham v. State*, 65 Neb. 394 (1902), 425.

CONCLUSION

Throughout this book, I have argued that the United States Supreme Court, in its majority *Dobbs v. Jackson Women's Health Organization*[1] decision overturning *Roe v. Wade*[2] and *Planned Parenthood of Southeastern Pennsylvania v. Casey*,[3] was grounded in an inarticulated but profound tradition of misogyny and patriarchy that hurts social progress in the United States, just as unacknowledged structural racism hurts social progress, limiting what our country can be.

More strongly, I have argued that *Dobbs* was not only wrong but awful and immoral; in a colloquial sense, I want to label it "legal malpractice." Reading it makes me feel like I am reading the infamous *Dred Scott v. Sanford* decision in which the Supreme Court declared that Black people have "no rights which the white man was bound to respect."[4] It is the totalitarianism (cloaked in democratic-sounding garb) of the reasoning and the unequivocal dismissal of women's interest that sickens me: "Women," said the *Dobbs* Court in essence, "you have no interest which men are bound to respect."

Throughout my study, I illustrated criticism, as I intend it, which encourages human progress through an engaged commitment and application of human agency and intelligence to solve social problems. Such analysis is both progressive and inclusive, forward-thinking and brave. Criticism works by reconsidering the "givenness" or taken-for-granted character of the social world: its concepts, understandings, cultural categories, etc. We see the world as "*given*" but criticism demonstrates that the world is "*taken*" (i.e., constructed) by interested cultural agents.[5] My criticism, as illustrated in this book, is an approach compatible with American pragmatism, which teaches that the world is not stable with fixed meanings that can be revealed through the "right" method or the proper religious faith. There is only a continuous quest to find workable solutions to life's many problems, which seem to be getting worse in recent years. The way to discover what is morally right or wrong is the same as when seeking truth: a good action is one that works to solve a given problem.[6] The goal of critical analysis is to work from within categories of existing thought (i.e., the "here and now" rather than the transcendental or metaphysical) to radicalize those categories, reveal their internal conditions and shortcomings, and demonstrate their unrecognized possibilities.

Admittedly, I could not rehash everything there is to say about how terribly un-American (by today's standards) and inhumane the Common Law Tradition (by *any* standard) regarding the status of women was, and how horribly women have been, and continue to be, treated in this country. Simply, women are often undervalued as human beings. I have taken the position, along with many scholars, that our society is misogynistic, that it is hostile to the development of young girls into healthy women, and one in which white men receive privilege at the expense of women and racial minorities. Women experience it as an everyday occurrence, a weight that presses upon them but often goes unaddressed or articulated. Year after year, it wears down, and tears down, a woman's psyche, deforming her soul and killing her dreams. Now that *Roe* and *Casey* have been eradicated by an angry and reactionary Court hell-bent on forcing a discredited and backward jurisprudence on the American people, that mistreatment and contempt for women will be heightened, and broadened, as groups holding terrible and cruel anti-womanist sentiments will be emboldened.[7]

While flawed in significant ways, *Roe* and *Casey* were foundational to bettering the social and legal conditions of women for nearly 50 years. That these decisions were not enough, few will disagree, but they were, in themselves, significant and appreciated. The fact that readers have been drawn to this book means they probably have more than a passing familiarity with the more well-known legal and/or social disabilities that women faced throughout history, as well as the challenges contemporary women face. I mostly cited from the cases that highlight and illustrate my argument that men, during the

Common Law Tradition (as well as before), had control over both women and their children, and part of that control was to decide whether a woman could have an abortion, and women had no say in the matter. After 50 years of *Roe*, that's what we are back to: men controlling women, devaluing women, putting women "in their place," appropriating their labor, and taking pleasure from their sexual subjugation.[8]

I am not a woman, but I do not have to be a woman to feel the outrage welling up inside of me. It is a visceral, maddening, bitter feeling of frustration and anger. And it is growing. I am not alone in feeling this way, and the more rightward moves the Supreme Court makes in the next few years, the more outrage this nation will experience. That will not be good for anyone. To quote William Butler Yeats from just after World War I, "The center does not hold."[9] I fear for our country.

In 2001, I graduated from Duke University School of Law (ranked #7) *magma cum laude*. I entered law school jaded and suspicious of legal institutions, the result of my childhood poverty being raised by a single mother, my youthful anarchist and socialist inclinations which I have never outgrown, and my doctoral studies involving rhetorical and critical theory. However, I left law school with more complicated feelings toward the law and our government. In better understanding the mechanism of power in this country, I grew to appreciate all the good things that can be and have been done with the law and how the "government" is really many different institutions and not a monolithic block. Above all, I (grudgingly) found respect for the ability of the Supreme Court, despite its past failures, to slowly advance the cause of human freedom and equality in this nation. I was proud of the times (far less than I would have liked) when members of the Court stood up to the backwardness and meanness of their eras and put this nation on a path to a better future, awestruck by its singular power at pivotal moments in history. If nothing else, law school showed me that the Supreme Court, at its best, is America at *its* best.

Now I am deeply, profoundly saddened, ashamed, and dejected. I have become angry and bitter in ways that I have not been for decades. The *Dobbs* decision broke my already jaded but hopeful heart. It destroyed my faith in the law and in the potential of this nation.[10] The *Dobbs* Court destroyed my slow-to-emerge optimism, precisely when such optimism is most needed, in the redemptive power of the law. I am also surprised and dismayed that woman, en masse (along with their male allies such as myself), have not shut down society over the *Dobbs* decision with massive waves of civil disobedience and acts of domestic disruption in what Cinzia Arruzza, Tithi Bhattacharya, and Nancy Fraser call a "radical refusal," a "withdrawing [of] housework, sex, and smiles."[11] It would be justified. It would be beautiful. It would make a difference. Perhaps I do not know where to look, but I do not see this positive disruption coming anytime soon. I see only the chaos and change from the rising vengeful right wing and the spasm of disgust and hatred they evoke. This keeps me up at night and glued to *The New York Times* each morning which I read on my phone before getting out of bed. This is a dreary, heavy existence. I do not feel free to laugh (how it pains me to write this).

I want to leave readers with a passage from a New Jersey court in 1972, striking down the conviction of a woman for being a "Common Scold," a gender crime in the Common Law Tradition. Only women could be convicted of this offense. As the court noted, "A Common Scold is a troublesome and angry woman, who, by brawling and wrangling among her neighbors, breaks the public peace, increases discord, and becomes a nuisance to the neighborhood."[12] To be convicted for being a "Common Scold" a woman had to be "habitually quarrelsome, noisy, and [of a] wrangling nature."[13] The offense was one of "habitual conduct," a pattern of behavior that was irksome to men, a continuity of bickering, scolding, and acting out of place. William Blackstone, after describing the crime of being Common Scold, describes the common law consequences:

> [She] shall be sentenced to be placed in a certain engine of correction called a trebucket, castigatory, or cucking-stool, which in the Saxon language signifies the scolding stool, though now it is frequently corrupted into ducking-stool, because the residue of the judgment is, that when she is so placed therein, she shall be plunged in the water for her punishment.[14]

Of course, we do not punish people like that anymore, but the myth of the "nag" remains, and many jokes are made at women's expense.[15] The point I want to make with this example is that, in every aspect of life, from where to live, what jobs she could have, to having a credit card, and in a hundred other areas, women needed the permission and protection of men to live their lives, and they were *not allowed to complain*. A good woman was a compliant woman, one who knew her place, and accepted her condition by keeping her mouth shut. Such compliancy may take different forms. One form, notes Catherine A. MacKinnon, "is that exploitation and degradation produce grateful complicity in exchange for survival. They produce self-loathing to the point of extinction of self, and it is respect for self that makes resistance conceivable."[16] Another less physical pressure for compliance is no less controlling, as John Stuart Mill pointed out:

> Men do not want solely the obedience of women, they want their sentiments. All men, except the most brutish, desire to have in the woman most nearly connected with them, not a forced slave, but a willing one; not merely a slave, but a favorite. They have, therefore, put every thing in practice to enslave their minds. The masters of women wanted more than simple obedience, and they turned the whole force of education to their purpose. All women are brought up from their very earliest years in the belief that their ideal of character is the very opposite to that of man; not self-will and self-government by self-control, but submission and yielding to the control of others.[17]

Compliancy in the face of something told to be fate is easy, if not mind-numbing. To thrive as a woman in patriarchy, that takes extraordinary effort and sacrifice. History is filled with such notable women, who suffered much to live life on their own terms, defying the patriarchy and its stultifying social and legal limitations, although the record is not as readily preserved as it would be in the case of men. The Common Law Tradition was like chaining an iron ball to a woman's leg, then dropping her into the ocean and scorning her for being unable to swim. Or, as woman right's activist Sarah Grimke put it:

> All history attests that man has subjected woman to his will, used her as a means to promote his selfish gratification, to minister to his sensual pleasures, to be instrumental in promoting his comfort; but never has he desired to elevate her to that rank she was created to fill. He has done all he could do to debase and enslave her mind; and now he looks triumphantly on the ruin he has wrought, and says, the being he has thus deeply injured is his inferior.[18]

Yet this changed; not as much as it needs to, but post-1970s America was different, *better*. The women's liberation movement and its crowning if not flawed achievement, *Roe v. Wade*, changed America for the better. The courts took a page, not from the decrepit reasoning of the *Dobbs* Court, but from the Court of Reason in the best Enlightenment sense of humanism over religion, intelligence over superstition, freedom over dependency, mutuality over hierarchy, and respect over disdain. *Roe* and its progeny stood for the change we desperately needed in this country, as did *Loving v. Virginia*,[19] *Lawrence v. Texas*,[20] and *Obergefell v. Hodges*[21] in their respective areas. As part of the revolution in women's rights during the 1970s, the court in *Palendrano* explained:

> One of the great virtues of the common law is its dynamic nature that makes it adaptable to the requirements of society at the time of its application in court. There is not a rule of the common law in force today that has not evolved from some earlier rule of common law, gradually in some instances, more suddenly in others, leaving the common law of today when compared with the common law of centuries ago as different as day is from night.[22]

Admittedly, the Constitution is old, and the Common Law Tradition is even older. While age may be a virtue for some things (i.e., a vintage automobile), an old book or old set of legal principles is not necessarily a *good* book or *good* principles—the age of a thing says nothing about its value to people living in the present. While the Common Law Tradition (or Bible) may have value to some people for some things, we no longer stone people to death for worshipping "false" gods, blasphemy, adultery, cursing one's parents, or even for being a rebellious child.[23] We do not hang children of the age of seven for stealing bread anymore, like we did under the Common Law Tradition, and we do not burn people suspected of being witches. The question of tradition, in all cases, is not age but *salience*, *applicability*, or *warrantability*. These sorts of things are part of the judicial "toolkit" by which judges balance society's need for both stability and change, for conserving the *best* of what we have accomplished as a society while freeing the future for us to do, and be, *better*. Such pragmatism is also an important part of the judicial function. For example, in 1829, the Supreme Court was faced with a Common Law Tradition limitation that discouraged land development at a time in our nation's history in which such development was most needed. The Court responded by simply ignoring the relevancy of the old English rule:

> The common law of England is not to be taken in all respects to be that of America. Our ancestors brought with them its general principles and claimed it as their birthright, but they brought with them and adopted only that portion which was applicable to their situation.[24]

In so doing, the Court ruled pragmatically in the interest of developing (or exploiting) our great natural resources in land and minerals.[25] It acknowledged that history is filled with bad ideas (or ideas that while once may have had a valid purpose, no longer serve that purpose) that people in later generations must leave behind. Supreme Court Justice Thurgood Marshall, the first African-American, and the most liberal, to serve on the high court, said as much when, in *declining* to speak at the 200th anniversary of the U.S. Constitution in 1987, remarked:

> I do not believe that the meaning of the Constitution was forever "fixed" at the Philadelphia Convention. Nor do I find the wisdom, foresight, and sense of justice exhibited by the Framers particularly profound. To the contrary the government they devised was defective from the start requiring several amendments, a civil war, and momentous social transformation to attain the system of constitutional government, and its respect for the individual freedoms and human rights, we hold as fundamental today. When contemporary Americans cite "The Constitution," they invoke a concept that is vastly different from what the Framers barely began to construct two centuries ago.[26]

That's what *Roe* represented as well, which was reemphasized in *Casey* and most recently in *Obergefell*. The reduction of women to their reproductive capacities is one of those *bad* ideas and practices we need to reject. As Mary E. Hawkesworth notes, "To claim that human anatomy dictates an invariant set of social relations and institutions is to misconstrue both the nature of humans and the nature of social organization. Humans have the capacity to choose how they wish to live."[27] *Roe* and *Casey* contributed to unpacking the full potential of women and helped some women (at least) leave behind outdated limitations and, in important ways, thrive.

But we can and *must* do better. That is why we need to move forward toward Reproductive Justice, so that all women, regardless of race and social class, can achieve the guarantees of liberty that men take for granted. Going backward serves no purpose but to demoralize and threaten all women and the men who work side-by-side with them to make this a better, more tolerant, and inclusive country. It also emboldens the reactionary forces that are threatening our democratic institutions and our personal liberties. As Martin Luther King Jr. famously said, "Injustice anywhere is a threat to justice everywhere. We are caught in an inescapable network of mutuality, tied in a single garment of destiny. Whatever affects one directly, affects all indirectly."[28] Women's rights are human rights and a threat to them is a threat to all our liberties as women and men.

In her "Statement on the Articles of Impeachment Delivered to the House Judiciary Committee on July 25, 1974," Democratic Representative Barbara Jordan, in one of the most eloquent examples of American political oratory, stood before the American people and demanded that President Richard Nixon be held accountable for his breaches of the public trust. Jordan, a black woman, was cognizant of her positionality: "I was not included in that 'We, the People.' I felt somehow for many years that George Washington and Alexander Hamilton just left me out by mistake."[29] She is kidding here; she knows that this was no oversight, but an *essential* part of our nation's design.

"But through the process of amendment, interpretation, and court decision I have finally been included in 'We, the People.'"[30]

Few readers of this book, and I hope, in this country, would disagree with Jordan and me that this change was a *good* thing and that it needs to *continue*. Jordan did not deny what was the past. She took it and forged a tool to construct a better future by focusing on the present: the change, the empowerment, the democracy emergent from the promises long delayed. Yet, Jordan would not compromise her demand for constitutional accountability. She *declared*, in a voice intended to reach across the decades, "If the impeachment provision in the Constitution of the United States will not reach the offenses charged here, then perhaps that eighteenth-century Constitution should be abandoned to a twentieth-century paper shredder!"[31] If Barbara Jordan were still alive, I like to think that she would approve of me when I say, in a voice nowhere near as eloquent as hers, that if women are still second-class citizens in the second quarter of the twenty-first century, then maybe the Constitution, written in the eighteenth century but reifying the values of even older periods, deserves a twenty-first-century shredding. If this sounds radical, I want you to think for a moment: Isn't that happening anyway with the current Supreme Court?

***

At last, we have come to the end of this book. The Supreme Court's *Dobbs* decision came down on June 24, 2022. Since then, I have spent nearly every waking moment anguishing over the outcome of that case. In my fall 2022 courses, the first semester after the *Dobbs* decision was released, it was all I could talk about. Both courses were about law, so it was not completely irrelevant, yet it became a discernable pattern (or idiosyncrasy) in both courses. In my Law and Diversity in U.S. History course, when I asked the class one day toward the end of the semester what the course was about, one student replied that it was about how the law always manages to "screw" women. That was not the answer I was expecting, as the course also deals with xenophobia, racism, and homophobia. Yet I must have, somehow, brought everything back to *Dobbs*.

Nearly my entire life has been lived under the conditions of reproductive freedom assured by *Roe*. While I am not capable of becoming pregnant, it has always been obvious to me that *Roe* was more important than the right, imperfectly expressed, to have an abortion. I knew, for example, that by protecting women from religiously imposed Christian limitations, that I enjoyed a degree of protection as a Jewish American. When I married my wife (who is from China) in 1996, in North Carolina, I was painfully aware that, but for *Loving*, our family would be vilified and the lives we were trying to build for ourselves nullified by operation of law under the guise of state-sanctioned religious bigotry. These are the types of things that happen when Christian extremists and other closed-minded bigots enact their "religious liberty" in the legal code.

Later came *Lawrence* and *Obergefell* which further entrenched these protections and the feeling of security I have. It is a time-honored insight that members of minority groups share (although not always acted upon), that a threat to any minority is a threat to all, and that everyone needs to stand up for the equality/equity and dignity of everyone else. There can be no exceptions. For equality/equity and dignity to mean anything, they must be *complete* in any society. There can be no second-class citizens in America. The fact that such "lesser" citizenship continues to exist in practice for many means that we progressives, interested in social justice and in the continuance of a liberal society, have our work cut out for ourselves.

Women and men have the power to change the world. Women have and must continue to take the lead, as collectively they are stronger than at any other time in history:

> The gloom and doom version of feminism has its numbers right, but it's all trees and no forest. American women have enormous power at their fingertips, particularly middle-class American women. They have more skill, more wealth, more political and consumer clout than ever before in history, more power than any group of women in the world. More power, if and when we choose to use it.[32]

For their part, men need to realize that women are our wives, daughters, sisters, lovers and friends. They are us and they are you. Their labor, intellect, creativity, and love all contribute to the success and health of our species. Men would be nothing without them. Men would not *be*. To hurt women is to hurt ourselves. To ill-treat women because they are women, to lord over them as men and to command them to do our bidding is a moral monstrosity of the greatest magnitude, a terrible habit that men have to unlearn in religion, politics, and law. That means changing the way we men interact with the world and our understanding of what it means to be men. Let's do it.

Notes

1 142 S.Ct. 2228 (2022).
2 410 U.S. 113 (1973).
3 505 U.S. 833 (1992).
4 60 U.S. 393 (1856), 407.
5 John Dewey, *The Quest for Certainty* (New York: Minton, Balch & Company, 1929), 178.
6 This view, originally articulated by William James in his *Pragmatism: A New Name for Some Old Ways of Thinking* (New York: Longmans, Green and Co., 1907), has been the subject of much critique. Indeed, the value of James' insight is dependent upon our ability to discern and articulate worthy "problems."
7 See Chris Stokel-Walker, "Anti-Feminism Is Route to Alt-Right," *New Scientist* 249 (2021): 12.
8 Catharine A. *Only Words* (Cambridge, MA: Harvard University Press, 1999).
9 "The Second Coming," *The Collected Poems of W.B. Yeats* (London, UK: Wordsworth Poetry Library, [1919]/1989), 158–159.
10 A wider discussion of how some legal educators feel deflated due to the current Supreme Court's alignment with the "policy priorities of the modern Republican Party," see Jesse Wegman, "The Crisis in Teaching Constitutional Law," *The New York Times*, February 26, 2024, https://www.nytimes.com/2024/02/26/opinion/constitutional-law-crisis-supreme-court.html.One professor, who has taught Constitutional Law for more than three decades, reported: "While I was working on my syllabus for this course, I literally burst into tears. I couldn't figure out how any of this makes sense. Why do we respect it? . . . I'm feeling very depleted by having to teach it."
11 *Feminism for the 99%: A Manifesto* (New York: Verso, 2019), 6–8. See also Masha Gessen, "The Abortion Protests in Poland Are Starting to Feel Like a Revolution," *The New Yorker*, November 17, 2020, https://www.newyorker.com/news/our-columnists/the-abortion-protests-in-poland-are-starting-to-feel-like-a-revolution.
12 *State v. Palendrano*, 120 N.J. Super. 336 (1972), 338.
13 Ibid.
14 *Commentaries on the Laws of England*, Book IV (New York: Oxford University Press, [1775]/2016), 111.
15 Michelle L. Bemiller and Rachel Zimmer Schneider, "It's Not Just a Joke," *Sociological Spectrum* 30, no. 4 (2010): 459–479, demonstrating how sexist jokes enact misogyny, reinforcing the sexual objectification of women, devaluing their abilities, and supporting violence against them.
16 *Feminism Unmodified: Discourses on Life and Law* (Cambridge, MA: Harvard University Press 1987), 61.
17 *The Subjection of Women* (Arlington Heights, IL: Harlan Davidson, [1869]/1980), 14–15.
18 *Letters on Equality of the Sexes and the Condition of Woman* (Boston: Isaac Knapp, 1838), 11.
19 388 U.S. 1 (1967), holding unconstitutional white-supremist anti-miscegenation laws that promote racial segregation of the family and intimate relationships by criminalizing interracial marriage and sexual intimacy between whites and members of other races.
20 539 U.S. 558 (2003), striking down anti-sodomy laws that criminalized same-sex intimacy.
21 576 U.S. 644 (2015), granting same-sex couples the right to marry.
22 *State v. Palendrano*, 342.

23 At one point, in England, there were 222 offenses characterized as capital crimes and the law was dubbed the "Bloody Code" by historians. John Walliss, *The Bloody Code in England and Wales, 1760–1830* (Cham, Switzerland: Palgrave Macmillan, 2018).

24 *Van Ness v. Pacard*, 27 U.S. 137, 144.

25 While endorsing the Court's pragmatism in adapting the Common Law Tradition to U.S. conditions, I realize that part of these "conditions" included the horrors of native genocide and the emergence and oppression of a working-class proletariat.

26 "Reflections on the Bicentennial of the United States Constitution," *Harvard Law Review* 101, no. 1 (1987): 2.

27 *Beyond Oppression: Feminist Theory and Political Strategy* (New York: Continuum, 1990), 81.

28 *Letter From a Birmingham Jail* (New York: Penguin Classics, [1964]/2018), 2.

29 Barbara Jordan, *Speaking the Truth with Eloquent Thunder*, ed. Max Herman (Austin: University of Texas Press, 2007), 27.

30 Ibid.

31 Ibid., 31.

32 Susan Estrich, *Sex & Power* (New York: Riverhead Books, 2000), 24.

BIBLIOGRAPHY

"Abortion Rights, May 2022: NPR/PBS NewsHour/Marist National Poll." Marist Poll. May 19, 2022. https://maristpoll.marist.edu/polls/npr-pbs-newshour-marist-national-poll-abortion-rights-may-2022/.

Abrams, Paula. "The Scarlet Letter: The Supreme Court and the Language of Abortion Stigma." *Michigan Journal of Gender & Law* 19, no. 2 (2013): 293–337.

Adams, Abigail. Abigail Adams to John Adams, March 31, 1776. In *The Adams Papers: Adams Family Correspondence*, *Founders Online*. https://founders.archives.gov/documents/Adams/04-01-02-0241.

Adams, Carole. *The Sexual Politics of Meat: A Feminist-Vegetarian Critical Theory*. New York: Continuum, 1990.

Adams, Char. "How Trump Ignited the Fight Over Critical Race Theory in Schools." *NBC News*, May 10, 2021. https://www.nbcnews.com/news/nbcblk/how-trump-ignited-fight-over-critical-race-theory-schools-n1266701.

Adams, John. "John Adams to Abigail Adams, April 14, 1776." In *Adams Family Papers: An Electronic Archive*. Massachusetts Historical Society. https://www.masshist.org/digitaladams/archive/.

Adams, John Quincy. "The Social Compact, Exemplified in the Constitution of the Commonwealth of Massachusetts." Transcript of speech given at the Franklin Lyceum, Providence, RI, November 25, 1842. https://archive.org/details/socialcompactexe00adam/page/n9/mode/2up.

Agamben, Giorgio. *Homo Sacer: Sovereign Power and Bare Life*. Translated by Daniel Heller-Roazen. Stanford, CA: Stanford University Press, 1998.

_______. *State of Exception*. Translated by Kevin Attell. Chicago: University of Chicago Press, 2005.

Alexander, Michelle. *The New Jim Crow: Mass Incarceration in the Age of Colorblindness*. New York: The New Press, 2010.

Ali, Lorraine, and Lisa Miller. "The Secret Lives of Wives." *Newsweek*, July 12, 2004.

Alito Jr., Samuel A. "Justice Alito Reflects on His Tenth Anniversary on #SCOTUS." Transcription of speech given at the Federalist Society's Texas Chapters Conference, September 21, 2015. https://joshblackman.com/blog/2015/09/21/justice-alito-reflects-on-his-tenth-anniversary-on-scotus/.

Alter, Charlotte. "The Failure of the Feminist Industrial Complex." *Time*, June 24, 2022. https://time.com/6190225/feminist-industrial-complex-roe-v-wade/.

American Social Hygiene Association. *Keeping Fit to Fight* (1917).

Armstrong, Gail. "Females Under the Law-'Protected But Unequal.'" *Crime & Delinquency* 23, no. 2 (1977): 109–120.

Armstrong, Karen. *The Gospel According to Woman: Christianity's Creation of the Sex War in the West*. Garden City, NY: Anchor Press, 1986.

Arruzza, Cinzia, Tithi Bhattacharya, and Nancy Fraser. *Feminism for the 99%: A Manifesto*. New York: Verso, 2019.

Atwood, Margaret. *The Handmaid's Tale*. New York: Anchor Books, [1986]/1998.

Balkin, Jack M., ed. *What* Roe v. Wade *Should Have Said: The Nation's Top Legal Experts Rewrite America's Most Controversial Decision*. New York: New York University Press, 2023.

Banner, Stuart. "When Christianity Was Part of the Common Law." *Law and History Review* 16, no. 1 (1998): 27–62.

_______. *The Decline of Natural Law*. New York: Oxford University Press, 2021.

Baron, Ava. "Protective Labor Legislation and the Cult of Domesticity." *Journal of Family Issues* 2, no. 1 (1981): 25–38.

Bartlett, Katharine T. "MacKinnon's Feminism: Power on Whose Terms?" *California Law Review* 75 (1987): 1559–1570.

Baumgardner, Jennifer, and Amy Richards. *Manifesta: Young Women, Feminism, and the Future*. New York: Farrar, Straus & Giroux, 2000.

Bax, Ernest Belfort. *The Fraud of Feminism*. London: Grant Richards, 1913.

Beatty, Jack. *Age of Betrayal: The Triumph of Money in America, 1865–1900*. New York: Vintage, 2008.

Bell, Derrick A. *Race, Racism, and American Law*. 4th ed. New York: Aspen Law, 2000.

Bemiller Michelle L., and Rachel Zimmer Schneider. "It's Not Just a Joke." *Sociological Spectrum* 30, no. 4 (2010): 459–479.

Berland, Lauren. *The Queen of America Goes to Washington City: Essays on Sex and Citizenship*. Durham, NC: Duke University Press, 1997.

Blackstone, William. *Commentaries on the Laws of England*. New York: Oxford University Press, [1775]/2016.

Blackwell, Elizabeth. *Pioneer Work in the Opening of the Medical Profession to Women*. London: Longsmans, Green, and Co., 1895.

Block, Walter E. "Evictionism and Libertarianism." *The Journal of Medicine and Philosophy* 39, no. 3 (2014): 248–257.

Bonilla-Silva, Eduardo. *Racism Without Racists: Color-Blind Racism and the Persistence of Racial Inequality in America.* 6th ed. New York: Rowman & Littlefield Publisher, 2021.

Bork, Robert. "Neutral Principles and Some First Amendment Problems." *Indiana Law Journal* 47, no. 1 (1971): 1–35.

Bouie, Jamelle. "The Real Threat to Freedom Is Coming from the States." *The New York Times*, May 26, 2023. https://www.nytimes.com/2023/05/26/opinion/freedom-states-rights.html#:~:text=Across%20the%20country%2C%20we%20are,is%20coming%20from%20the%20states.

Brandeis, Louis. *Women in Industry: Decision of the United States Supreme Court in Curt Muller vs. State of Oregon: Upholding of the Oregon Hour Law for Women and Brief for the State of Oregon* (1908).

Bredbenner, Candice Lewis. *A Nationality of Her Own: Women, Marriage, and the Law of Citizenship*. Berkeley: University of California Press, 1998.

Brennan Jr., William J. "Speech to the Text and Teaching Symposium." Transcript of speech given at Georgetown University, October 12, 1985, Washington, DC. From Occasional Paper No. 2, in *The Great Debate: Interpreting Our Written Constitution*. https://fedsoc.org/commentary/publications/the-great-debate-justice-william-j-brennan-jr-october-12-1985.

Bres, Rose. *Maids, Wives, and Widows: The Law of the Land and of the Various States As It Affects Women*. New York: E.P. Dutton & Company, 1918.

Bridges, Khiara. *Reproducing Race: An Ethnography of Pregnancy as a Site of Racialization*. Berkeley: University of California Press, 2011.

Bronner, Stephen Eric. *The Bigot: Why Prejudice Persists*. New Haven, CT: Yale University Press, 2015.

_______. *Ideas in Action: Political Tradition in the Twentieth Century*. Lanham, MD: Rowman & Littlefield, 1999.

Brownmiller, Susan. *Against Our Will: Men, Women, and Rape*. New York: Penguin Books, 1975.

_______. "Under Law, Rape Was at First a Crime Only Against a Father's Property, But That Has Changed." *The New York Times*, October 1, 1975.

Burnett, James Compton. *Organ Diseases of Women*. Philadelphia, PA: Boericke & Tafel, 1897.

Cahn, Edmond Nathaniel. "Justice Black and First Amendment Absolutes: A Public Interview." *New York University Law Review 37* (1962): 552–554.

Caldwell, Christopher. "The Roots of our Partisan Divide." In *Imprimis: A 50th Anniversary Collection*, edited by Douglas A. Jeffrey. Hillsdale, MI: Hillsdale College Press, 2022.

Caldwell, Taylor. "They're Spoiling Eve's Great Con Game." *American Opinion* (September 1970): 6.

Carter, Jimmy. "Losing My Religion for Equality." *The Age*, July 15, 2009. https://www.theage.com.au/politics/federal/losing-my-religion-for-equality-20090714-dk0v.html.

Cawston, Amanda. "The Feminist Case Against Pornography: A Review and Re-Evaluation." *Inquiry* 62, no. 6 (2019): 624–658.

Césaire, Aimé. *Discourse on Colonialism*. New York: Monthly Review Press, [1955]/2000.

Chapkis, Wendy. *Beauty Secrets: Women and the Politics of Appearance*. Boston: South End Press, 1986.

Chemerinsky, Erwin. *The Case Against the Supreme Court*. New York: Penguin Books, 2014.

_______. *Worse Than Nothing: The Dangerous Fallacy of Originalism*. New Haven, CT: Yale University Press, 2022.

Chen, David W. "15 States Shut Out Food Aid for 8 Million Children." *The New York Times*, January 12, 2024. https://www.nytimes.com/2024/01/12/us/school-lunches-assistance-republicans.html?searchResultPosition=1.

Chesler, Phyllis. *Patriarchy: Notes of an Expert Witness*. Monroe, ME: Common Courage Press, 1994.

Christiaens, Tim. "Financial Neoliberalism and Exclusion with and Beyond Foucault." *Theory, Culture & Society* 36, no. 4 (2019): 95–116.

Clarke, Edward H. *Sex in Education*. Cambridge, MA: Houghton, Mifflin, 1873.

Clarke, Walter. "Social Reasons for Medical Prophylaxis." *Social Hygiene* 5, no. 1 (January 1919): 41–48.

Cleveland, Grover. "Would Woman Suffrage Be Unwise?" *The Ladies Home Journal*, October 1905.

Cobbe, Frances. *Criminals, Idiots, Women, and Minors. Is the Classification Sound? A Discussion on the Laws Concerning the Property of Married Woman*. Manchester, UK: A. Ireland and Co., 1869.

Coggan, Sharon L. *Sacred Disobedience: A Jungian Analysis of the Saga of Pan and the Devil*. Lanham, MD: Lexington Books, 2020.

Cole, Kirsti and Holly Hassel, eds. *Surviving Sexism in Academia: Strategies for Feminist Leadership*. New York: Routledge, 2017.

Collins, Patricia Hill. *Black Feminist Thought: Knowledge, Consciousness, and the Politics of Empowerment*. New York: Routledge, [1990]/2022.

Comstock, Anthony. *Traps for the Young*. New York: Funk & Wagnalls Co., 1884.

Conyngton, Mary. *Senate Report on Condition of Woman and Child Wage-Earners in the United States v. 15: Relation Between Occupation and Criminality of Women*. Washington, DC: Government Printing Office, 1911.

Cooper, Thomas. *Law of Libel and the Liberty of the Press*. New York: G.F. Hopkins & Son, 1830.

Corbin, Caroline Mala. "The Supreme Court's Facilitation of White Christian Nationalism." *Alabama Law Review* 71 (2019): 833–866.

Crawford, Neta C. "Human Cost of the Post-9/11 Wars: Lethality and the Need for Transparency." Watson Institute at Brown University. November 2018. https://watson.brown.edu/costsofwar/files/cow/imce/papers/2018/Human%20Costs%2C%20Nov%208%202018%20CoW.pdf.

Crenshaw, Kimberly W. *On Intersectionality: Essential Writings*. New York: The New Press, 2017.

Critchlow, Donald. *Phyllis Schlafly and Grassroots Conservatism: A Woman's Crusade*. Princeton, NJ: Princeton University Press, 2005.

Crook, John. "*Patria Potestas*." *The Classical Quarterly* 17, no. 1 (1967): 113–122.

Cross, Christina J., Paula Fomby, and Bethany Letiecq. "Interlinking Structural Racism and Heteropatriarchy: Rethinking Family Structure's effects on Child Outcomes in a Racialized, Unequal Society." *Journal of Family Theory & Review* 14, no. 3 (2022): 482–501.

Cruikshank, Alfred B. *Popular Misgovernment in the United States*. New York: Moffat, Yard, & Company, 1920.

Curry-Ledbetter, Campbell. "Women's Suffrage in New Jersey 1776–1807: A Political Weapon." *Georgetown Journal of Gender and the Law* 21 (2019): 705–723.

Dalin, David G. *Jewish Justices of the Supreme Court: From Brandeis to Kagan*. Waltham, MA: Brandeis University Press, 2017.

Daly, Mary. *Beyond God the Father*. Boston: Beacon Press, 1993.

_______. *The Church and the Second Sex*. Boston: Beacon Press, 1986.

Darnall, William Edgar. "The Pubescent Schoolgirl." *American Gynecological and Obstetrical Journal* 18 (1901): 488–493.

Davis, Angela. *Women, Race & Class*. New York: Vintage, 1983.

de Beauvoir, Simone. *The Second Sex*. New York: Vintage, [1952]/1989.

de Grazia, Edward. *Girls Lean Back Everywhere: The Law of Obscenity and the Assault on Genius*. 2nd ed. New York: Vintage, 1993.

Derr, Mary Krane, Linda Naranjo-Huebel, and Rachel MacNair. *Pro-Life Feminism: Yesterday and Today*. New York: Sulzberger & Graham Publishers, 1995.

DeSilver, Drew. "Proposed Amendments to the U.S. Constitution Seldom Go Anywhere." *Pew Research Center*, April 12, 2018. https://www.pewresearch.org/fact-tank/2018/04/12/a-look-at-proposed-constitutional-amendments-and-how-seldom-they-go-anywhere/#:~:text=Of%20the%20roughly%2012.

"Devastatingly Pervasive: 1 in 3 Women Globally Experience Violence." *WHO News Release*, March 9, 2021. https://www.who.int/news/item/09-03-2021-devastatingly-pervasive-1-in-3-women-globally-experience-violence.

Dewey, John. *A Common Faith*. New Haven, CT: Yale University Press, 1934.

_______. *The Quest for Certainty*. New York: Minton, Balch & Company, 1929.

Donovan, Josephine. *Feminist Theory: The Intellectual Traditions*. 3rd ed. New York: Continuum, 2000.

Dube, Kate. "What Feminism Means to Today's Undergraduates." *Chronicle of Higher Education* 50, no. 41 (June 2004). http://chronicle.com/article/What-Feminism-Means-to-Todays/8838/.

Dudziak, Mary L. "Desegregation as a Cold War Imperative." *Stanford Law Review* 41, no. 1 (1988): 61–120.

Dworkin, Andrea. *Intercourse*. New York: Basic Books, 1987.

Early, Joseph E. *Because of Eve: Historical and Theological Survey of the Subjugation of Women in the Christian Tradition*. Irvine, CA: Universal Publishers, 2022.

Ehrenreich, Barbara, and Deirdre English. *For Her Own Good: 150 Years of the Experts' Advice to Women*. New York: Anchor Books, 1978.

Elkins, Caroline. *Legacy of Violence: A History of the British Empire*. New York: Alfred A. Knopf, 2022.

Ellerbe, Helen. *The Dark Side of Christian History*. San Rafael, CA: Morningstar Books, 1995.

Emerson, Ralph Waldo. *Essays and Addresses*. Chicago: Scott, Foresman and Company 1907.

Erler, Edward J. "Does Diversity Really Unite Us? Citizenship and Immigration." In *Imprimis: A 50th Anniversary Collection*, edited by Douglas A. Jeffrey, 228–236. Hillsdale, MI: Hillsdale College Press, 2022.

Estrich, Susan. *Sex & Power*. New York: Riverhead Books, 2000.

Evans, Elrena, and Carolina Grant, eds. *Mama PhD: Women Write about Motherhood and Academic Life*. New Brunswick, NJ: Princeton University Press, 2008.

Faiez, Rahim. "UN: Afghanistan Is World's Most Repressive Country for Women." *Associated Press*, March 8, 2023. https://apnews.com/article/taliban-afganistan-women-rights-united-Nations-591c39436d53f83e5a0c423c5e06891c.

Falconer, Martha. "The Part of the Reformatory Institution in the Elimination of Prostitution." *Social Hygiene* 5, no. 1 (January 1919): 160–166.

Fisher, Max. "Scalia Says Constitution Doesn't Protect Women from Gender Discrimination." *The Atlantic*, January 4, 2011. https://www.theatlantic.com/politics/archive/2011/01/scalia-says-constitution-doesn-t-protect-women-from-gender-discrimination/342789/.

"Forced Pregnancy: A Commentary on the Crime in International Criminal Law." Amnesty International. June 30, 2020. https://www.amnesty.org/en/wp-content/uploads/2021/05/IOR5327112020ENGLISH.pdf.

Ford, Matt. "Samuel Alito Believes That Christians Are Oppressed in America." *The New Republic*, August 2, 2022. https://newrepublic.com/article/167266/samuel-alito-religious-freedom-doctrine.

Forell, Caroline, and Donna Matthews. *A Law of her Own: The Reasonable Woman as a Measure of Man*. New York: New York University Press, 2000.

Foster, Diana Greene. *The Turnaway Study: Ten Years, a Thousand Women, and the Consequences of Having—or Being Denied—an Abortion*. New York: Simon and Schuster, 2020.

_______, Sarah E. Raifman, Jessica D. Gipson, Corinne H. Rocca, and M. Antonia Biggs. "Effects of Carrying an Unwanted Pregnancy to Term on Women's Existing Children." *The Journal of Pediatrics* 205 (2019): 183–189.

Foucault, Michel. *The Foucault Reader*. New York: Vintage Books, 2010.

_______. *Language, Counter-Memory, Practice: Selected Essays and Interviews*. Ithaca, NY: Cornell University, 1977.

_______. *Security, Territory, Population: Lectures at the Collège de France 1977–1978*. New York, NY: Picador, 2009.

Freud, Sigmund. *The Future of an Illusion*. New York: W.W. Norton & Company, [1927]/1961.

Fried, Marlene Gerber, Elena Gutiérrez, Loretta Ross, and Jael Silliman. *Undivided Rights: Women of Color Organizing for Reproductive Justice*. Chicago, IL: Haymarket Books, 2016.

Friedan, Betty. *The Feminine Mystique*. New York: Dell Publishing, 1963.

_______. "Our Revolution Is Unique." In *American Political Thought*. 5th ed., by Kenneth M. Dolbeare and Michael S. Cummings, 450–454. Washington, DC: CQ Press, 2004.

Fuller, Lon L. "Positivism and Fidelity to Law—A Reply to Professor Hart." *Harvard Law Review* 71 (1957): 630–672.

Gallaher, Ruth A. *Legal and Political Status of Women in Iowa*. Iowa City: State Historical Society of Iowa, 1918.

Geis, G. "Lord Hale, Witches, and Rape." *British Journal of Law and Society* 5, no. 1 (1978): 26–44.

Gentry, Caron E. "Misogynistic Terrorism: It Has Always Been Here." *Critical Studies on Terrorism* 15, no. 1 (2022): 209–224.

Geraghty, Jim. "Ruth Bader Ginsburg's Unexpected Legacy." *National Review*, June 24, 2022. https://www.nationalreview.com/corner/ruth-bader-ginsburgs-unexpected-legacy/.

Gessen, Masha. "The Abortion Protests in Poland Are Starting to Feel Like a Revolution." *The New Yorker*, November 17, 2020. https://www.newyorker.com/news/our-columnists/the-abortion-protests-in-poland-are-starting-to-feel-like-a-revolution.

Gibson, Katie L. "The Rhetoric of *Roe v. Wade*: When the (Male) Doctor Knows Best." *Southern Communication Journal* 73, no. 4 (2008): 312–331.

Gilder, George. *Wealth and Poverty*. New York: Regnery Gateway, [1981]/2012.

Ginsburg, Ruth Bader. "Some Thoughts on Autonomy and Equality in Relation to *Roe v. Wade*." *North Carolina Law Review* 63, no. 2 (1985): 375–386.

———. "Speaking in a Judicial Voice." *New York University Law Review* 67, no. 6 (1992): 1185–1209.

Glaspell, Susan K. *Her America: "A Jury of Her Peers" and Other Stories*. Iowa City: University of Iowa Press, 2010.

Greenway, John. *American Folksongs of Protest*. Philadelphia: University of Pennsylvania Press, 1953.

Gresko, Jessica. "Amid Ethics Issues, Supreme Court Justices Say No Fix Needed." *PBS News Hour*, season 49, aired April 26, 2024, on Rocky Mountain PBS. https://www.pbs.org/newshour/politics/amid-ethics-issues-supreme-court-justices-say-no-fix-needed.

Grimke, Sarah. *Letters on Equality of the Sexes and the Condition of Woman*. Boston: Isaac Knapp, 1838.

Gross, Terry. *All I Did Was Ask: Conversations with Writers, Actors, Musicians, and Artists*. New York: Hyperion, 2004.

Guha, Nayanika. "In Multiple States, Rapists Can Sue Their Victims for Parental Custody." *Prism*, March 22, 2022. https://www.who.int/news/item/09-03-2021-devastatingly-pervasive-1-in-3-women-globally-experience-violence.

Gupta, Alisha Haridasani. "Is the Legal System an Effective Solution to Domestic Violence?" *The New York Times*, December 15, 2020. https://www-nytimes-com.aurarialibrary.idm.oclc.org/2020/12/15/us/domestic-violence-fka-twigs-shia-labeouf.html?searchResultPosition=1.

Haas, Michaela. "When Your Rapist Demands Custody." *Mother Jones*, September/October 2019.

Hacker, Meg. "When Saying 'I Do' Meant Giving up Your U.S. Citizenship." *Prologue* (2014): 56–61.

Hale, Matthew. *Pleas of the Crown*. London, [1736]/1847.

Hall, G. Stanley. "The Ideal School as Based on Child Study." *The Review of Education* 7, no. 3 (1901): 88–94.

Hamilton, Matt. "Brock Turner to be Released from Jail After Serving Half of Six-Month Sentence in Stanford Sexual Assault Case." *Los Angeles Times*, August 30, 2016. https://www.latimes.com/local/lanow/la-me-ln-brock-turner-release-jail-20160829-snap-story.html.

Han, Zoe. "States That Restrict Access to Abortion Have Higher Rates of Maternal and Infant Mortality, Study Finds." *Market Watch*, December 16, 2022. https://www.marketwatch.com/story/states-that-restrict-access-to-abortion-have-higher-rates-of-maternal-and-infant-mortality-study-finds-11671202629?siteid=.

Hand, Learned. "75th Anniversary Address to the Legal Aid Society of New York." Transcript of speech given at the Waldorf Astoria, New York, NY, February 16, 1951. https://orinkerrblog.files.wordpress.com/2018/06/learned-hand-address-1.pdf.

_______. "'The Spirit of Liberty': I Am an American Day Address." Transcript of speech given for the "I Am an American Day" event in Central Park, New York, NY, 1944. http://www.digitalhistory.uh.edu/disp_textbook.cfm?smtID=3&psid=1199.

Harding, Kate. *Asking for It: The Alarming Rise of Rape Culture—And What We Can Do About It*. Boston: Da Capo Lifelong Books, 2015.

Harrison, John. "The Lawfulness of the Reconstruction Amendments." *The University of Colorado Law Review* 68 (2001): 375–462.

Hasinoff, Amy Adele. *Sexting Panic: Rethinking Criminalization, Privacy, and Consent*. Urbana, IL: University of Illinois Press, 2015.

Hawkesworth, Mary E. *Beyond Oppression: Feminist Theory and Political Strategy*. New York: Continuum, 1990.

Häyry, Matti. "*Roe v. Wade* and the Predatory State Interest in Protecting Future Cannon Fodder." *Cambridge Quarterly of Healthcare Ethics* (2022): 1–9.

Heckel, Sally, dir. *A Jury of Her Peers*. New York: Women Make Movies, 2005. DVD, 30 min.

Himmelstein, Jerome L. "The Social Basis of Antifeminism: Religious Networks and Culture." *Journal for the Scientific Study of Religion* 25, no. 1 (1986): 1–15.

Hirschon, Renée, ed. *Women and Property-Women as Property*. New York: Routledge, [1984]/2023.

Hoagland, Sarah Lucia. *Lesbian Ethics: Toward New Value*. Palo Alto, CA: Institute of Lesbian Studies, 1990.

Hodge, Hugh L. *On Criminal Abortion: Lecture Introductory to the Course on Obstetrics, and Diseases of Women and Children*. Philadelphia, PA: T.K. and P.G. Collins, 1854–1855.

Hoffman, Lauren, Osub Ahmed, and Bela Salas-Betsch. *State Abortion Bans Will Harm Women and Families' Economic Security Across the U.S.* Center for American Progress, August 25, 2022. https://www.americanprogress.org/article/state-abortion-bans-will-harm-women-and-families-economic-security-across-the-us/.

hooks, bell. *Feminist Theory: From Margin to* Center. Boston, MA: South End Press, 1984.

Horowitz, Daniel. *Betty Friedan and the Making of "The Feminine Mystique": The American Left, the Cold War, and Modern Feminism*. Amherst: University of Massachusetts Press, 2000.

Hull, Akasha Gloria, Patricia Bell-Scott, and Barbara Smith, eds. *All the Women Are White, All the Blacks Are Men, But Some of Us Are Brave*. Old Westbury, NY: The Feminist Press, 1982.

Hunter, James Davison. *Culture Wars: The Struggle to Define America*. New York: Basic Books, 1991.

"The Hypocrites' Club." *The Economist*, March 13, 2008. https://www.economist.com/united-states/2008/03/13/the-hypocrites-club.

Irons, Peter. *A People's History of the Supreme Court*. New York: Penguin, 2006.

Isherwood, Lisa, and Dorothea McEwan. *Introducing Feminist Theology*. Sheffield, UK: Sheffield Academic Press, 1993.

James, William. *Pragmatism: A New Name for Some Old Ways of Thinking*. New York: Longmans, Green and Co., 1907.

_______. *The Will to Believe*. New York: Longmans, Green and Co., 1897.

Jefferson, Thomas. "Thomas Jefferson to Samuel Kercheval, July 12, 1816." In *American History from Revolution and Reconstruction to Beyond: The Letters of Thomas Jefferson 1743–1826*. https://www.let.rug.nl/usa/presidents/thomas-jefferson/letters-of-thomas-jefferson/.

_______. "Thomas Jefferson to Samuel Kercheval, September 5, 1816." In *National Archives: Founders Online*. https://founders.archives.gov/documents/Jefferson/03-10-02-0255.

Jeffreys, Sheila. *Anticlimax: A Feminist Perspective on the Sexual Revolution*. Washington Square: New York University Press, 1991.

Jeffries, Stuart. "Are Women Human? Interview With Catharine A. McKinnon." *The Guardian*, April 5, 2006. https://www.theguardian.com/world/2006/apr/12/gender.politicsphilosophyandsociety.

Johnson, Lyndon B. "To Fulfill These Rights." Transcript of commencement address given at Howard University, Washington, DC, June 4, 1965. https://www.presidency.ucsb.edu/documents/commencement-address-howard-university-fulfill-these-rights.

Jones, Rachel K., and Doris W. Chiu. "Characteristics of Abortion Patients in Protected and Restricted States Accessing Clinic-Based Care 12 Months Prior to the Elimination of the Federal Constitutional Right to Abortion in the United States." *Perspectives on Sexual and Reproductive Health* 55, no. 2 (2023): 80–85.

_______, Lori F. Fohwirth, and Anne M. Moore. "'I Would Want to Give My Child, Like, Everything in the World': How Issues of Motherhood Influence Women Who Have Abortions." *Journal of Family Issues* 29, no. 1 (2008): 79–99.

Jordan, Barbara. *Speaking the Truth with Eloquent Thunder*, edited by Max Herman. Austin: University of Texas Press, 2007.

Kafka, Franz. *The Metamorphosis*. New York: Modern Library, [1915]/1972.

Kaufman, Risa, Rebecca Brown, Catalina Martínez Coral, Jihan Jacob, Martin Onyango, and Katrine Thomasen. "Global Impacts of *Dobbs v. Jackson Women's Health Organization* and Abortion Regression in the United States." *Sexual and Reproductive Health Matters* 30, no. 1 (2022): 1–10.

Keyssar, Alexander. *The Right to Vote: The Contested History of Democracy in the United States*. New York: Basic Books, 2000.

Kimport, Katrina, Tracy A. Weitz, and Lori Freedman. "The Stratified Legitimacy of Abortions." *Journal of Health and Social Behavior* 57, no. 4 (2016): 503–516.

King, Martin Luther Jr. "I Have a Dream." *Negro History Bulletin* 31, no. 5 (May 1, 1968): 16–17.

_______. *Letter From a Birmingham Jail*. New York: Penguin Classics, [1964]/2018.

Kline, Marlee. "Race, Racism, and Feminist Legal Theory." *Harvard Women's Law Journal* 12 (1989): 115–150.

Kyvig, David E. *Explicit and Authentic Acts: Amending the U.S. Constitution, 1776–1995*. Lawrence: University Press of Kansas, 1996.

Laird, Pamela Walker. *Pull: Networking and Success Since Benjamin Franklin*. Cambridge, MA: Harvard University Press, 2007.

Langmaid, Virginia. "Study of Wealthy Nations Finds American Women Most Likely to Die of Preventable Causes, Pregnancy Complications." *CNN*, April 5, 2022. https://www.cnn.com/2022/04/05/health/us-women-health-care/index.html.

"Lawyer Calls Bush a 'Christian Taliban' Panel Examines the Blurring Line Between Church, State." *The Stamford Advocate*, January 21, 2005.

Leavitt, Judith Walzer. *Brought to Bed: Childbearing in America, 1750 to 1950*. New York: Oxford University Press, 1986.

Lens, Vicki. "'Deconstructing the Administrative State': Legal Trends and Consequences." *Journal of Sociology & Social Welfare* 50, no. 2 (2023): 35–51.

Leonard, Devin. *Neither Snow nor Rain: A History of the United States Postal Service*. New York: Grove Press, 2016.

Lerner, Gerda. *The Creation of Patriarchy*. New York: Oxford University Press, 1986.

Lerner, Seth. *Tradition*. New York: Oxford University Press, 2016.

Levinson, Stanford. *Written in Stone: Public Monuments in Changing Societies*. Durham, NC: Duke University Press, 1998.

Lewis, Bernard. *What Went Wrong? Western Impact and Middle Eastern Response*. New York: Oxford University Press, 2002.

Lin, Tom C. W. "Americans, Almost and Forgotten." *California Law Review* 107, no. 4 (2019): 1249–1302.

Llewellyn, Karl. *The Bramble Bush*. New York: Oceana Publications, 1930.

Loan, Karen. "Sotomayor Felt 'Shell-Shocked' After U.S. Supreme Court's Abortion Decision." *Reuters*, January 4, 2023. https://www.yahoo.com/news/sotomayor-felt-shell-shocked-u-213826007.html.

Locke, John. *Two Treatises of Government, a Critical Edition*. Cambridge, UK: Cambridge University Press, [1689]/1963.

Longwell, Marjorie. "The American Woman: Then and Now." In *The Equal Rights Amendment, Hearings Before the Subcommittee on Constitutional Amendments of the Committee on the Judiciary United States Senate* (1970).

López, Francesca, Alex Molnar, Royel Johnson, Ashley Patterson, LaWanda Ward, and Kevin Kumashiro. *Understanding the Attacks on Critical Race Theory*. National Education Policy Center, 2021.

López, Ian Haney. *White by Law: The Legal Construction of Race*. New York: New York University Press, 2006.

Luker, Kristin. *Abortion and the Politics of Motherhood*. Berkeley: University of California Press, 1984.

Mac Donald, Heather. "The Negative Impact of the #MeToo Movement." In *Imprimis: A 50th Anniversary Collection*, edited by Douglas A. Jeffrey. Hillsdale, MI: Hillsdale College Press, 2022.

MacKinnon, Catharine A. *Are Women Human? And Other International Dialogues*. Cambridge, MA: Harvard University Press, 2006.

_______. "Feminism, Marxism, Method, and the State: An Agenda for Theory." *Signs* 7, no. 3 (1982): 515–544.

_______. *Feminism Unmodified: Discourses on Life and Law*. Cambridge, MA: Harvard University Press 1987.

_______. *Only Words*. Cambridge, MA: Harvard University Press, 1999.

_______. "Reflections on Sex Equality Under Law." *The Yale Law Journal* 100, no. 5 (1991): 1281–1328.

_______. *Sexual Harassment of Working Women: A Case of Sex Discrimination*. New Haven: Yale University Press, 1979.

_______. *Toward a Feminist Theory of the State*. Cambridge, MA: Harvard University Press, 1991.

_______. *Women's Lives, Men's Laws*. Cambridge, MA: Harvard University Press, 2007.

Mahdawi, Arwa. "A Republican Theme on Abortions: 'It's OK for Me, Evil for Thee.'" *The Guardian*, August 25, 2018. https://www.theguardian.com/world/2018/aug/25/a-republican-theme-on-abortions-its-ok-for-me-evil-for-thee.

Maier, Steven F., and Martin E. P. Seligman. "Learned Helplessness at Fifty: Insights from Neuroscience." *Psychological Review* 123, no. 4 (2016): 349–367.

Main, Thomas J. *The Rise of Illiberalism*. Washington, DC: Brookings Institution Press, 2022.

Mann, Susan Archer, and Douglas J. Huffman. "The Decentering of Second Wave Feminism and the Rise of the Third Wave." *Science & Society* 69, no. 1 (2005): 56–91.

Mansbridge, Jane J. *Why We Lost the ERA*. Chicago: University of Chicago Press, 1986.

Mansfield, Edward. *The Legal Rights, Liabilities and Duties of Women*. Salem, MA: Jewett and Co., 1845.

Marshall, Susan E. "Keep Us on the Pedestal: Women Against Feminism in Twentieth-Century America." In *Women: A Feminist Perspective*, edited by Jo Freeman, 568–581. Mountain View, CA: Mayfield, 1995.

Marshall, Thurgood. "Reflections on the Bicentennial of the United States Constitution." *Harvard Law Review* 101, no. 1 (1987): 1–5.

Mather, Cotton. *Wonders of the Invisible World*. New York: Bell Publishing Company, [1693]/1900.

Matusow, Allen J. *The Unraveling of America: A History of Liberalism in the 1960s*. Athens, GA: The University of Georgia Press, [1984]/2009.

Mayeri, Serena. "How Abortion Rights Will Die a Death by 1,000 Cuts." *The New York Times*, August 30, 2018. https://www.nytimes.com/2018/08/30/opinion/brett-kavanaugh-abortion-rights-roe-casey.html.

McBrien, J. L. "Moral Training Thru the Agency of the Public School." Transcript of address given at the National Education Association, Journal of the Proceedings and Addresses of the Forty-Fifth Annual Meeting, Los Angeles, CA, July 8–12, 1907.

McKenzie, Andrea. "'This Death Some Strong and Stout Hearted Man Doth Choose': The Practice of *Peine Forte et Dure* in Seventeenth- and Eighteenth-Century England." *Law and History Review* 23, no. 2 (2005): 279–313.

Melillo, Gianna. "US Ranks Worst in Maternal Care, Mortality Compared With 10 Other Developed Nations." *American Journal of Managed Care*, December 3, 2020. https://www.ajmc.com/view/us-ranks-worst-in-maternal-care-mortality-compared-with-10-other-developed-nations.

Mill, John Stuart. *The Subjection of Women*. Arlington Heights, IL: Harlan Davidson, [1869]/1980.

Mills, C. Wright. *The Sociological Imagination*. New York: Oxford University Press, [1959]/2000.

Mohr, James C. *Abortion in America: The Origins and Evolution of National Policy, 1800–1900*. New York: Oxford University Press, 1978.

Morgan, Robin. *Going Too Far: The Personal Chronicle of a Feminist*. New York: Vintage Books, 1978.

Muller, Robert T. "Childfree Women Are Still Subjected to Stigma." *Psychology Today*, March 11, 2022. https://www.psychologytoday.com/us/blog/talking-about-trauma/202203/childfree-women-are-still-subjected-stigma.

Murray, Melissa. "Race-ing *Roe*: Reproductive Justice, Racial Justice, and the Battle for *Roe v. Wade*." *Harvard Law Review* 134, no. 6 (2021): 2025–2102.

Mutcherson, Kimberly. "Beyond Roe: Imagining the Future of Scholarship on Reproduction." *Women's Rights Law Reporter* 35 (2013): i–viii.

Nathanson, Bernard. "Operation Rescue: Domestic Terrorism or Legitimate Civil Rights Protest?" *The Hastings Center Report* 19, no. 6 (1989): 28–32.

Newitz, Annalee. "The 19th-Century Troll Who Hated Dirty Postcards and Sex Toys." *The New York Times*, September 20, 2019. https://www.nytimes.com/2019/09/20/opinion/sunday/mens-rights-activists-comstock.html.

Nie, Jing-Bao. "The Problem of Coerced Abortion in China and Related Ethical Issues." *Cambridge Quarterly of Healthcare Ethics* 8, no. 4 (1999): 463–475.

Niebuhr, Reinhold. *Major Works on Religion and Politics*. New York: The Library of America, 2015.

Nietzsche, Friedrich. *On the Genealogy of Morals*. Translated by Walter Kaufmann. New York: Vintage Books, [1887]/1989.

_______. *The Portable Nietzsche*. Translated by Walter R. Kaufmann. New York: Modern Library, 1977.

Noble, Alan. "The Evangelical Persecution Complex." *The Atlantic*, August 4, 2014. https://www.theatlantic.com/national/archive/2014/08/the-evangelical-persecution-complex/375506/.

Norton, Caroline. *The Separation of the Mother and Child By the Law of "Custody of Infants" Considered*. London: Roake and Varty, 1838.

Ojanuga, Durrenda. "The Medical Ethics of the 'Father of Gynecology,' Dr. J. Marion Sims." *Journal of Medical Ethics* 19, no. 1 (1993): 28–31.

Orwell, George. "Politics and the English Language." *Horizon* 13, no. 73 (January 1946): 252–265.

_______. *Why I Write*. New York: Penguin Books, [1946]/2005.

Packard, Elizabeth. *Modern Persecution, or Married Woman's Liabilities*. Vol. II. Hartford, CT: Case, Lockwood & Brainard, 1874.

Parkhurst, Charles. *Talks to Young Women*. New York: Curtis Publishing, 1897.

Peach, Lucinda J. "From Spiritual Descriptions to Legal Prescriptions: Religious Imagery of Woman as 'Fetal Container' in the Law." *Journal of Law and Religion* 10, no. 1 (1993): 73–93.

Perry, Louise. *The Case Against the Sexual Revolution*. Cambridge, UK: Polity, 2022.

Pheterson, Gail. "Alliances Between Women: Overcoming Internalized Oppression and Internalized Domination." *Signs* 12, no. 1 (1986): 146–160.

Pike, Gregory K. "Coerced Abortion—The Neglected Face of Reproductive Coercion." *The New Bioethics* 29, no. 2 (2022): 85–107.

Pliley, Jessica Rae. "Any Other Immoral Purpose: The Mann Act, Policing Women, and the American State, 1900–1941." PhD dissertation, Ohio State University, 2010.

Pollard, J. F. "Fascism and Catholicism." In *The Oxford Handbook of Fascism*, edited by R. J. B. Bosworth, 166–184. Oxford University Press, 2019.

Postel, Danny. "Last Words from Richard Rorty." *The Progressive*, June 2007. https://progressive.org/magazine/last-words-richard-rorty/.

Pracher, Maria. "The Marital Rape Exemption: A Violation of a Woman's Right of Privacy." *Golden Gate University Law Review* 11, no. 3 (1981): 717–757.

Proffatt, John. *Woman Before the Law*. New York: G.P. Putnam's Sons, 1874.

Prosser, William L. *Prosser on Torts*. 3rd ed. St. Paul, MN: West Publishing Co., 1964.

Ravkind, William M. "Comment, Justifiable Homicide in Texas." *Southwestern Law Journal* 13 (1959): 508–524.

Reiss, Fraidy. "At 19, I Was Forced to Marry a Stranger and Was Sexually Assaulted Every Month for 12 Years." *Huffpost Personal*, January 9, 2024. https://www.huffpost.com/entry/fraidy-reiss-forced-marriage_n_6592d981e4b0bf73e176edb9.

Reyes, Christopher. *In His Name*. Vol. 4. Bloomington, IL: Trafford Publishing, 2014.

Richardson, James L. *Contending Liberalisms in World Politics*. Boulder, CO: Lynne Rienner Publishers, 2001.

Ricoeur, Paul. *Freud and Philosophy: An Essay on Interpretation*. New Haven, CT: Yale University Press, 1970.

Rissman, Kelly. "Thirteen-Year-Old Girl is Forced to Give Birth Under Mississippi Abortion Ban." *Independent* (UK), August 14, 2023. https://www.independent.co.uk/news/world/americas/teen-girl-mississippi-abortion-ban-b2392968.html.

Roberts, Dorothy. "Reproductive Justice, Not Just Rights." *Dissent* 62, no. 4 (2015): 79–82.

Robinson, Kimberly Strawbridge. "Congress Can't Force Ethics Code on Supreme Court, Alito Says." *Bloomberg Law*, July 28, 2023, https://news.bloomberglaw.com/us-law-week/congress-cant-force-ethics-code-on-supreme-court-alito-says.

Robinson, Lelia. *The Law of Husband and Wife*. Boston: Lee and Shepard, 1889.

Rocca, Corinne H., Goleen Samari, Diana G. Foster, Heather Gould, and Katrina Kimport. "Emotions and Decision Rightness Over Five Years Following an Abortion: An Examination of Decision Difficulty and Abortion Stigma." *Social Science & Medicine* 248 (2020): 1–8.

Rodin, Judith, L. Silberstein, and R. H. Striegel-Moore, "Women and Weight: A Normative Discontent." In *Nebraska Symposium on Motivation, 1984, Volume 32: Psychology and Gender*, edited by Theo B. Sonderegger, 267–307. Lincoln, NE: University of Nebraska Press, 1985.

Rorty, Richard. *Achieving Our Country*. Cambridge, MA: Harvard University Press, 1998.

Ross, Fred A. *Slavery Ordained of God*. Philadelphia: J.B. Lippincott & Co., 1859.

Rothbard, Murray. *For a New Liberty: The Libertarian Manifesto*. 2nd ed. Auburn, AL: Ludwig von Mises Institute, [1973]/2006.

Rouse, Stella, and Shibley Telhami. "Most Republicans Support Declaring the United States a Christian Nation." *Politico*, September 21, 2022. https://www.politico.com/news/magazine/2022/09/21/most-republicans-support-declaring-the-united-states-a-christian-nation-00057736.

Russell, Arlie, and Anne Machung, *The Second Shift: Working Parents and the Revolution at Home*. New York: Avon Books, 1990.

Russell, Bertrand. *Marriage & Morals*. New York: Liveright Publishing, 1957.

_______. *Skeptical Essays*. London: Routledge, [1928]/1993.

_______. *Unpopular Essays*. New York: Routledge, [1950]/2009.

Russell-Brown, Katheryn. "Go Ahead and Shoot-The Law Might Have Your Back." In *Deadly Injustice: Trayvon Martin, Race, and the Criminal Justice System*, edited by Devon Johnson, Amy Farrell, and Patricia Y. Warren, 115–145. New York: New York University Press, 2015.

Saad, Lydia. "Broader Support for Abortion Rights Continues Post-*Dobbs*." *Gallup*, June 14, 2023. https://news.gallup.com/poll/506759/broader-support-abortion-rights-continues-post-dobbs.aspx.

Sacks, Kenneth S. *Understanding Emerson: "The American Scholar" and His Struggle for Self-Reliance*. Princeton, NJ: Princeton University Press, 2003.

Said, Edward W. *Representations of the Intellectual*. New York: Vintage, 1994.

Salvatore, Diane. Interview with Barack and Michelle Obama. *Ladies' Home Journal*, September 2008. http://www.lhj.com/lhj/printableStory.jsp?Storyid=/templatedata/lhj/story/data/1217259570907.xml&catref=lhj117.

Sanger, Margaret. "Margaret Sanger Answers Questions on Abortion-An MSPP Exclusive." In *The Margaret Sanger Papers Project Newsletter* #60. New York University, 2012.

_______. *Woman and the New Race*. New York: Brentano's Publisher, 1920.

Sartre, Jean Paul. *What Is Literature?* New York: Routledge, 2001.

Scalia, Antonin. "The Disease as Cure: 'In Order to Get beyond Racism, We Must First Take Account of Race.'" *Washington University Law Quarterly* 147 (1979): 147–157.

_______. "Judicial Adherence to The Text of Our Basic Law: A Theory of Constitutional Interpretation." Transcript of lecture given at Catholic University of America, October 18, 1996. https://www.proconservattive.net/PCVol5Is225ScaliaTheoryConstlInterpretation.shtml.

Schlafly, Phyllis. *Feminist Fantasies*. Dallas, TX: Spence Publishing Company, 2003.

_______. *The Power of the Positive Woman*. New Rochelle, NY: Arlington House, 1977.

_______. "What's Wrong with 'Equal Rights' for Women?" Iowa State University: Archives of Women's Political Communication. January 1, 1972. https://awpc.cattcenter.iastate.edu/2016/02/02/whats-wrong-with-equal-rights-for-women-1972/#:~:text=This%20respect%20is%20part%20and,He%20created%20us%20this%20way.

Sheffield, Carole J. "Sexual Terrorism." In *Women: A Feminist Perspective*. 5th ed., edited by Jo Freeman, 1–21. Mountain View, CA: Mayfield Publishing, 1995.

Shore, Jennifer. "Rape Culture in America." *Focus for Health Foundation* (December 9, 2019). https://www.focusforhealth.org/rape-culture-in-america/.

Shorter, Edward. *Women's Bodies: A Social History of Women's Encounter with Health, Ill-Health and Medicine*. New York: Routledge, 2017.

Slater, Philip. *The Pursuit of Loneliness*. Boston: Beacon Press, 1970.

Smith, Rogers M. "'One United People:' Second-Class Female Citizenship and the American Quest for Community." *Yale Journal of Law and the Humanities* 1, no. 2 (1989): 229–293.

Sohn, Amy. *The Man Who Hated Women: Sex, Censorship, and Civil Liberties in the Gilded Age*. New York: Farrar, Straus and Giroux, 2021.

Spettel, Sarah, and Mark Donald White. "The Portrayal of J. Marion Sims' Controversial Surgical Legacy." *The Journal of Urology* 185 (2011): 2424–2427.

Stanton, Elizabeth Cady. *The Woman's Bible*. Amherst, NY: Prometheus Books, [1895]/1999.

"Statement on Boxing." World Medical Association. October 1983, revised October 2017. https://www.wma.net/policies-post/wma-statement-on-boxing/.

Steinem, Gloria. "If Men Could Menstruate." *Women's Reproductive Health* 6, no. 3 ([1978]/2019): 151–152.

_______. *Revolution from Within: A Book of Self-Esteem*. Boston: Little, Brown and Company, 1992.

Stern, Karl. *The Flight from Woman*. St. Paul, MN: Paragon House, [1965]/1985.

Stern, Scott Wasserman. "The Long American Campaign against Venereal Disease and Its Carriers." *Harvard Journal of Law and Gender* 38 (2015): 373–436.

Stokel-Walker, Chris. "Anti-Feminism Is Route to Alt-Right." *New Scientist* 249 (2021): 12.

Story, Joseph. *The Miscellaneous Writings of Joseph Story*. Cambridge, MA: Houghton and Haywood.

Straus, Murray A. "Sexual Inequality, Cultural Norms, and Wife-Beating." In *Women into Wives: The Legal and Economic Impact of Marriage*, edited by James Robert Chapman and Margaret Gates, 59–77. Beverly Hills, CA: Sage, 1977.

Stub, Whitney. *Perversion for Profit: The Politics of Pornography and the Rise of the New Right*. New York: Columbia University Press, 2013.

Suk, Julie. *After Misogyny: How the Law Fails Women and What to Do About It*. Berkeley, CA: University of California Press, 2023.

Suliman, Adela, and Timothy Bella. "GOP Rep. Boebert: 'I'm Tired of This Separation of Church and State Junk.'" *The New York Times*, June 28, 2022, https://www.washingtonpost.com/politics/2022/06/28/lauren-boebert-church-state-colorado/.

Sultan, Aisha. "Could You Go to Prison for Having a Miscarriage?" *St. Louis Post Dispatch*, December 11, 2023. https://www.stltoday.com/news/local/column/aisha-sultan/sultan-could-you-go-to-prison-for-having-a-miscarriage/article_a5af41d0-9504-11ee-b4e8-33a37eee5d89.html.

Swartz, Omar. "Hierarchy Is Not Harmony: A View of the Traditional Chinese Family." In *Chinese Communication Studies: Contexts and Comparisons*, edited by Xing Lu, Wenshan Jia, and D. Ray Heisey, 119–133. Westport, CT: Greenwood Press, 2002.

_______. *In Defense of Partisan Criticism: Communication Studies, Law, & Social Analysis*. New York: Peter Lang, 2005.

_______. "Merger Doctrine." In *The Social History of American Families*, edited by Marilyn J. Coleman and Lawrence H. Ganong, 866–867. Thousand Oaks, CA: Sage, 2014.

_______. "Toward a Critique of Normative Justice: Human Rights and the Rule of Law." *Socialism & Democracy* 18 (2004): 185–209.

_______ and Lucy W. McGuffey. "Migrating Pedagogy in American Universities: Cultivating Moral Imagination and Social Justice." *Communication Education* 67, no. 1 (2018): 102–109.

_______ and Candice Nunag Tardio. "Gender, Education and Careerism: The Recurring 'Conflict' Between Ovaries and Brains in the 19th and Early 20th Centuries." In *Emerging Strategies for Public Education Reform*, edited by Marquis C. Grant, 235–252. Hershey, PA: IGI Global, 2021.

_______ and Candice Nunag Tardio. "Propter Defectum Sexus and the Stalled Gender Revolution." In *Women and Inequality in the 21st Century*, edited by Brittany C. Slatton and Carla D. Brailey, 24–39. New York: Routledge, 2019.

Sweeney, Dennis M. "Commentary: June 1 Marks Anniversary of Having Women on Maryland Juries." *The Daily Record*, May 21, 2010. https://thedailyrecord.com/2010/05/31/june-1-marks-anniversary-of-having-women-on-maryland-juries/.

Switzer, Kathrine. *Marathon Woman: Running the Race to Revolutionize Women's Sports.* New York: Carroll & Graf, 2007.

Taub, Nadine, and Elizabeth M. Schneider. "Women's Subordination and the Role of Law." In *The Politics of Law*. 2nd ed., edited by David Kairys. New York: Pantheon, 1990.

Thomas, Clarence. "Faith and Reasoning are Mutually Reinforcing." In *Imprimis: A 50th Anniversary Collection*, edited by Douglas A. Jeffrey, 134–137. Hillsdale, MI: Hillsdale College Press, 2022.

Thomas, William. *The Unadjusted Girl.* Boston: Little, Brown, and Company, 1923.

Tompkins, Phillip K. "Communication, Charity, Social Justice, and the Abolition of Homelessness." In *Social Justice and Communication Scholarship*, edited by Omar Swartz, 53–75. New York: Routledge, 2012.

_______. "Using Communication Research to Mitigate Homelessness: Emergence from Outreach Work." *Spectra* 47, no. 1, May 2011.

Treisman, Rachel. "States with the Toughest Abortion Laws Have the Weakest Maternal Supports, Data Shows." August 18, 2022, in *National Public Radio's Special Series: Reproductive Rights in America*. https://www.npr.org/2022/08/18/1111344810/abortion-ban-states-social-safety-net-health-outcomes.

Tseelon, Efrat. *The Masque of Femininity: The Presentation of Woman in Everyday Life*. Thousand Oaks, CA: Sage, 1995.

U.S. Congress. Senate. Committee on the Judiciary. *Confirmation Hearing on the Nomination of Samuel A. Alito Jr. to be an Associate Justice of the Supreme Court of the United States*, 109th Cong., January 31, 2006.

U.S. Congress. Senate. Committee on the Judiciary. *Confirmation Hearing on the Nomination of Ruth Bader Ginsburg to be an Associate Justice of the Supreme Court of the United States*, 103rd Cong., August 3, 1993.

U.S. Court of Appeals. Second Circuit. *Remarks at Proceedings of a Special Session of the United States Court of Appeals for the Second Circuit in Commemoration of Judge Learned Hand's Completion of Fifty Years of Federal Service* (1959).

Van Pachterbeke, Matthieu, Christopher Freyer, and Vassilis Saroglou. "When Authoritarianism Meets Religion: Sacrificing Others in the Name of Abstract Deontology." *European Journal of Social Psychology* 41, no. 7 (2011): 898–903.

Walker, Barbara G. *Restoring the Goddess: Equal Rites for Modern Women*. New York: Prometheus Books, 2000.

Walker, Timothy. *Introduction to American Law*. Boston: Charles C. Little and James Brown, 1837.

Wall, L. L. "The Medical Ethics of Dr. J. Marion Sims: A Fresh Look at the Historical Record." *Journal of Medical Ethics* 32, no. 6 (2006): 346–350.

Wallace-Wells, Benjamin. "How a Conservative Activist Invented the Conflict Over Critical Race Theory." *The New Yorker*, June 18, 2021. https://www.newyorker.com/news/annals-of-inquiry/how-a-conservative-activist-invented-the-conflict-over-critical-race-theory.

Walliss, John. *The Bloody Code in England and Wales, 1760–1830*. Cham, Switzerland: Palgrave Macmillan, 2018.

Walter, Nicole. "My Abortion at 11 Wasn't a Choice. It Was My Life." *The New York Times*, August 18, 2022. https://www.nytimes.com/2022/08/18/opinion/abortion-pregnancy-child-roe.html.

War Department. *Committee on Protective Work for Girls: Commission on Training Camp Activities*. Washington, DC, 1917.

Wegman, Jesse. "The Crisis in Teaching Constitutional Law." *The New York Times*, February 26, 2024. https://www.nytimes.com/2024/02/26/opinion/constitutional-law-crisis-supreme-court.html.

Weigel, Gabriela, Laurie Sobel, and Alina Salganicoff. "Criminalizing Pregnancy Loss and Jeopardizing Care: The Unintended Consequences of Abortion Restrictions and Fetal Harm Legislation." *Women's Health Issues* 30, no. 3 (2020): 143–146.

Weiner, Eric. "The Long, Colorful History of the Mann Act." March 11, 2008, in *National Public Radio's All Things Considered*. https://www.npr.org/transcripts/88104308.

West, Thomas G. "The Liberal Assault on Freedom of Speech." In *Imprimis: 50th Anniversary Collection*, edited by Douglas A. Jeffrey, 210–220. Hillsdale, MI: Hillsdale College Press, 2022.

White, James Boyd. *When Words Lose Their Meaning: Constitutions and Reconstitutions of Language, Character, and Community*. Chicago: University of Chicago Press, 1984.

Whitman, James Q. *Hitler's American Model: The United States and the Making of Nazi Race Law*. Princeton: Princeton University Press, 2017.

Whitman, Walt. *The Portable Walt Whitman*. New York: Penguin Classics, 2003.

Willingham, Leah. "Gender Divide Prominent as Male-Dominated Legislatures Debate Abortion." *PBS*, September 24, 2022. https://www.pbs.org/newshour/politics/gender-divide-prominent-as-male-dominated-legislatures-debate-abortion.

Wilson, Woodrow. *The New Freedom: A Call for the Emancipation of the Generous Energies of a People*. New York: Doubleday, Page, and Company, 1913.

"Women: Trouble for ERA." *Time*, February 19, 1973.

Yeats, William Butler. "The Second Coming." In *The Collected Poems of W.B. Yeats*, 158–159. London, UK: Wordsworth Poetry Library, [1919]/1989.

Younge, Gary. "Archbishop Desmond Tutu: The Secrets of a Peacemaker." *The Guardian*, May 22, 2009. https://www.theguardian.com/books/2009/may/23/interview-desmond-tutu.

Zaitchik, Alan. "Viability and the Morality of Abortion." *Philosophy & Public Affairs* 10, no. 1 (1981): 18–26.

Zaleski, Sam. "More Republican Women Than You Think Have Had Abortions. Here's How I Know." *Politico*, July 31, 2022. https://www.politico.com/news/magazine/2022/07/31/republican-women-have-abortions-too-00048632.

Zaremby, Justin. *Legal Realism and American Law*. New York: Bloomsbury Academic, 2014.

Ziegler, Mary. "Women's Rights on the Right: The History and Stakes of Modern Pro-Life Feminism, 1968 to the Present." *Berkeley Journal of Gender, Law & Justice* 28 (2013): 232–268.

Zinn, Howard. A *People's History of the United States*. New York: Harper Perennial Modern Classics, [1980]/2015.

_______. *The Politics of History*. 2nd ed. Urbana: University of Illinois Press, 1990.

Cases

303 Creative v. Elenis, 143 S.Ct. 2298 (2023).

Abrams v. United States, 250 U.S. 616 (1919).

Adarand Constructors v. Peña, 515 U.S. 200 (1995).

American Booksellers Association v. Hudnut, 771 F.2d 323 (1985).

Bailey v. State, 215 Ark. 53 (1949).

Baker v. Carr, 369 U.S. 186 (1962).

Baker v. Nelson, 409 U.S. 810 (1972).

Bedan v. Turney, 99 Cal. 649 (1893).

Benson v. Remington, 2 Mass. 113 (1806).

Board of County Commissioners v. Umbehr, 518 U.S. 668 (1996).

Bowers v. Hardwick, 478 U.S. 186 (1986).

Bradley v. State, 1 Miss. 156 (1824).

Bradwell v. Illinois, 83 U.S. 130 (1873).

Bray v. Alexandria Women's Health Clinic, 506 U.S. 263 (1993).

Breedlove v. Suttles, 58 S.Ct. 205 (1937).

Briggs v. State, 29 Ga. 723 (1860).

Burger v. State, 238 Ga. 171 (1977).

Chapman v. Mitchell, 23 N.J. Misc. 358 (1945).

Chapman v. Phoenix National Bank, 85 N.Y. 437 (1881).

Commonwealth v. Daniel, 430 Pa. 642 (1968).

Dobbs v. Jackson Women's Health Organization, 142 S.Ct. 2228 (2022).

Dred Scott v. Sandford, 60 U.S. (19 How.) 393 (1857).

Employment Division, Department of Human Resources of Oregon v. Smith, 494 U.S. 872 (1990).
Foster v. Alston, 7 Miss. (6 Howard) 406 (1842).
Geduldig v. Aiello, 417 U.S. 484 (1974).
Goesaert v. Cleary, 335 U.S. 464 (1948).
Gompers v. United States, 233 U.S. 604 (1914).
Gonzales v. Carhart, 550 U.S. 124 (2007).
Grigsby v. Reib, 105 Tex. 597 (1913).
Harris v. McRae, 448 U.S. 297 (1980).
Hoyt v. Florida, 368 U.S. 57 (1961).
In re Bushbey, 112 N.Y.S. 262 (1908).
In re Goodell, 39 Wis. 232 (1875).
J. E. B. v. Alabama, 511 U.S. 127 (1994).
Johnson v. McIntosh, 21 U.S. 543 (1823).
King v. DeManneville, 102 Eng. Rep. 1054 (1804).
Kirchberg v. Feenstra, 450 U.S. 455 (1981).
Konigsberg v. State Bar of California, 366 U.S. 36 (1961).
Korematsu v. United States, 323 U.S. 214 (1944).
Lafler v. Athletic Board, 536 F. Supp. 104 (1982).
Lawrence v. Texas, 539 U.S. 558 (2003).
Lochner v. New York, 198 U.S. 45 (1905).
Loper Bright Enterprises v. Raimondo, 143 S.Ct. 2429 (2024).
Loving v. Virginia, 388 U.S. 1 (1967).
MacKenzie v. Hare, 239 U.S. 299 (1915).
Maher v. Roe, 432 U.S. 464 (1977).
McFall v. Shrimp, 10 Pa. D. & C.3d 90 (1978).
Michael M. v. Superior Court, 450 U.S. 464 (1981).
Miller v. State, 9 Ga. App. 599 (1911).
Minor v. Happersett, 88 U.S. 162 (1875).
Missouri v. Holland, 252 U.S. 416 (1920).
Moore v. City of East Cleveland, 431 U.S. 494 (1977).
Muller v. Oregon, 208 U.S. 412 (1908).
National Federation of Independent Businesses v. Sebelius, 567 U.S. 519 (2012).
New State Ice Co. v. Liebmann, 285 U.S. 262 (1932).
Obergefell v. Hodges, 576 U.S. 644 (2015).
Parents Involved in Community Schools v. Seattle School District, 551 U.S. 701 (2007).
Planned Parenthood of Southeastern Pennsylvania v. Casey, 505 U.S. 833 (1992).
Plessy v. Ferguson, 163 U.S. 537 (1896).
Price v. State, 18 Tex. Ct. App. 474 (1885).
Prigg v. Pennsylvania, 41 U.S. 539 (1842).
Perez v. Sharp, 198 P.2d 17 (1948).
Reed v. Reed, 404 U.S. 71 (1971).
Reed v. State, 123 Tex. Crim. 348 (1933).
Reynolds v. United States, 98 U.S. 145 (1879).

Ritter v. Ritter, 31 Pa. 396 (1858).
Robinson's Case, 131 Mass. 376 (1881).
Roe v. Wade, 410 U.S. 113 (1973).
Shaw v. Shaw, 17, Conn. 189 (1845).
Shaw v. State, 510 S.W. 2d 926 (1974).
Shelby County v. Holder, 570 U.S. 529 (2013).
Silverman v. Campbell, 486 S.E.2d (1997).
Slaughter-House Cases, 83 U.S. 36 (1873).
Smith v. Nicholas Building Company, 93 Ohio St. 101 (1915).
State v. Hall, 187 So. 2d 861 (1966).
State v. Hunter, 208 Or. 282 (1956).
State v. Emery, 224 N.C. 581 (1944).
State v. Limon, 280 Kan. 275 (2005).
State v. Palendrano, 120 N.J. Super. 336 (1972).
Students for Fair Admissions v. Harvard, 600 U.S. 181 (2023).
Taylor v. Louisiana, 419 U.S. 522 (1975).
Taylor's Case, 86 Eng. Rep. 189 (K.B. 1676).
Territory v. Armstrong, 28 Haw. 88 (1924).
The Civil Rights Cases, 109 U.S. 3 (1883).
Thornburgh v. American College of Obstetricians and Gynecologists, 476 U.S. 747 (1986).
Torcaso v. Watkins, 367 U.S. 488 (1961).
United States v. Cruikshank, 92 U.S. 542 (1876).
United States ex rel. Robinson v. York, 281 F. Supp. 8 (D. Conn. 1968).
United States v. St. Clair, 291 F. Supp. 122 (S.D.N.Y. 1968).
Van Ness v. Pacard, 27 U.S. 137 (1829).
Yania v. Bigan, 397 Pa. 316 (1959).
Youngstown Sheet & Tube Co. v. Sawyer, 343 U.S. 579 (1952).
Washington v. Harper, 494 U.S. 210 (1990).
Wenham v. State, 65 Neb. 394 (1902), 425.
West Virginia State Board of Education v. Barnette, 319 U.S. 624 (1943).
White v. Fleming, 522 F.2d 730 (1975).
Winston v. Lee, 470 U.S. 753 (1985).

ABOUT THE AUTHOR

Omar Swartz is an interdisciplinary scholar with a J.D. (*magna cum laude*) from Duke University and a PhD from Purdue University (Communication). From 2010–2024 he was Director of the Master of Social Science program and runs the Law Studies major and minor at the University of Colorado Denver where he has been on the faculty since 2001 (currently in the Department of Political Science). He has written or edited 14 books and more than 120 essays, book chapters, encyclopedia entries, and reviews. In addition to teaching graduate and undergraduate courses on Law and Diversity in U.S. Legal History, Professor Swartz teaches Constitutional Law, the First Amendment, and Foundations and Theories in Interdisciplinary Studies. In 2013 he received the "Ally of the Year Award" from the CU Denver Women's Resource Center and, in 2017, earned the Graduate School Dean's Masters Mentoring Award.

INDEX

www.ingramcontent.com/pod-product-compliance
Ingram Content Group UK Ltd.
Pitfield, Milton Keynes, MK11 3LW, UK
UKHW021032041026
15470UKWH00014B/1487

9 783034 353878